Developing a Digital National Library for Undergraduate Science, Mathematics, Engineering, and Technology Education

Report of a Workshop

National Research Council

Center for Science, Mathematics, and
Engineering Education

NATIONAL ACADEMY PRESS
Washington, D.C.   1998

NATIONAL ACADEMY PRESS • 2101 CONSTITUTION AVENUE, NW • WASHINGTON DC 20418

NOTICE: The project that is the subject of this report was approved by the Governing Board of the National Research Council, whose members are drawn from the councils of the National Academy of Sciences, the National Academy of Engineering, and the Institute of Medicine. The members of the committee responsible for the report were chosen for their special competences and with regard for appropriate balance.

This report has been reviewed by a group other than the authors according to procedures approved by a Report Review Committee consisting of members of the National Academy of Sciences, the National Academy of Engineering, and the Institute of Medicine.

The National Research Council (NRC) is the operating arm of the National Academies Complex, which includes the National Academy of Sciences, the National Academy of Engineering, and the Institute of Medicine. The National Research Council was organized in 1916 by the National Academy of Sciences to associate the broad community of science and technology with the Academy's purposes of furthering knowledge and providing impartial advice to the federal government. Functioning in accordance with general policies determined by the Academy, the Council has become the principal operating agency of both the National Academy of Sciences and the National Academy of Engineering in providing services to the government, the public, and the scientific and engineering communities. The Council is administered jointly by both Academies and the Institute of Medicine. Dr. Bruce M. Alberts, President of the National Academy of Sciences, and Dr. William Wulf, President of the National Academy of Engineering, also serve as chairman and vice chairman, respectively, of the National Research Council.

The Center for Science, Mathematics, and Engineering Education (CSMEE) was established in 1995 to provide coordination of all the National Research Council's education activities and reform efforts for students at all levels, specifically those in kindergarten through twelfth grade, undergraduate institutions, school-to-work programs, and continuing education. The Center reports directly to the Governing Board of the National Research Council.

This study by CSMEE was conducted under a grant from the National Science Foundation to the National Academy of Sciences/National Research Council (DUE-9727710). Any opinions, findings, or recommendations expressed in this report are those of the participants in the workshop and the authors and do not necessarily reflect the views of the National Science Foundation.

Additional copies of this report are available from the National Academy Press, 2101 Constitution Avenue, NW, Lock Box 285, Washington, DC 20055. (800) 624-6242 or (202) 334-3313 (in the Washington Metropolitan Area)

Library of Congress Cataloging-in-Publication Data

Developing a digital national library for undergraduate science,
  mathematics, engineering, and technology education : report of a
  workshop / National Research Council, Center for Science,
  Mathematics, and Engineering Education, Computer Science and
  Telecommunications Board.
    p.   cm.
  Includes bibliographical references.
  ISBN 0-309-05977-1 (pbk.)
    1. Education libraries—United States—Congresses. 2. Scientific
libraries—United States—Congresses. 3. Science—Study and
teaching—United States—Computer network resources—Congresses.
4. Digital libraries—United States—Congresses. I. Center for
Science, Mathematics, and Engineering Education. II. National
Research Council (U.S.). Computer Science and Telecommunications
Board.
  Z675.P3D48 1998
  026.5—dc21   97-45304
                                           CIP

This report is also available online at http://www.nap.edu.

Printed in the United States of America.

DEVELOPING A DIGITAL NATIONAL LIBRARY FOR UNDERGRADUATE SCIENCE, MATHEMATICS, ENGINEERING, AND TECHNOLOGY EDUCATION

STEERING COMMITTEE

JACK M. WILSON, Rensselaer Polytechnic Institute, Chair
DENICE D. DENTON, University of Washington
HARVEY KEYNES, University of Minnesota
JAMES W. SERUM, Hewlett-Packard Company

Staff

JAY B. LABOV, Co-Study Director, Center for Science, Mathematics, and Engineering Education

HERBERT S. LIN, Co-Study Director, Computer Science and Telecommunications Board

NANCY L. DEVINO, Senior Staff Officer, Center for Science, Mathematics, and Engineering Education

GAIL E. PRITCHARD, Research Assistant, Center for Science, Mathematics, and Engineering Education

KATHLEEN JOHNSTON, Editorial Associate, Center for Science, Mathematics, and Engineering Education

TERRY K. HOLMER, Project Assistant, Center for Science, Mathematics, and Engineering Education

CATHERINE Y. BELL, Administrative Assistant, Center for Science, Mathematics, and Engineering Education

CENTER FOR SCIENCE, MATHEMATICS, AND ENGINEERING EDUCATION

TABLE OF CONTENTS

Developing a Digital National Library for Undergraduate Science, Mathematics, Engineering, and Technology Education

EXECUTIVE SUMMARY

A central role of the National Science Foundation (NSF) is to support the improvement of science, mathematics, engineering, and technology (SME&T) education for all students in the United States at all grade levels. In its quest to catalyze and sustain educational reform at the undergraduate level, the NSF issued a report in 1996 on the status of undergraduate SME&T education (National Science Foundation, 1996b). That report called for fundamental changes in the ways in which SME&T subjects are taught and urged the agency to sponsor the development of "a national electronic library for validating and disseminating successful educational practices" (National Science Foundation, 1996b, page 72) and to "provide specific problem training sessions for faculty across institutions, in topics such as how to do inquiry and collaborative learning in large 'lecture' classes, how to assess learning outcomes, and how to document learning gains at the departmental and institutional levels" (National Science Foundation, 1996b, page 72).

Digital libraries[1] are currently under construction for a number of scientific research communities with support from the NSF, the National Aeronautics and Space Administration (NASA), and the Department of Defense's Advanced Research Projects Agency (DARPA). The Library of Congress also is developing a digital library to disseminate its vast holdings more readily.

---

[1] Dr. Christine Borgman, UCLA, offered the following definition as determined by participants at the UCLA/NSF Workshop, "Social Aspects of Digital Libraries": "[Workshop participants] determined that digital libraries encompass two complementary ideas: 1. Digital libraries are a set of electronic resources and associated technical capabilities for creating, searching, and using information. In this sense they are an extension and enhancement of information storage and retrieval systems that manipulate digital data in any medium (text, images, sounds, static or dynamic images) and exist in distributed networks. The content of digital libraries includes data, metadata that describe various aspects of data (e.g., representation, creator, owner, reproduction rights), and metadata that consists of links or relationships to other data or metadata, whether internal or external to the digital library; and 2. Digital libraries are constructed—collected and organized— by a community of users, and their functional capabilities support the information needs and uses of that community. They are a component of communities in which individuals and groups interact with each other, using data, information, and knowledge resources and systems. In this sense they are an extension, enhancement, and integration of a variety of information institutions as physical places where resources are selected, collected, organized, preserved, and accessed in support of a user community. These information institutions include, among others, libraries, museums, archives, and schools, but digital libraries also extend and serve other community settings, including classrooms, offices, laboratories, homes, and public spaces." (Borgman et al., 1996)

This report is available on line at http://www.gslis.ucla.edu/DL/UCLA_DL_REPORT.html.

Given the potential of digital libraries to provide rapid access to large amounts of information and the research base on digital libraries that these other projects already had generated, the NSF's Division of Undergraduate Education asked the National Research Council's (NRC) Center for Science, Mathematics, and Engineering Education (CSMEE) to undertake a study that would 1) explore the feasibility of establishing a digital National Library for undergraduate SME&T education and 2) examine various challenges that would have to be overcome in order to build a library that is both educationally innovative and cost effective.

In collaboration with the NRC's Computer Science and Telecommunications Board (CSTB), CSMEE responded to NSF's request by forming a project steering committee consisting of representatives from the NRC's four postsecondary boards and committees (Mathematical Sciences Education Board, Board on Engineering Education, Committee on Undergraduate Science Education, and the Committee on Information Technology). The Steering Committee, in turn, commissioned ten "white papers" from individuals with expertise in SME&T education, technological aspects of digital libraries, library science, and economic and legal aspects of this rapidly evolving area of knowledge and research. These commissioned papers (revisions of which are reprinted in Appendix A of this report) served as the basis for plenary and break-out discussions at a workshop that was held at the National Academy of Sciences on August 7-8, 1997. Some 50 guests from academe, digital library initiatives, private laboratories, private foundations, research and teaching libraries, and the commercial publishing sector participated in this workshop.

ISSUES CONSIDERED

The issues that these papers and workshop participants considered are diverse and exceedingly complex. They include the following:

Curricular, Pedagogical, and User Issues
(e.g., Who is the potential user population? What types of materials should be included? What impact can be expected?)

Logistic and Technology Issues
(e.g., What kinds of editorial oversight are needed? What kinds of technology are currently available to build such a national library (NL)? How can a multi-year project like this adapt to new technologies that may emerge?)

Economic and Legal Issues
(e.g., How can we estimate or measure the costs and benefits of establishing an NL? What are the long-term financial implications? How could intellectual property, copyright, and "fair use" issues be resolved?)

At the workshop, Steering Committee Chair Jack Wilson also charged participants with trying to arrive at answers to the following cross-cutting questions:

Is an NL a good idea for improving undergraduate SME&T education?
Is an NL a better idea than other initiatives that might compete for the same funds?
If the NSF does commit to supporting the proposed NL, then what kinds of information and issues will it need to consider so that the project can be undertaken efficiently and cost effectively?

Accordingly, this report provides a detailed summary of the presentations at the workshop and a synthesis of the discussions that were generated there. The report also identifies those issues on which workshop participants were able to reach substantial agreement and those which remained unresolved by the conclusion of the meeting. The report presents the conclusions of members of the Steering Committee who attended the workshop and provides a number of recommendations to the NSF from the entire Steering Committee about both the value and feasibility of proceeding with this project.

OVERVIEW OF CONCLUSIONS
The conclusions of the workshop are organized here by major issues addressed.

Users and Needs
These issues pervaded the entire workshop. A broad agreement developed that faculty engaged in SME&T education would be included among the primary users targeted by an NL. Workshop participants also concurred that the central focus of an NL should be to improve and enhance learning of SME&T.

Nevertheless, there was considerable divergence of opinion about the extent to which an NL also should provide learning resources directly to undergraduate students and possibly other users (e.g., advanced high school students, adults engaged in distance learning through a university program, lifelong learners seeking information on specific topics, or those wishing to increase their understanding and appreciation of SME&T in general). There also was a divergence of opinion about how often these "student users" would access an NL.

Most workshop participants agreed that the establishment of an NL could potentially be a useful tool for improving undergraduate SME&T education. However, some workshop participants noted that a large part of the SME&T teaching community has not yet felt a sense of urgency about the need for reform. Indeed, for the most part, participants believed that the workshop discussions had not made a convincing case that an NL was an essential component of SME&T education reform. However, some workshop participants and commissioned papers pointed out that, in addition to providing high-quality materials for improving learning of SME&T, an NSF-sponsored initiative to support an NL could have an important impact on undergraduate SME&T education by underscoring and showcasing the importance of educational reform in highly tangible ways. On the other hand, funds used to support an NL would then not be available to support other educational initiatives, and there is no current analysis available that indicates the relative efficacy of an NL compared to alternatives.

Because only a few science and mathematics teaching faculty and undergraduate students were present at the workshop (a list of workshop participants and their institutional affiliations is provided in Appendix C; biographical sketches of workshop participants are in Appendix D), it is not clear to what extent the proposed NL actually would be utilized by faculty to improve their teaching of SME&T courses or by other stakeholders of a larger NL. Input and advice from potential users also will be critical for designing and developing an NL's content.

Content

There was considerable discussion about what kinds of information the proposed NL should contain. Workshop participants agreed that an NL could offer a large variety of materials, such as digitized text (e.g., from professional journals, course syllabi, student works-in-progress, reports about the outcomes and evaluation of SME&T education projects that have been funded by NSF and other grantmaking agencies), videos and still images, instructional software and simulations, and anything else of relevance that could be stored digitally. However, there was little agreement about which classes of these materials an NL should make available, either immediately or in the future. In part, these disagreements were related to the issue of who the primary users of an NL will be. Thus, defining the intended audience for any NL initiative will aid in making decisions about its content. Discussion focused on several important issues related to content:

1. Should an NL commission and store discipline-based source content or serve primarily as a cataloging resource that electronically "points" users to information stored on other computers and hard copy? A broad agreement developed that, at a minimum, an NL should contain pointers to useful materials. Pointers are much less expensive to create and maintain than stored source content, more easily allow for contributions from a wider spectrum of interests and organizations in the SME&T community, and minimize current legal challenges related to intellectual property rights, copyright law, and licensing agreements. However, an NL could face several important constraints if it were to rely exclusively on the use of pointers rather than commissioning and storing at least some materials. Until consistently reliable software is available to enable an NL's registry to update the addresses of materials stored elsewhere on the Internet, tracking the location of materials will be problematic. An NL's ability to catalyze development of or to exert quality control over materials specifically suited to this medium could be very limited. Also, an NL's holdings should reach a "critical mass" of quality materials that will attract wide usership; whether the quality and quantity of materials currently on the Internet is sufficient to reach this "critical mass" in different subject areas must be determined.

2. Should an NL simply make materials available (either directly or by pointing to other Web sites), such as traditional libraries do now, or allow users to add materials to a library? Contributed materials might include such items as new teaching tools and modules or annotations (e.g., reviews, comments by users, supplemental information) about materials already available from an NL.

3. Who should exert editorial oversight of the proposed NL's contents? What types of standards should be estab-

lished for accepting materials for an NL? Minimum standards and strategies for including materials and the level of editorial oversight would likely be very different if an NL were simply to point to other resources rather than storing and disseminating them directly to users. Different standards also would have to be developed for accepting materials that have undergone peer review vs. materials that have not been subjected to such scrutiny (e.g., course syllabi, courseware applications, annotations and discussions about other materials included in the proposed NL). The workshop participants broadly agreed that some mechanism for distinguishing formally reviewed from unreviewed material would be necessary, both from the standpoint of the user and for the credibility of the proposed NL itself.

4. *Who should create content for an NL?* Here there was fairly broad agreement that creators could include faculty, publishers, professional societies, and students. The issue of who creates content for an NL also relates to the issue of "critical mass." If the information in an NL is not sufficient in quantity or quality, user disappointment followed by disuse are likely consequences. All of these issues have implications for what materials are placed into an NL and how long they are archived.[2]

5. *What kinds of tools will be needed to facilitate browsing and searching of an NL by users?* Experience with currently available search engines for the Internet clearly indicates that simple keyword searches, though sometimes useful, are inadequate when searching through large volumes of information. Development of interactive, "intelligent" tools that facilitate searching for materials, especially those that have been designed to exploit an NL's specific electronic capabilities, should be an important component in any design of an NL for undergraduate SME&T education.

6. *Is the proposed NL a library?* Most workshop participants agreed that an NL for undergraduate SME&T education certainly would embrace many of the characteristics of traditional libraries. However, this resource also could incorporate many other features not found in traditional libraries, such as the capacity for the NL's users to add materials and to work interactively with and upgrade materials already in the NL. Thus, workshop

---

[2]In this report, "to archive" and/or "to serve as an archival function" mean to preserve in readable form over the long term any material determined to have enduring value. "To store" and "to preserve" are used in this report in a technological sense, as in to save copies offline of material no longer in active use but possibly desirable at some future date.

participants suggested, and the Steering Committee concurs, that a better set of descriptors be devised to reflect more accurately this resource's vision and objectives and to convey better to users how it might be utilized.

Economic and Legal Issues

In addition to focusing on the potential value or desirability of an NL for undergraduate SME&T education, the workshop also addressed a number of economic and legal issues. These topics were considered by workshop participants primarily in the context of the implementation and deployment of this resource. The following issues were raised.

1. Economic issues: While government agencies and private foundations might provide key start-up funding for an NL, workshop participants agreed that this resource would eventually need to become financially self-sustaining. However, there was no general agreement about how best to address questions of economic viability and sustainability.

2. Legal issues: Workshop participants identified a number of legal issues that would need to be solved before the proposed NL could become operational. These include

- *Intellectual Property (IP).* IP issues in the context of an NL are similar to those that any online provider of content faces. However, inclusion of some types of material (e.g., course notes) may not be as problematic as other materials because remuneration to the authors or developers is not necessarily involved.
- *Liability.* NL materials that involve some potential risk to users (e.g., instructions for performing undergraduate laboratory exercises) may involve liability for those responsible for administering the proposed NL initiative or for the authors and creators of materials to whom an NL points.
- *Privacy.* To the extent that students use materials or information found in an NL (e.g., an online diagnostic test), well-meaning faculty may be interested in the extent and nature of such usage. Obtaining such information might impinge on students' expectations for privacy.

Workshop participants concluded that these issues could not be solved independently for the proposed NL. Rather, a regime of general law and practice will evolve as online publishing and dissemination of information becomes more extensive. An NL for undergraduate SME&T education will have to be flexible enough to accommodate a wide range of possible legal regimes and challenges.

3. Technology issues: Workshop participants discussed many technology-related issues, including

- *The need for an NL to be oriented to satisfying user needs rather than to being a vehicle for advancing the creation of technology or research about digital libraries.* Any technologies employed by an NL also should be developed and deployed to accommodate the needs of users. Associated with this requirement, some workshop participants questioned the conventional wisdom of making the proposed NL available exclusively via the Internet. Because some institutions of higher education in the United States and other parts of the world do not now enjoy access to the Internet and others have only limited access through data lines that would require too much time for the downloading of large applications or data sets, important issues of equity and access must be considered carefully and addressed. Other formats, such as CD-ROM sets, might be considered as components of vehicles for disseminating information from any NL initiative (although interactivity could be compromised compared to access to the Internet). Workshop participants also noted that the development of Internet II could possibly restrict access to an NL only through selected colleges and universities.[3,4] Again, equity of access

---

[3]President William Clinton's announced goals for the "Next Generation" Internet initiative are as follows: 1. Connect universities and national labs with high-speed networks that are 100 to 1,000 times faster than today's Internet. These networks will eventually be able to transmit the contents of the entire Encyclopedia Britannica in under a second; 2. Promote experimentation with the next generation of networking technologies. For example, technologies are emerging that could dramatically increase the capabilities of the Internet to handle real-time services, such as high-quality videoconferencing; and 3. Demonstrate new applications that meet important national goals and missions. Higher speed, more advanced networks will enable a new generation of applications that support scientific research, national security, distance education, environmental monitoring, and health care. (Smith and Weingarten, 1997)

[4]A reviewer of this report, who must remain anonymous under the Report Review Guidelines of the National Research Council, wrote to disagree with the workshop discussion regarding lack of wide accessibility to Internet II: This person indicated that his institution has had access to the Very Broadband Network Service (VBNS), the precursor of Internet II, for some time. The institution has a switch that routes outgoing messages to the VBNS or the Commodity Internet (Internet I), depending on the destination. No one on the Commodity Internet has had problems reaching this reviewer or others at this university. The reviewer acknowledged that there may be issues of performance between Internet I and II, particularly if streaming audio or video applications are developed, but this reviewer does not believe that access will be an issue.

---

should be an important consideration in any discussions of delivery systems for this NL.

- *An NL for undergraduate SME&T education should employ technologies that are adaptive, flexible, and responsive to unforeseen user needs and problems.* New applications and modules should be designed to operate with software that is widely available for other applications (e.g., commonly used spreadsheets). This design would reduce the time required for users to learn how to work with such materials. An NL initiative also will need to deal with content prepared to run on older computers and software platforms that may be incompatible with newer hardware and software platforms.

- *Technology employed in the proposed NL should be developed with advice and oversight from the professional communities who are most knowledgeable about how people both organize and use information: librarians and social and behavioral scientists.* Without these informed perspectives, an NL is not likely to optimize opportunities for teaching and learning.

STEERING COMMITTEE RECOMMENDATIONS

Workshop participants generally agreed that the idea of an NL for SME&T education was sufficiently promising that the NSF should pursue it further, and the Steering Committee concurs. Although workshop participants did not agree on specific next steps, the Steering Committee makes the following recommendations based on information in the commissioned papers and presentations and discussions at the workshop to guide the NSF's planning for an NL initiative and its issuance of one or more request for proposals (RFPs). The Steering Committee recommends that these steps be acted upon sequentially. The recommendations that are summarized below parallel the discussion in the "Synthesis and Conclusions" sections of the report, and readers should consult that section for additional details. The following text is cross-referenced to relevant text in that section.

1. Clarify the potential customers of an NL for undergraduate SME&T education (page 47)

1.1 Because workshop participants were unable to delineate the stakeholders or to specify the content for this proposed NL, the NSF should do so. The level of funding that the agency can devote to this project may dictate the breadth of the proposed NL's users, and that, in turn, may help with content decisions. However, the Steering Committee recommends that, *prior to making final decisions about this issue*, the NSF should make a concerted effort to bring together in a series of focus groups representatives from *all* communities that might be an NL's likely users and service providers. Focus groups should be small and should be structured to encourage participants to discuss freely 1) their requirements for resources and tools that would help them improve teaching and learning of undergraduate SME&T, and 2) the ways in which the digital National Library could address those requirements. At a minimum, participants in these focus groups should include

- *College and university SME&T faculty from all types of post-secondary institutions*, including two-year colleges, undergraduate liberal arts colleges, predominantly undergraduate comprehensive universities, and research universities.
- *College and university SME&T faculty at different stages of their academic careers.*
- *College and university faculty involved with research and practice in science and mathematics education, including the preparation of future K-12 teachers.*
- *SME&T faculty from middle- and high-schools across the United States.*
- *Undergraduate students* from different types of colleges and universities. This group should include both "traditional" and "non-traditional" students.
- *Graduate and postdoctoral students* who are likely to enter careers in academe also should be consulted since they will define future needs of faculty.
- *Librarians.*
- *Social and behavioral scientists* with expertise in organizational constructs and in the ways in which people learn new information.
- *Computer and information system specialists* with specific experience with digital libraries.
- *Directors of college and university information technology services.*
- *Representatives from the commercial publishing sector.*
- *Representatives from professional SME&T societies.*
- *Representatives from the private non-profit sector,* such as foundations.

1.2 The Steering Committee suggests that two different types of focus group meetings be held. Some focus groups should concentrate on receiving input from single communities, especially SME&T faculty and students. Others should involve people from many or all of the aforementioned sectors in crosscutting sessions, with the primary objectives of having convenors listen and respond to the ideas and expressed needs of potential users.

1.3 The Steering Committee recommends that NSF also might employ the services of one or more professional organizations to organize these focus groups, to facilitate discussions within the groups and to prepare an independent assessment of user needs and desires based on the group discussions.

2. Articulate priorities for content, technological considerations, and economic and legal models before committing to the establishment of an NL (page 48)

The Steering Committee can offer no specific recommendations about whether the proposed NL should commission the creation and storage of materials vs. developing a sophisticated system of pointers to materials that reside and are maintained elsewhere. Differences in cost between the two systems, evolving legal precedents with respect to copyright and fair use of materials, and the emergence of new technologies that may overcome some of the limitations of pointing to information stored elsewhere all must be factored into the final structure of an NL. Moreover, these parameters are likely to change during the development phase of the project. Ongoing advice from appropriate experts in all of these fields is warranted if the project proceeds.

2.1 The Steering Committee recommends that the proposed NL be viewed primarily as a resource for improving and inspiring *learning* of undergraduate SME&T rather than merely as a means to promote more effective *teaching* of these subjects. If an NL is to be a central component of current efforts to reform and improve undergraduate SME&T education, it must offer more than teaching tools alone. The NSF should appoint a Board of Overseers consisting of acknowledged experts in SME&T education, library sciences, and digital libraries that is charged to work with a broad spectrum of intended users and the other stakeholders *before* decisions are made about what kinds of materials should be placed into the proposed NL. If an NL initiative cannot afford to support all areas of SME&T, then the Board should decide on the initial areas of focus and look to expand coverage as the project develops.

2.2 Steering Committee members also agree with many workshop participants and recommend that an NL should strive to focus on collecting or pointing to materials that either are inaccessible through other media formats or are so innovative that they are unlikely to be commercially available or viable in the short-term. Because a "critical mass" of materials is vitally important to the success of an NL, the acquisition of such innovative new materials will likely need to be balanced with more traditional materials, at least initially.

2.3 The Steering Committee recommends that the NSF emphasize involvement by professional SME&T societies in developing content that could be appropriate for an NL. Many of these organizations already have produced materials that might be incorporated into an NL at little or no cost. By promoting the development of these kinds of teaching and learning tools and by officially recognizing their members who do so, professional societies could become key catalysts in changing the culture of higher education to embrace as legitimate scholarly activities the promotion and evaluation of teaching and the promotion of effective learning by students.

2.4 The Steering Committee recommends that an NL should provide information about and access to projects in undergraduate SME&T education that the NSF and other agencies have supported financially.

2.5 The Steering Committee recommends that the NSF also seek a new, more encompassing descriptor for this project. Workshop participants recognized, and the Steering Committee concurs, that "Digital National Library" or "National Library"—the terms that have been most commonly used to describe this entity—may be more confusing than enlightening to anyone who envisions the potential stakeholders in this project and the services it may provide. Any NL initiative is likely to transcend the functions of many conventional libraries. A more appropriate descriptor might help to focus the higher education community on the need for such a resource and its importance.

3. Develop and issue one or more RFPs to establish an NL for undergraduate SME&T education

As the NSF receives additional input from stakeholders about the goals of and need for an NL (via Recommendations 1 and 2), the scope and potential cost of the project should become clearer. During the workshop, Steering Committee Chair Jack Wilson charged participants with trying to arrive at answers to the following major crosscutting questions: 1) Is an NL a good idea for improving undergraduate SME&T education and 2) Is an NL a better idea than other initiatives that might compete for the same funds? *If the NSF is convinced on the basis of its explorations that it can answer these questions in the affirmative, then the question of how to implement this project should become the central focus.* Options for proceeding at that point would include

Option 1:   Undertaking a single, large initiative that would result in an operational NL within several years.

Option 2:   Undertaking several smaller initiatives for shorter periods of time (12-24 months). These initiatives might be competitive and operate independently of each other or they might be components of some larger cooperative agreement. These various models for establishing an NL could then be evaluated against each other, with a final coordination of best practices that might lead to a single, integrated project.

3.1   Given the tremendous complexity of this project and the number of communities that must be directly involved if it is to have any chance for success, the Steering Committee recommends that NSF consider adopting *Option 2*. Steering Committee members envision that the smaller initiatives suggested in *Option* 2 might be incorporated into a program similar to those that the NSF's Division of Undergraduate Education has sponsored in recent years to change the ways in which chemistry and calculus are taught. Optimally, this new initiative would incorporate many similar components, including those delineated in Recommendations 3.2 and 3.3 below.

3.2   The Steering Committee recommends that the NSF, in following through with Recommendation 3.1, should develop an RFP articulating the need for and issues involving the establishment of an NL as outlined in this report. The RFP would encourage diverse groups of stakeholders to focus on some subset of the issues. Collaboration among stakeholders and interdisciplinary approaches to address the questions posed here would be encouraged. Preproposals could be sought, with funds then awarded to successful groups to encourage them to develop full proposals.

Depending on the funds available, the NSF might then award larger contracts to one or more groups to tackle specific issues or sets of issues. Each of these final awardees would be expected to inform each other of their progress and problems through routine communications, reports, and through meetings of teams convened on a regular basis (at least annually).

3.3 Because the central concern of workshop participants was to define the users of and the need for an NL for undergraduate SME&T education, the Steering Committee recommends that RFPs for preproposals not be formulated until the NSF sponsors the focus groups described above. Feedback and evaluation of information from these groups of users and providers could then serve as the basis for constructing RFPs that would help eventual awardees to address specifically the established needs and requirements of potential NL users.

INTRODUCTION

BACKGROUND

One of the key missions of the National Science Foundation (NSF)'s Directorate for Education and Human Resources is the improvement of undergraduate science, mathematics, engineering, and technology (SME&T) education. Through its Division of Undergraduate Education, the NSF has supported the development of innovative SME&T curricula, research on the processes by which students learn about SME&T, professional development in teaching and pedagogy for both university faculty and future teachers of grades K-12 in the SME&T disciplines, and the upgrading and improvement of undergraduate SME&T laboratories.

Despite efforts by individuals and calls for improvement from prestigious national organizations (e.g., Clinton and Gore, 1994; National Research Council, 1991, 1995, 1996a; National Science Foundation, 1992, 1996b; Project Kaleidoscope, 1991, 1997), progress in the reform and improvement of undergraduate SME&T education often has been agonizingly slow. Among the many reasons the improvement of SME&T education has not progressed more rapidly are a reward and incentive system that often emphasizes research productivity over excellence in teaching, a lack of attention during postbaccalaureate and postdoctoral training to effective approaches in teaching and learning, changing demographics and levels of pre-college preparation in SME&T among undergraduate student populations, and shrinking institutional budgets.

During the past three decades, the NSF and other public and private sources have provided hundreds of millions of dollars to support the development of classroom and laboratory programs and materials that could, if widely disseminated and adopted, help change how undergraduates in the United States learn about SME&T. However, many college and university faculty are either unaware of these resources, have difficulty accessing them, or resist their use. As a result, too many faculty continue to spend considerable time and effort "reinventing" courses, course materials, and laboratory programs that are already available to them and could be adapted to their own teaching situations.

"[T]he most crucial task now facing the NSF and other funders is the conversion of innovation to broad and sweeping change. We know a good deal about what works well for SME&T students. It will require deep commitment to integrate the best of these innovations into the ongoing life of undergraduate SME&T education, thereby effecting the comprehensive educational change that is needed."

JOAN GIRGUS (NATIONAL SCIENCE FOUNDATION, 1996b, P. 43)

Today, an individual faculty member who is interested in changing the way he or she teaches SME&T has no central "single point of contact" to begin a search for useful ideas. Journals oriented toward education in the various SME&T disciplines are a place to start but are generally found *in toto* only in print and therefore are time consuming to search. Because many such resources are published by disciplinary professional societies, they may not emphasize interdisciplinary approaches to teaching and learning that are being recommended by reformers of undergraduate SME&T education. Moreover, journal articles usually do not contain discussions of techniques and materials that have *not* worked in authors' classrooms and laboratories (which would allow readers either to avoid repeating these activities and procedures or to modify them). Many more innovations are never disseminated or published.

Electronic searching may rapidly yield additional information not found in printed literature or in other, less traditional sources. However, many faculty are not well versed in using electronic tools for searching, and currently available search engines may not be sophisticated enough to narrow a search to information that is truly useful to educators. In addition, search engines that provide hundreds or thousands of "hits" on a topic can be more discouraging than helpful. As a result, many individual educators and institutions that support their efforts to improve undergraduate SME&T education believe that reform efforts need an easily accessible and searchable source of courses, laboratories, and other programs that have been used successfully in a variety of educational settings, as well as objectively evaluated for their effectiveness. A recent report recommended that NSF should

> Provide additional leadership for change in undergraduate SME&T education, beyond program funding, specifically:
>
> 1. Together with other major players (such as the NRC, AAAS, ERIC, and the National Library of Medicine), explore the establishment of a national electronic system for validating and disseminating successful educational practices …
>
> 3. Provide specific problem-solving training sessions for faculty across institutions, in topics such as how to do inquiry and collaborative learning in large "lecture" classes, how to assess learning outcomes, and how to document learning gains at the departmental and institutional levels.

NATIONAL SCIENCE FOUNDATION, 1996b, P. 72

The development of a digital National Library (NL) may be one approach to disseminating and evaluating such information. Digital libraries are large-scale collections of information where materials are stored or referred to in electronic format and delivered to users through dedicated lines or, increasingly, over the Internet.[1] Within the past

decade, the quantity and variety of digital information sources have grown rapidly. Ongoing innovations in information technologies and increased support by the public and private sectors for providing rapid access to large amounts of information in virtually all areas of knowledge have led to the development of a wide range of autonomous, often unconnected and uncoordinated digital collections and services by businesses, organizations, and educational institutions (Bishop, 1995). These digital databases and other electronic resources serve as repositories for all types of information that increasingly can be searched both within and across collections (Schatz and Chen, 1996).

"Innovations and successes in education need to spread with the speed and efficiency of new research results."

NATIONAL RESEARCH COUNCIL, 1996a, P. 6

Ample evidence now exists to indicate that the day-to-day operation of a business or practice of a scientific field can be transformed through the use of electronically mediated communications—most notably electronic mail and applications of the World Wide Web. Such communications enable those actively engaged in business or academic disciplines to receive more information more rapidly

---

[1] Dr. Christine Borgman, UCLA, offered the following definition as determined by participants at the UCLA/NSF Workshop, "Social Aspects of Digital Libraries": "[Workshop participants] determined that digital libraries encompass two complementary ideas: 1. Digital libraries are a set of electronic resources and associated technical capabilities for creating, searching, and using information. In this sense they are an extension and enhancement of information storage and retrieval systems that manipulate digital data in any medium (text, images, sounds, static or dynamic images) and exist in distrib-

uted networks. The content of digital libraries includes data, metadata that describe various aspects of data (e.g., representation, creator, owner, reproduction rights), and metadata that consists of links or relationships to other data or metadata, whether internal or external to the digital library; and 2. Digital libraries are constructed—collected and organized—by a community of users, and their functional capabilities support the information needs and uses of that community. They are a component of communities in which individuals and groups interact with each other, using data, information, and knowledge resources and systems. In this sense they are an extension, enhancement, and integration of a variety of information institutions as physical places where resources are selected, collected, organized, preserved, and accessed in support of a user community. These information institutions include, among others, libraries, museums, archives, and schools, but digital libraries also extend and serve other community settings, including classrooms, offices, laboratories, homes, and public spaces." (Borgman et al., 1996)

This report is available on line at http://www.gslis.ucla.edu/DL/UCLA_DL_REPORT.html.

than ever before. Even with relatively unsophisticated search engines, finding electronic information online has become an important part of the daily routine of business people, scientists, and engineers.

By accelerating the dissemination of research findings, digital libraries are having a major impact in fields such as physics and computer science. The benefits of such instantaneously available sources of information are apparent to the scientific and engineering research communities and to the agencies that support them. In response, the NSF, the Department of Defense Advanced Research Projects Agency (DARPA), and the National Aeronautics and Space Administration (NASA) are developing a major joint research initiative in digital libraries (the Digital Library Initiative). This initiative currently consists of projects at six universities and more than 75 partner organizations whose primary focus is to advance research on issues associated with constructing a digital national library for research communities (National Science Foundation, 1997).[2] Research from these initiatives has begun to point the way to how to store, manage, and retrieve large quantities of highly heterogeneous information (e.g., text, graphics, animations, software, etc.). These new tools and techniques go far beyond the simple subject or keyword searches on which today's Internet search engines are based.

Digital libraries also might benefit the scientific, mathematics, and engineering communities that are engaged in higher education. With the computerization of college and university campuses across the United States and the concurrent increase in access to the World Wide Web, postsecondary SME&T faculty and students are increasingly likely to need, appreciate, and use high-quality material made available to them over the Internet (National Research Council, 1994; Resmer, 1997). In the past five years alone, the Internet has provided tools and challenges in instructional methods, curriculum development, and research unparalleled in any comparable historical period in the United States (Daniel, 1996; Laurillard, 1993). Indeed, information technology has the potential to restructure fundamentally methods and processes of teaching and learning both in- and outside of the school and uni-

versity environments (e.g., Panel on Educational Technology, 1997).

Many electronic databases currently exist for both the K-12 and undergraduate SME&T communities (e.g., ERIC, sponsored by the U.S. Department of Education; NASA's Web sites; databases and other resources available from the American Association for the Advancement of Science, National Geographic Society, National Science Teachers Association, Project Kaleidoscope, Howard Hughes Medical Institute, the NRC's Committee on Undergraduate Science Education, GenenTech, and numerous professional scientific, mathematics, and engineering societies). These databases are operated and maintained independently of each other, updated at varying intervals, and directed toward different user audiences. Because sponsoring organizations decide which materials they will make available at their sites, the type and quality of information can vary considerably. The potential for these databases and emerging digital libraries in various research communities to serve as prototypes or models for a national repository of information for the undergraduate SME&T communities warrants additional discussion and consideration.

PROCESS

With such history and promising research results from other realms in hand, it is not surprising that the NSF might look to these experiences and experiments to address a fundamental reality of much of undergraduate SME&T education: most innovation undertaken by institutions and individual faculty members in SME&T education cannot readily build on the efforts of others.

The undergraduate SME&T education community has long articulated the need for a national resource that would provide ready access to a comprehensive and dynamic collection of high-quality educational materials. In response, the NSF has considered soliciting proposals to design, construct, and administer a National Library for Undergraduate Science, Mathematics, Engineering, and Technology Education as an enterprise that eventually would be self-sustaining. A broad vision for what such a library for undergraduate SME&T education might include was articulated in a conceptual plan envisioned by the National Science Foundation:

---

[2]Additional information on the Digital Library Initiative is available on line at http://dli.grainger.uiuc.edu/national.htm.

"The National Library will utilize advanced information technologies to provide ready access to and use of a large and distributed resource of current and future educational products and materials for undergraduate science, mathematics, engineering, and technology (SME&T) education. In addition to high quality learning and teaching resources supported by a solid base of research, these materials would include assessment and evaluation instruments and results that would inform current and future practice.

"The Library will achieve this vision by developing robust procedures and protocols to: 1) "capture" best educational practices and materials; 2) review and validate materials to ensure that the highest standards are maintained; 3) provide ready identification and retrieval of materials and information about materials through effective indexing and linking; and 4) offer a dynamic and interactive environment that will encourage broad participation in educational initiatives. It is expected that the National Library of Undergraduate Science Education will serve the nation as the premier provider of effective educational resources."

H. RICHTOL, NATIONAL SCIENCE FOUNDATION
(PERSONAL COMMUNICATION)

Motivated by this vision, the NSF's Division of Undergraduate Education asked the National Research Council (NRC) to examine various issues associated with the establishment of a digital National Library (NL) to support undergraduate SME&T education. In response, under the auspices of the NRC's Center for Science, Mathematics, and Engineering Education (CSMEE) and the Computer Science and Telecommunications Board (CSTB), the NRC established a steering committee to oversee this project. The Steering Committee consisted of representatives from each of the NRC's committees and boards that deal with some aspect of postsecondary SME&T education (Committee on Undergraduate Science Education, Mathematical Sciences Education Board, Board on Engineering Education, and the Committee on Information Technology). The Steering Committee commissioned a series of papers from acknowledged experts in SME&T education, digital library and electronic information technologies, and economic and legal

aspects of digitizing and posting information (e.g., intellectual property rights, copyright law).

The commissioned papers, revisions of which are reprinted in this report as Appendix A, served as the basis for discussion at the workshop that was held August 7-8, 1997, in Washington, D.C. at the National Academy of Sciences. (See Appendix B for the Workshop Agenda.) Fifty-four invited participants and more than twenty observers from the Division of Undergraduate Education and other Directorates of the NSF attended this workshop.[3] As an open meeting, the workshop was also attended by several members of the press and other interested parties. (Names and institutional affiliations of invited participants, steering committee members, and NSF and other observers who attended the workshop are listed in Appendix C. Biographical sketches of Steering Committee members and invited participants are provided in Appendix D.)

PROJECT FOCI

Given the potential cost of establishing a digital National Library for undergraduate SME&T education and the many issues associated with doing so, the workshop organizers attempted to provide focus to the commissioned papers and to workshop discussions by providing authors and workshop participants with the following questions:

Curricular, Pedagogical, and User Issues

- Who and how large is the potential user populations? What is the evidence that faculty and students would utilize this resource?
- What impact can be expected from a digital National Library (NL) for improving undergraduate science, mathematics, engineering and technology (SME&T) education?
- What types of materials should be included?
- What other kinds of support would users need to integrate materials from a library into their courses and curricula and to use them effectively and wisely?

---

[3]NSF staff were present at all plenary and break-out sessions. They did not participate in discussions but did offer background information and answered specific questions that were raised by participants or facilitators.

- How might decisions about the scope and nature of the content of curricular and pedagogic materials for inclusion in the proposed NL be made? Who should be involved in making such decisions?
- How can an NL respond to changes in curriculum and pedagogy? Should materials be removed from the proposed NL as curriculum and pedagogy evolve? Who should make these decisions?

Logistic and Technology Issues

- What kinds of editorial oversight are needed to build, maintain, and expand an NL?
- What kinds of technology are currently available to construct and store information in an NL?
- Would information be stored in centralized computers or dispersed at many sites? How would architecture affect search and delivery of stored materials?
- How can a multiyear project like this predict, adapt to, and take advantage of new technology that may emerge while an NL is being built? How can it continue to evolve over time as new generations of hardware and software take the place of earlier tools in use?

Economic and Legal Issues

- How can we estimate or measure the costs and benefits of establishing an NL for undergraduate SME&T education?
- Are there alternative or complementary approaches for improving undergraduate SME&T education with the resources that would have to be committed to an NL?
- How much would it cost to maintain and regularly upgrade an NL? How much money should be budgeted to purchase new hardware and software to run the proposed NL as information technology advances in the future? What are the long-term financial implications for hardware and software to support advances both in technology and pedagogy?
- Could an NL eventually become financially self-sufficient?
- Who might take over the costs if the government does not continue its support?

ORGANIZATION OF THE PROJECT

Organization of Commissioned Papers and Workshop Discussions

Authors of commissioned papers were asked to focus their comments as well as their questions and talking points on one of the three major topics outlined above as project foci. Some authors concentrated their efforts on delineating the issues in one major topic, and some discussed additional topics. Commissioned papers were distributed to registered participants a week before the workshop. Following the workshop, authors were given the opportunity to revise their papers which are reprinted in Appendix A of this report.

The workshop agenda of plenary and break-out sessions allowed participants first to consider and articulate the user, pedagogical, technical, economic, and legal issues that the NSF would need to consider should the agency decide to pursue the establishment of an NL for SME&T education. With the discussion from Day 1 as background, participants then proceeded on Day 2 to address *whether* the NSF should move forward with this project, given the large amounts of money that would be required and the other ways in which these funds might be spent by the Division of Undergraduate Education to improve undergraduate SME&T education.

When registering for the workshop, participants were asked to prioritize their preferences for participation in the workshop's two days of break-out sessions. Each session was based on one of the three foci articulated earlier. Because most participants have expertise in more than one of these major areas, they were assigned to attend a break-out session dealing with their second choice topic on the first day and their first choice topic during the second day of the workshop. To allow for continuity of discussions between the first and second days, the same facilitators moderated the same break-out sessions both days. Reports from the break-out groups are summarized in the body of this report.

ORGANIZATION OF THE REPORT

This report is based largely, but not exclusively, on the papers commissioned for the workshop and on the discussions and conclusions that emerged from the workshop itself. The commissioned papers as revised by authors following the workshop are reprinted intact in Appendix A, so the body of this report does not summarize them systematically. However, authors of and topics in commissioned papers occasionally were the focus of discussion during the workshop and so appear in that context. Other sources of information include published literature that was made available by participants during the workshop, additional feedback and comments from workshop participants after the workshop, and the other references that are cited herein.

Participants in this workshop were charged with examining a broad spectrum of issues, and many perspectives were expected. To provide readers of this report with the breadth and richness of those perspectives and insights, first a detailed overview and synopsis is provided of major themes from presentations by plenary speakers, from discussions that followed plenary presentations and reports from break-out sessions, and from general discussions throughout the workshop. The workshop's major themes are then organized and synthesized into critical issues and questions concerning 1) Curricular, Pedagogical, and User Issues; 2) Logistic and Technology Issues; and 3) Economic and Legal Issues. Finally, conclusions from the workshop and recommendations from the Steering Committee based on all the information at hand are provided.

References to specific programs and initiatives that were discussed by workshop participants are included throughout this report. These programs are cited for information purposes only and do not imply endorsement by the National Research Council.

SUMMARY OF THE WORKSHOP

INTRODUCTORY REMARKS

Using the themes described in the project foci section of this report, Jack Wilson, Chair of the Steering Committee, opened the workshop on August 7, 1997, by asking participants to be able to answer the following major crosscutting questions by the end of the workshop:

Is an NL a good idea for improving undergraduate SME&T education?

Is the proposed NL a better idea than other initiatives that might compete for the same funds?

If the NSF does commit to supporting an NL, what kinds of information and issues will it need to consider so the project can be undertaken efficiently and cost effectively?

Hal Richtol, Director of the Laboratory and Technology Development Section of NSF's Division of Undergraduate Education and Program Officer for an NL initiative, spoke next. He noted that there have been many important innovations in SME&T education during the past 30 years. These innovations have led to a broad spectrum of educational materials and methodologies for use by both faculty and students and an expanded research base to support local and national efforts to improve teaching and learning. Richtol noted that while much of this progress has been catalyzed by sponsoring agencies (both public and private), a great deal of progress also has been the result of dedicated individual faculty members working without formal support to improve their courses and programs, and some of their work goes unrecorded. Given that many innovations are never disseminated, Richtol said that the NSF felt that there would be great value in developing an electronic system that could serve both as a central repository for existing materials and as a reliable gateway to other collections of materials and ideas. This system also might serve as a forum for both faculty and students for the submission of project materials or information for formal review and evaluation—a venue for the systematic generation and preservation of informed discussion and review

of educational material and a quality control agent for what is posted to the system. Faculty might then sample from these resources to determine suitability for their programs and institutions, communicate their findings to broader audiences, and participate in far-reaching discussions, current thinking, and debate about undergraduate SME&T education. This system also could prove very useful both to the K-12 educational community and to the concerns of business and industry as they work with the undergraduate sector to address such issues as school-to-work transitions, partnerships between these communities, and communicating the value of undergraduate SME&T education to the public at large.

Richtol reiterated Wilson's message that the NSF needs advice from workshop participants about whether or not to proceed with the concept of an NL as an educational infrastructure for faculty, students, and the public. If the NSF does proceed with this project, how should it be developed and by whom? What kind of entity would administer and manage an NL so that it might eventually become a self-sustaining enterprise? Richtol emphasized that consideration of these complex issues will go well beyond this workshop and any developmental efforts that might occur over the next year, five years, or during the next decade.

Plenary Sessions, Day 1

Following introductory remarks, the remainder of the morning of Day 1 was devoted to formal remarks by eight workshop participants. The speakers had been selected by the Steering Committee and NRC staff to provide a variety of perspectives. Some speakers had written commissioned papers; others had not.

These formal remarks were offered in two plenary sessions of four speakers each. Each speaker answered questions following her/his presentation. General discussion ensued after each plenary session.[4]

---

[4]The number of participants who wanted to offer comments following the first set of plenary speakers exceeded the time available for discussion. Thus, some comments intended for the first session

Session I: Presentations
The first session presentations were given by:

William Arms, Corporation for National Research Initiatives

Miriam Masullo, T.J. Watson Research Center, IBM Research Center

Michael Raugh, Interconnect Technologies Corporation

Lee Zia, Department of Mathematics, University of New Hampshire

William Arms spoke on three themes:
First, although he believes there is a need for a resource such as a digital National Library, Arms concluded that the commissioned papers collectively had not yet made a convincing case for how any NL initiative could benefit undergraduate education and urged participants to focus on this issue during the workshop. He pointed out that some of the commissioned papers suggested that libraries traditionally have not been central to undergraduate science education in many institutions of higher education. In trying to decide how to make the case for an NL, Arms provided two examples of how technology has added value to undergraduate education, sometimes in ways that were unexpected and unanticipated. In both examples (a distance learning program at the British Open University and the introduction of technology to all facets of undergraduate education at Carnegie-Mellon University), success was realized, Arms said, because the faculty at both institutions (the users) took control of the projects and shaped them to fit user needs. In both cases, faculty emphasized how the technology could best be employed to abet teaching and learning. Subsequent studies have indicated that these tools also have enabled teaching and research to be more closely conjoined than in the past because faculty have found they can use the same tools for teaching as for research. Arms emphasized that the undergraduate SME&T community must articulate a vision of how computing can be best employed in undergraduate education and that such a vision could be best articulated by teaching faculty. He noted that teaching faculty were underrepresented at the workshop.

Second, Arms addressed the issue of a "library without collections." He suggested that, unlike contemporary libraries and electronic databases where information is housed in a building or stored and distributed from a central computer, an NL project should look seriously at a structure that would guide users to collections of materials that are located and maintained elsewhere. Pointers might refer to commercially available materials, online collections, curricula (e.g., the online collection of curricula provided by the Mathematics Department at Dartmouth College[5]), and course notes and modules. The function of an NL would be to identify, evaluate, review, and index these materials.

Third, Arms emphasized that developing and maintaining an NL will be technically difficult. If an NL is to provide a high-quality service to users, it will be absolutely necessary to find people who are dedicated to the service aspects of putting the technology together. Users must define how the technology is employed; technology must not dictate how a library can and cannot be utilized.

Miriam Masullo continued the discussion of the role of an NL with respect to teaching and learning. She agreed with several authors of commissioned papers that the term "library," as applied to an NL project, places limitations on what this entity might become and how it might evolve. In contrast, if a digital library is defined as "a class of tools that includes capturing, authoring, storing, managing, searching, organizing, retrieving, indexing, sharing, and collaborating, we are probably talking about computer science and several other disciplines as well."

Masullo next described some of her experiences with digital libraries in K-12 education in the United States and similar projects around the world. Her experience convinces her that such entities will be built in unexpected places and in the near future because the enabling technology is now available. She thinks that it is justified to associate a sense of urgency with the proposed NL project.

---

were made during the discussion period following the second set of plenary presentations, resulting in overlap of issues between the plenary sessions. For the sake of clarity, comments from general discussions following both plenary sessions are summarized in a single section of this report. Comments are grouped by the issue raised rather than by the session during which the comment was offered.

[5]Available on-line at http://math.dartmouth.edu/math/courses.html.

However, Masullo emphasized that the focus should be on how to organize information in this new medium. If traditional transport and dissemination mechanisms are changed, new problems could emerge that could frustrate users and discourage use of an NL. In short, much more attention should be paid to how people acquire and use information from computers and networks.

Masullo also raised the issue of equity of access to information in an NL and how information in an NL might be distributed to or shared with other countries. After working with UNESCO on such issues, Masullo said that while the Internet is probably the delivery vehicle of choice for the United States and more developed nations, it may not be the avenue for distributing information to other parts of the world. However, if information from an NL is to be globally accessible, then transport parameters must be changed. If these parameters are changed, many other features of the system also may have to be altered, resulting in a multitude of technological issues to be resolved before the system can be used. Different delivery mechanisms also might have a severe impact on the quality of service, again raising the important issue of equity of access. Masullo disagreed with the notion that the challenge of the "have-nots" will be resolved with more sustained connectivity because she has not seen this happen to date with today's network technology.

Masullo also urged the group to think about what the term "national" actually connotes. Is an NL to be constructed primarily for use by people in the United States or will it be our contribution to the international dissemination of information electronically? How inclusive would an NL be? Many other countries are investing heavily in similar kinds of information infrastructures. If the United States means to be first in this new means of disseminating information, it also might eventually be left behind.

Masullo also emphasized that other countries (e.g., Singapore, Brazil, Chile, Malaysia, and Egypt) are investing hundreds of millions to billions of dollars each in their projects and choosing to focus on dedicated education infrastructures rather than "information superhighways." She advocated that the United States consider this emphasis as it develops its own facilities.

Michael Raugh described himself as an academic mathematician "who happened to wander on to the Internet one day" and who then formed a company to create digital libraries. His company currently is building a digital library for research and development in aviation safety information for the Federal Aviation Administration. Raugh reiterated Arms' point that it is difficult to build a digital library. He added that librarians already know this. Whether traditional or digital, libraries are complex structures that involve curating content, indexing, cataloging, abstracting, and providing for preservation. Raugh said that the issues of preservation of materials and other similar long-term issues have not yet been addressed seriously by the cooperative federal agency initiative that is involved with constructing the other aforementioned digital libraries.

Lee Zia addressed Arms' challenge to articulate a need or use for an NL. He pointed out that some of the commissioned papers suggested that faculty would be the primary users of this resource. Other papers stated that students should be the targeted clients. Zia felt that targeting an NL either to faculty or to students establishes a dichotomy that should be avoided since both faculty and students are two groups of *learners*. By focusing on the needs of learners, the dichotomy between serving the needs of faculty vs. students disappears.

"To teach is to learn twice."

JOSEPH JOUBERT, AS QUOTED BY LEE ZIA

There are examples of materials that achieve what Zia envisions, but he also agreed with Richtol that much of this work is being carried out by individuals. Technology has allowed people to rethink not only what they are teaching but also how they are teaching it and, more importantly, how their students are learning and interacting with the content. He also agreed with commissioned paper authors and previous speakers that the use of the term "library" evokes an image that is hard to alter, and he advocated finding an alternative term.

Zia emphasized that the proposed project, if properly designed to support learning and focus on the needs of diverse learners, could provide unprecedented opportunities for *all* students, not just the top students in a class, to engage more in the inquiry process and in research.

Zia then provided an example of how he might use information technology in his classroom to enhance student understanding of complex concepts such as differential equations—courseware that would allow students to venture well beyond reading about particular concepts and descriptions of the equations involved. With the courseware he envisioned, students could manipulate the initial conditions and parameters of the equation and instantaneously see the consequences of their manipulations. They could then apply their work to other, related systems in biology or chemistry to better understand how differential equations are employed in those other disciplines.

However, such outstanding programs require an enormous commitment of creative time and effort, not to mention technological manipulation so that they will operate on a variety of hardware platforms. Because such resources still are not widely available (and are seldom evaluated systematically for their ability to improve learning), not all students may have access to or benefit from them.

Are faculty members willing to make the required investments of time and effort to produce and use such materials? Will students use and benefit from such efforts? Zia did not offer specific answers but, rather, closed by saying that he believes there is a definite need for this resource and that the NSF should continue to pursue the concept of an NL for undergraduate SME&T education.

Session II: Presentations
The second session presentations were given by:

Mary Case, Office of Scholarly Communication, Association of Research Libraries
Michael Lesk, Bellcore
Francis Miksa, Graduate School of Library and Information Science, University of Texas at Austin
Nisha Vora, Association of American Publishers

Mary Case began by stating that if the agenda for an NL is not broad or visionary enough to stir people to create and use this facility, it is unlikely that any agency will be able to overcome the chal-

lenges and face the issues required to get the job accomplished. Case sees an NL as an entity that will 1) improve SME&T education; 2) attract more students to careers in these fields; and 3) by virtue of the first two, strengthen the United States' position in the global marketplace. However, she added that it also is important to develop an educated citizenry in SME&T to understand the importance of research. Case said that any NL initiative should take into account the billions of dollars that colleges and universities already have spent in computer hardware, software, and networking and find ways to use that existing infrastructure to better educate undergraduates.

Case pointed to the general agreement that collaborative activity is one of the most effective ways for students to learn and noted that such collaborative learning could take place in a research setting. In fact, many in higher education are promoting research by undergraduates. Given this, an NL could serve in part as a learning laboratory for undergraduates. It could be an active environment that provides resources, tools, and collaborative opportunities to support teaching, learning, and the creation of new knowledge by both faculty and students. The resources that might be incorporated into such an NL include primary research resources, raw data, published literature, reference sources, courseware, interactive modules that allow users to manipulate data, computer-aided design, lab simulations, and virtual reality applications. Case advocated an NL that supports multimedia, makes research tools available electronically, provides tools for users to create papers and courseware, and allows users to videoconference. She added that the enterprise is not worth pursuing if it does not take advantage of the interactiveness of these resources.

Meanwhile, the library community continues to struggle with many of these same issues. Case said it will be critical to bring people with this experience and perspective into discussions about the nature and course of development of an NL. Construction of an NL also must be examined in light of the funding crisis in higher education. The Council for Aid to Education predicts a $38 billion shortfall in funding for higher education by the year 2015. This shortfall, coupled with spiraling costs and the volume of new materials in SME&T that libraries must purchase, will have a grave impact on how universities organize themselves, how teaching is done, and what the higher education and library communities can afford to do.

An NL also must address other legislative and technical challenges. Likely to contain both public domain and proprietary resources, an NL should nonetheless work to insure that all materials associated with it are available for all educational purposes. An NL system must recognize the need to compensate authors and publishers, to allow robust educational and research uses, and to keep all of this "affordable." Real issues of intellectual property rights, copyright, and other legal challenges will need to be addressed before materials are made available to users through any new NL system.

Finally, Case stated that construction of an NL must accompany cultural changes in higher education so that the system of promotion and tenure values teaching as much as it does research and other types of scholarship. As with scientific research, the realm of higher education needs to find ways to evaluate the contributions of individuals in a highly collaborative environment. In many ways, these types of social and cultural issues can be more difficult than the technical ones, Case observed. Maintaining peer review and having support from national organizations like the NSF, professional and scholarly societies, and approval by colleges and universities will be very important to this effort, she added.

"In many ways, the social and cultural issues are often more difficult than the technical [ones]."

MARY CASE, PLENARY SESSION II

Michael Lesk began his presentation by displaying recent data from NSF on the number of bachelor's degrees awarded in different areas of SME&T (e.g., see Figure 1, from National Science Foundation, 1996a). With the exception of the life and agricultural sciences, the number of degrees awarded in engineering, mathematics, and computer science has been declining in recent years. The number of degrees awarded in the clinical sci-

ences has remained low. Furthermore, most of the advanced students in SME&T are not coming from U.S. undergraduate institutions. For example, more than half of the Ph.D.s awarded in mathematics have gone to individuals who are not U.S. citizens.

Many people already are using what amounts to a digital library. It is called the World Wide Web. Importantly, Lesk said, arguments remain about how best to use the material one can make available in this way. Computer-aided instruction traditionally has been factual in nature or has encouraged drill. Most researchers agree that students learn better with applications that enhance creativity and make locating information easy. Bellcore has performed studies showing that people who have to answer questions to problems can do so 25% faster and 25% more accurately if they search a digital book rather than a paper text (Egan et al., 1991). Other, similar studies have measured student learning using electronic text and hypermedia (e.g., Friedman et al., 1989; Marchionini, 1994), although very few definitive reports exist about the efficacy of this process. The upshot is that an NL may not be able to achieve its mission simply by providing scans of information from textbooks; rather, new types of materials will be needed, as well as more usable and searchable traditional materials.

While some have predicted that the cost of digitizing information will become prohibitive, Lesk reported that current prices for scanning books range from 8.5 cents to 40 cents per page ($25 to $120 for a typical SME&T book). More important than cost are educational content and benefit. Is it educationally beneficial to digitize existing materials? Perhaps, Lesk said, since undergraduates resort to the Internet so frequently to find information. Lesk advocated that underlying any discussion of digitizing and storing information should be the question of whether doing so will enhance education and whether we can measure that enhancement.

Francis Miksa began by saying that after having read the commissioned papers and listening to comments all morning, he had arrived at a "state of ignorance" about the proposed NL project. The more people talked about it, the less he felt he knew about it.

As a librarian and professor of library science, Miksa said he found the prospect and reality of

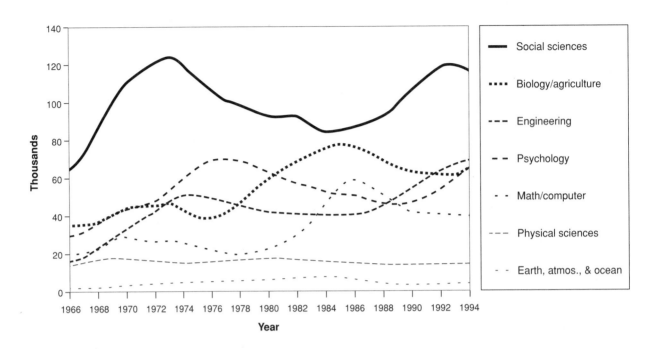

FIGURE 1. Science and engineering bachelors degrees awarded, by major field: 1966-1994. Reprinted from Chart 2, National Science Foundation (1996a).[6]

delivering information electronically tremendously exciting. He characterized it as an idea whose time has come, whether people like it or not. However, there is a difference between electronic delivery of information *per se* and the concept of a digital library, Miksa said. The latter is informed ultimately by the idea of the library, which has a long history. In its present context, a library is a function of a series of value-adding activities that are performed with respect to media, information, and the housing of various media containing information. Traditionally, librarians have performed these activities. In short, a library is not, by any definition, an inert mass of things that have been collected and indexed; rather, it is a process of adding value to that mass.

In a digital library, the roles of librarians include value-adding activities such as selecting information sources from among all those available and acquiring them in digital form, organizing those sources of information into an intellectually cohesive structure, providing assistance to others in finding and using such resources, and preserving information as required. Perhaps the newest challenge imposed by

digital libraries, Miksa said, is the potential for combining the concepts of publishing and electronic commerce. Another challenge to consider for the proposed NL project is the need for it to be constructed in a manner that supports its primary purpose of improving undergraduate SME&T education specifically and the educational process in general. All other parameters must flow from that purpose. This premise will cause such questions to arise as, What actually goes on in undergraduate education? What kinds of information-bearing entities are used in that process? How are they used?

Miksa said that what should be happening in undergraduate education is enhancement of the process of discovery by students. He noted that this notion is similar to the idea expressed in John Jungck's commissioned paper of a direct and conscious confrontation with ignorance and Harold Billing's idea of students as mavericks who contribute to the digital library in addition to using it (see Appendix A). Despite his opinion, however,

[6]Available online at http://www.nsf.gov/cgi-bin/getpub?nsf96139.

Miksa cautioned that an NL whose primary focus is on discovery might attract only a small number of users. Given the general temperament of people when they are students and the myriad conditions under which they attend school and pursue education, the discovery approach alone may be insufficient to meet the needs of this diverse group. Undergraduate education should be structured to allow students to experience the discovery of new knowledge.

Nisha Vora explained that her role at the American Association of Publishers (AAP) is to work with anti-piracy enforcement and copyrights. She expressed concern that with the explosive growth of information technology, a project like an NL for undergraduate SME&T education would need to be thoroughly informed about and respect copyright law and licensing. She advocated discussions about how to balance the interests of teachers, students, and proprietors when such a project is developed. She also advocated the need to look at existing laws and models for guidance.

Vora addressed the misconceptions that copyright holders want to "lock everything up" and do away with the doctrine of fair use or that educators only want materials to be free of charge. She returned to the idea of balance, with publishers and higher education working together to resolve such misconceptions. Vora said that opportunities exist to provide vast amounts of resources and tools and to facilitate creativity and communication among students, teachers, and other scholars around the world.

Vora noted that legislation is being proposed and negotiations are going forward regarding issues of database protection and fair use. She said the publishing community has interests on both sides of these issues because publishers that create database directories are pulling their raw data from other sources. Thus, both publishers and authors are users as well as holders of copyrights.

Vora mentioned that AAP is addressing a problem that affects most electronic databases and libraries: keeping URLs current. In collaboration with William Arms' group (CNRI), AAP is developing a *digital object identifier*, an electronic "license plate" that stays with a digital object and allows businesses and others to identify and track the object wherever it moves on the Internet. This device, if

successful, could be immensely important in the maintenance and curation of information in an NL for undergraduate SME&T education.

In closing, Vora emphasized the need to promote the incentive for creativity and development of new materials while at the same time protecting what already has been developed.

General Discussion, Day 1
The following questions and discussion points emerged after the plenary presentations on Day 1.

Is there a need for an NL?
William Arms was concerned that all of the discussion to this point had focused on what an NL for undergraduate SME&T education could do for other people, not the participants themselves. Were participants convinced that they could be better teachers if they had ready access to an NL? Robert Lichter addressed Arms' concern by stating that not enough potential users of an NL were present at the workshop.[7]

Elizabeth Dupuis was uncertain about who would use this proposed NL and whether it actually would improve undergraduate education in ways that other programs and resources could not. She pointed out that some workshop participants saw this as a resource for faculty, while others felt that students should be the primary beneficiaries. What is placed into a library will, in large part, depend upon the resolution of this issue, Dupuis maintained.

Lorraine Normore emphasized the importance of knowing who the users of an NL for undergraduate SME&T education will be and how they currently obtain information. Science students today use textbooks as primary sources for finding information. In contrast, people at the graduate level and beyond do not rely on textbooks for such purposes. These people are using the Internet and other information sources to generate new ideas. There currently is no common mechanism for getting undergraduates to work as graduate students and others do. Rather than saying that an NL should contain information from or pointers to textbooks, we should work to change the process of

---

[7]In organizing this workshop, the NRC issued invitations to some 180 people, many of whom are academics in a wide variety of SME&T disciplines.

learning so that we foster the kinds of thinking and work habits that trained scientists and technologists ultimately will need to use.

Francis Miksa urged NSF to proceed modestly with the project, at least in the near future. Although an NL is a wonderful goal, Miksa outlined an alternative project. He suggested focusing on mathematics, engineering, and technology as central loci for this initiative. Faculty, students, librarians, and computer technologists all would be key players in establishing such an NL initiative. These groups would work together within disciplines to catalog (with editorial comment) information that is available and appropriate to the discipline, whether it is available on the Internet or not. Tools would be employed to preserve Internet materials that are deemed worthy of preserving, to catalogue and track them automatically, and to remove more ephemeral materials. These groups would develop standardized vocabulary, thesauruses, and syntax methodologies for their disciplines so that users could find information more accurately and easily. The project also would proceed as existing libraries do to sort, catalogue, and disseminate information.

Amanda Spink pointed out that ongoing experiments with digital libraries on individual university campuses could inform the present project and ultimately be integrated with it. Jack Wilson agreed, saying that this project should tie into those other projects being sponsored by the NSF and private foundations.

How large is the potential audience of users?
Roberta Lamb urged the workshop participants to think beyond faculty and current undergraduates as the primary users of an NL. She said that an NL also should be useful and accessible to continuing learners. Because many people reenter the realm of education after their initial formal education has ended, these students blur the boundaries between learners and workers and between teachers and learners. Ruth Seidman also emphasized the importance of constructing an NL to include materials that will transcend the undergraduate years and be valuable to people who wish to revisit subjects or explore new topics later in life, especially since careers and disciplines change often and rapidly.

Gordon Freedman reminded the workshop participants that by the time any NL initiative is well established, it will be serving a primary audience that is 12 years old today. Therefore, the project must account for the ways in which these students will work when they reach college age. The spectrum of students is very broad, ranging from those who will be able to create three-dimensional models on computers to those who think that they will not be able to participate in our society at all. Taking into account the current status of K-12 education and the students who are in it now will be vitally important to the future success of an NL.

Content of and access to the proposed NL
Michael Lesk suggested that many undergraduates now rely on the World Wide Web for most or all of the information that they research. Thus, we should ask not whether we will have a digital library for undergraduates but what its content will be. What would we like to see in an NL that is better than what is on the Internet now? Students will use online information, but which information will they seek out?

Gordon Freedman said that the primary issue is less about content than an access system that is sufficiently standardized and universally available so that any high school teacher or college professor could find desired information. What universality can be applied to an NL so the least amount of time will be spent in acquiring appropriate and relevant information? Similarly, Nabil Adam noted that developers of materials appropriate for the proposed NL initiative will need to have development tools that allow them to spend most of their creative energies on content rather than on issues of a technical or technological nature.

Edward Fox said that at his institution and all over the world, people are creating rich curricula and learning tools at many different levels, ranging from some that are commercially available to local innovations that could be adopted and adapted elsewhere. Students at his institution have begun to depend on these resources, and data collected there indicate that these resources are effective for enhancing student learning. A major question is how such resources can be distributed. Some authors of materials refuse to make them available without compensation or to provide them to entities that do not have mechanisms in place for peer review and evaluation.

Wayne Wolf felt that there should not be a "go/no go" decision from the workshop about whether to establish an NL or what it should look like. The proposed NL should have some uncertainty built into it (as do conventional libraries) so that students will learn that there often is no single answer or solution to a problem. Students then would need to deal with information as professional scientists and engineers do. Ronald Stevens expanded on this point, saying that another potential use for an NL would be to point out what is *not* known. For example, an NL could point to emerging concepts, disagreements, and conflicts in new disciplines. A compilation of such emerging information could be a great resource for researchers and others who want to examine "cutting edge" information about specific topics or scientific disciplines.

Wayne Wolf said that an NL that served to point to repositories of books available in other libraries would not be very useful. Rather, an NL should help users find information about emerging new topics that are not readily or easily available elsewhere. Students find such topics very interesting, and faculty should have a resource that permits easy access to such supporting materials. While some of this kind of information already is available on the Internet, an NL could formalize its indexing and evaluation. An NL also should make sure that the users substantially benefit by computerized access to information. Searching speed should be high and access rapid. Effective dissemination tools are important for the proposed NL, Wolf said.

Jack Wilson expanded on Wolf's comments by saying that another advantage of electronic media beyond rapid access is the ability to offer continuous annotation and review of materials. Such interactivity among users is very difficult to achieve in a traditional, text-based library setting. As Zia mentioned during his presentation, there also should be opportunity for users to interact with and change the parameters of the materials they are using.

Clifford Lynch spoke on the issue of undergraduate students both as creators and users of content. He questioned how much dynamic, meaningful content undergraduates, especially those at the beginning of their undergraduate careers, actually could produce. Lynch also pointed out that as it is structured currently, much of higher education does not stress such modes of teaching and learning for the vast majority

of undergraduate students. Much current learning is textbook-based. Given that cultural change in education often is slow, Lynch asked how an NL could be constructed to enhance the kinds of educational experiences that are now offered to most undergraduates. Jack Wilson responded that, at his institution, teams of undergraduates, graduate students, and faculty author electronic materials. However, undergraduates do much of the work. Graduate students and faculty may be responsible for quality control and overall direction of the project, but undergraduates play important roles in the process. James Davis said that when he was at Cornell University, undergraduates in computer science did not create content, but they provided public, electronic annotation of existing materials and the courses in which they were enrolled. Student commentaries also included discussions of the processes of learning.

Christine Borgmann again raised the issue first articulated by William Arms about building an NL that accommodates the ways in which users would actually employ the resources. She emphasized that surprisingly little research has been done at the nexus of information seeking and problem solving. However, an NSF-sponsored conference held a year ago examined the social aspects of digital libraries, such as learner-centered designs, information life cycles, and incentives for using, preserving, and creating information (Borgmann et al., 1996). Other initiatives similar to the present one are under way and are addressing similar issues. How can this workshop carve out a specific niche for undergraduate SME&T education without duplicating other efforts? The current project, if funded, must coordinate its efforts with those other projects and learn from their research and experience. If the community waits to move forward until it resolves how students actually will use information in an electronic environment, the proposed NL for undergraduate SME&T education might never be built.

Robert Lichter reminded workshop participants that we cannot predict what information will be important to archive[8] for use 100 years from now,

---

[8]In this report, "to archive" and/or "to serve as an archival function" mean to preserve in readable form over the long term any material determined to have enduring value. "To store" and "to preserve" are used in this report in a technological sense, as in to save copies offline of material no longer in active use but possibly desirable at some future date.

and so we must build this uncertainty into the equation of what is selected for inclusion in an NL. Hard and fast decisions should not be made that would limit what is going to be important for the next generation of educational leaders who are today's 12 year olds (or even younger), and whose focus on teaching and learning is likely to be very different from ours.

"[W]e do not want to make hard and fast decisions that are going to limit what is going to be important for the next generation of educational leaders. [Those future leaders] are today's 12 year olds, whose focus on teaching and learning is likely to be very different from ours."

R. LICHTER, WORKSHOP PARTICIPANT

Tora Bikson countered that while people tend to view archivists as individuals who try to keep and preserve everything, archivists actually work systematically to determine what is and what is not worth keeping. For instance, when a new library is established or materials from a new area of knowledge are collected, archivists may apply a generous retention policy to all of those materials for a few years. These materials may then be evaluated to determine what is worth retaining in the long term. Such decisions are typically made on classes of items rather than on individual items. Bikson suggested that similar procedures be applied to materials in an NL. For example, she thought that annotations by students about the efficacy of a particular learning process might be valuable for several years but then could be removed as the process to which they refer evolves and new comments are added. Decisions about selective long-term retention are particularly important for an NL because of the cost of maintaining older digital materials in formats that can be accessed with contemporary software.

Is the proposed NL really a library?
Francis Miksa suggested that a useful analogy for the Internet is a publishing realm or publishing empire rather than a library. A library makes informed decisions about its own physical collections and catalogs, as well as connections to other paper and electronic resources. A library is not the same as a publishing realm. Thus, it would be helpful to all concerned to develop different terminology to describe this proposed NL. Barbara Polansky expanded on an idea in James Keller's commissioned paper by agreeing that we should focus on encouraging creative thinking rather than simply on constructing a library. She suggested that this entity be seen more as a national electronic resource locator to materials in many realms that helps users gain access to the materials themselves or to the authors of those materials. Peter Graham agreed, saying that the library community has been looking at very similar issues involving the blurring of the distinction between how libraries use information and what is happening outside the control and influence of library structures. Graham felt that the entity at hand is less a library than what might be called "a reserve book room in electronic form." In short, an NL should be more a mechanism and structure for accessing information.

Timothy Ingoldsby countered that an NL should serve as more than a pointer to other sites and sources. It also should serve as a "repository of last resort" for projects that are especially innovative or on the cutting edge of a discipline or pedagogy but not yet developed sufficiently to attract a commercial publisher or major funding.

Robert Lichter, as president of a private foundation, said that an important additional function of an NL would be to allow educators to realize that many good ideas and materials are already available for use. This knowledge alone could save potential developers of materials from "reinventing the wheel" and significantly reduce the amount of money expended by funders on projects that replicate earlier efforts. Lichter felt that this is a nontrivial issue that has to be factored into the economic equation of an NL as well as into resolution of issues of content, evaluation, and access.

Tora Bikson emphasized the need to pay careful attention to acquisition and evaluation processes. Currently, it is very difficult to search large databases or electronic clearinghouses unless the user is armed with sufficient information about references or keywords before beginning a search.

"A library without organization is the World Wide Web. A library without content is a building."

JACK WILSON, WORKSHOP CHAIR

What is the meaning of "national" in NL?

Christine Borgmann revisited Miriam Masullo's discussion of what is implied by use of the term, "national." In central and eastern Europe, individual governments view national libraries as their nation's contributions to the world. Is the workshop's view of an NL that of an entity by and for the United States or are we actually thinking about building the United States' contribution to the international information infrastructure for undergraduate SME&T education? Edward Fox replied that government agencies such as the NSF have provided millions of dollars for the exploration of educational and research components of digital libraries and that while a "national" digital library should be international, the United States must play an active leadership role in the process. Any NL initiative also must be for the national benefit of the United States. In another take on the meaning of "national" in this context, Borgmann added that the term implies that other agencies with overlapping interests in education (e.g., FIPSE, the Department of Education's Fund for the Improvement of Postsecondary Education) should team with the NSF to pursue their parallel goals and objectives.

Technology/economic issues

James Davis expressed concern that many of the programs and other materials either available or being written now will not be usable in three years because of rapidly changing technology. It is difficult to think of a library that contains content that "self-destructs" at every release of a new computer operating system. Richard Furuta emphasized that if the proposed NL is to be established, the planners must work with existing technology that can serve all potential users over the next several years while building a system that still will provide the same services on computer platforms 20 and more years from now. On the other hand, Robert Lichter urged

that the technology associated with an NL be dictated by the needs of users rather than vice versa.

Keith Stubbs asked what role Internet II[9] might play in the development of an NL. Since it is supposed to be accessible only by institutions of higher education, placing the proposed NL on this platform could immediately limit what materials go into it. Internet II also would create problems of access for users such as lifelong learners and those involved with continuing education. While undergraduates can put anything they author onto Internet I, their access to Internet II might be more restricted. Stubbs concluded that the development of Internet II needs to be monitored carefully for its potential impact on an NL for undergraduate SME&T education.[10]

Robert Panoff pointed out the high costs of digitizing materials that are now in other formats. Moreover, digitized materials have to be placed into a format that can be readily searched and that is reliable, robust, and accessible to all people through existing hardware and software systems. Tora Bikson expanded on this concern, saying that many organizations that are now preserving documents digitally are finding that maintenance costs are great because of the constant need for technology

---

[9]President William Clinton's announced goals for the "Next Generation" Internet initiative are as follows: 1) Connect universities and national labs with high-speed networks that are 100 to 1,000 times faster than today's Internet. These networks will eventually be able to transmit the contents of the entire Encyclopedia Britannica in under a second; 2) Promote experimentation with the next generation of networking technologies. For example, technologies are emerging that could dramatically increase the capabilities of the Internet to handle real-time services, such as high-quality videoconferencing; and 3) Demonstrate new applications that meet important national goals and missions. Higher speed, more advanced networks will enable a new generation of applications that support scientific research, national security, distance education, environmental monitoring, and health care. (Smith and Weingarten, 1997)

[10]A reviewer of this report, who must remain anonymous under the Report Review Guidelines of the National Research Council, wrote to disagree with the workshop discussion regarding lack of wide accessibility to Internet II: This person indicated that his institution has had access to the Very Broadband Network Service (VBNS), the precursor of Internet II, for some time. The institution has a switch that routes outgoing messages to the VBNS or the Commodity Internet (Internet I), depending on the destination. No one on the Commodity Internet has had problems reaching this reviewer or others at this university. The reviewer acknowledged that there may be issues of performance between Internet I and II, particularly if streaming audio or video applications are developed, but this reviewer does not believe that access will be an issue.

upgrades (e.g., conversion) to retain these documents in an interactively usable, manipulable form. Another serious problem is maintaining dynamic links and pointers among documents. Currently available technology does not make this task easy or inexpensive.

Harvey Keynes said that although many materials are available on the Internet, not much is developed to the point that faculty can use them well or on short notice in their classrooms. Getting faculty to create useful, content-rich materials will require external funding so they can devote large blocks of time to their projects.

Clifford Lynch again raised the issue of whether an NL should commission the creation of new content or organize and point to existing materials. If the decision is for the former, then much of the financial support from the NSF and elsewhere must be devoted to producing this content, at least toward the beginning of the project. Some examples of attempts to create content already exist. The NSF-sponsored Synthesis Coalition allows engineering faculty access to the National Engineering Education Delivery System (NEEDS) database of objects and materials that they can use in their courses.[11] This project has shown that it is costly to translate such a concept into usable content because faculty have had to invest a lot of time to adapt the material that was made available to them. Lynch expressed concern about the problems with scaling up to produce content for an NL that covers all areas of SME&T. Brandon Muramatsu agreed with Lynch's assessment of the problem. Muramatsu has been involved with a project to develop a database of engineering courseware (NEEDS). One question has been, How does another instructor or student take a piece of courseware and easily adapt it to her/his own use and teaching/learning objectives? Muramatsu said that a large problem has been the lack of instructor's guides and clear articulation of the learning goals of the software. Without such supplemental materials, much of the content of an NL may have only limited use and success in enhancing teaching and learning.

Tora Bikson agreed that even well planned interactive materials that are produced de novo by one person are difficult for others to use. Bikson said that RAND research on building educational resources for teaching and learning high school science suggests that it is best to create new materials on top of existing, common software packages that then are used in a variety of contexts. People who are familiar with the basic package will not have as many problems in getting the new innovation to work as those who are unfamiliar with the software platform. In addition, both written and electronic documentation are more likely to be provided with commonly used platforms, whereas educators are reluctant to spend the time and effort producing such documentation for their own software creations. Finally, this approach enables students to learn authentic skills—ones that transfer to veridical contexts of use. An educational interface developed for a standard Geographic Information Systems, for instance, allowed students to master some of the inquiry techniques employed by social demographers (McArthur et al., 1995).[12]

Intellectual property issues

Robert Panoff expressed concerns about how copyright law might impede the development of content for an NL. There are many examples of students authoring materials that could be used in an NL, and they should be encouraged. However, because students are transient at an institution, their contributions raise concerns about intellectual property rights. Even if students create materials, faculty ultimately must take responsibility for the use of these materials in their classrooms. If the proposed NL is to be a dynamic entity, Panoff said that ways must be found for users to take, use, and mold available materials without having to be concerned about who owns the intellectual property involved. When and how should materials developed by others be made available for fair use?

Shamkant Navathe revisited the issue of archiving features of an NL with respect to copyright and other intellectual property rights. He proposed a multitiered architecture for an NL, where one tier would archive journals, conference proceedings, working papers, and reports. This tier would be subject to all copyright and other laws governing

---

[11]Information on the Synthesis Coalition is available online at http://www.synthesis.org, and information on NEEDS is available on line at http://www.needs.org.

---

[12]Available online at http://www.rand.org/hot/mcarthur/Papers/esscots.html.

intellectual property. Other tiers, or layers, might contain unreferenced materials and possibly "exploratory materials" made available for use and revision but not subjected to the same level of legal scrutiny or archived as meticulously as materials in the first tier.[13]

Richard Furuta suggested that issues regarding copyright, fair use, and intellectual property transcend this particular project. They are so important and encompassing and have such widespread commercial implications that they will be addressed in other realms. This initiative should track those efforts and plan the development of an NL to take into account and incorporate the legal precedents that will inevitably emerge regarding these issues.

Edward Fox was pleased that publishers were well represented at the workshop. Many digital library conferences in the past have had no representation from the publishing community. Fox suggested that the NRC broker a highly publicized collaborative agreement or arrangement between universities and publishers to work together on resolving the issues of fair use and intellectual property rights that were raised at this workshop. If an arrangement were struck, the proposed NL could tap into a vast resource of materials that is now largely unavailable, such as the information contained in the more than 200,000 graduate and undergraduate theses produced in the United States. each year. With support from FIPSE, an initiative is currently under way to build a national digital library of theses and dissertations.[14]

In counterpoint, Ronald Stevens said he has heard that approximately 80% of people who earn a Ph.D. never publish their dissertations, which calls into question the usefulness of at least some of the materials that are being produced. In addition, the most prestigious journals typically accept only between 10% and 20% of submissions. So, professional publishing is a mature field that selects the best materials submitted. If the proposed NL becomes a new professional model where many more additional contributions are

included within it, the overseers of this resource must worry about maintaining the quality of information that becomes available. This issue also applies to teaching materials. If virtually everything is made available, will teaching suffer as a result? Any NL initiative must consider what kinds of standards for quality and rigor it will set before accepting materials.

An NL and the culture of higher education
Francis Miksa asked how the creation of teaching materials intersects with the tenure process at postsecondary institutions. At his institution, there is "slow movement" toward giving credit for the creation of teaching and learning materials. Is this a trend at other colleges and universities? Jack Wilson responded that much work is now going on in this area. Rather than teaching per se, Wilson emphasized that the discussion at hand is really about professional development and the recognition of this kind of work as another form of scholarship. Wilson agreed that the reward system has to change.

Straw Poll and Results
During the first day's plenary session, participants requested a straw poll about whether or not NSF should support the establishment of an NL for undergraduate SME&T education and what its purpose might be. The resolution on which the vote was taken read as follows:

> NSF should provide funding and coordination for a national initiative to support undergraduate education with at least the following components: 1) collecting and preserving important content, especially that which emerges as part of normal research in educational enterprises; 2) supporting development of virtual library collections; and 3) applying components 1) and 2) to enhance learning.

The outcome of the vote was 25 in favor, 1 opposed, and 16 undecided. Jack Wilson interpreted the vote as indicating that participants are committed to having NSF do something in this realm but that they are not completely certain what should be done. It should be noted that a second straw poll was not taken at the end of the workshop.

---

[13]This idea was developed further in an afternoon break-out session. A more detailed plan for this proposal can be found in Tables 1 and 2 on page 35.

[14]National Digital Library of Theses and Dissertations Initiative. For more information, contact: http://www.ndltd.org.

REPORTS FROM BREAK-OUT SESSIONS, DAY 1

Four break-out groups met during the afternoon of Day 1 of the workshop. One group each focused on "Curricular, Pedagogical, and User Issues" and "Economic and Legal Issues." Two groups considered "Logistic and Technology Issues." Each break-out group appointed one or more members to report their group's discussions and findings.

Curricular, Pedagogical, and User Issues

Given the issue discussed earlier in the day regarding whether this project should be considered a library in the traditional sense, this break-out group worked to find a different name for an NL.[15] They also discussed issues of audience, the kinds of materials that should be placed in this facility, the kinds of controls and governance needed for what is placed into, maintained by, and supported in an NL, and how to maintain user interest in and support of this enterprise.

The group decided that an NL should definitely target the needs of SME&T faculty. Some people felt that it also should be aimed at students, although others in the group worried that few students would utilize it if the materials focused primarily on needs of faculty. However, government agencies, foundations, publishers, and other commercial interests also would have to find benefit from the development of an NL for undergraduate SME&T education for it to succeed. The proposed NL must provide a clear, compelling message to its community of users about its objectives and how the materials contained within it contribute to those objectives.

The proposed NL project should take advantage of and learn from existing quality control programs for making decisions about materials to be included. In addition, an NL should incorporate and promote materials that have been created based on existing national education standards (e.g., National Council of Teachers of Mathematics *Standards in Mathematics* and the National Research Council's *National Science Education Standards*).[16] An NL should

serve other interests, such as policy-making organizations in individual states and in the federal government. Importantly, an NL should focus on providing materials that target specific goals for improving teaching and learning that could not be undertaken without it. Finally, outcome measures for success of the proposed NL should be developed at the beginning of the initiative, with input from the community of users.

Expanding on Shamkant Navathe's comments, the group also produced the following two tables of "things" that might be placed into an NL (Table 1) and tools that could be made available to users of an NL for producing their own materials (Table 2):

In Table 1, "Formal Materials" refers to resources, many of which already are online. Incorporating such materials into an NL would require licensing agreements with many different publishers and other proprietors. Materials listed under "Archival Materials" would be suitable for more permanent types of cataloging, indexing, and storage. "Other Refereed Materials" would include those that have undergone less scrutiny via formal refereeing processes. Some materials, such as software that has been peer-reviewed prior to its release, might fall within either of these two categories.

Under the "Informal Materials" heading are unrefereed, exploratory, and experimental resources. These kinds of materials might originate from both faculty and students and include items such as course syllabi, laboratory exercises, computer applications, and theses and other papers produced by students that are available for sharing, interactive commentary, and further development. How this material would be submitted and posted to an NL is an open question. The group felt that the NSF should support projects for various models of NL governance boards. These boards would experiment with criteria for including materials in an NL in the same time frame as other components of the system were developing (see "Recommendations," page 53). The group did not attempt to identify these criteria.

As Table 2 shows, the group thought that the proposed NL also must provide tools that allow users to work from and contribute to it effectively. "Creation and Authoring" tools would enable contributors to produce materials with standardized software that is easy to use. "Usage" tools would facilitate rapid searching and browsing of the pro-

---

[15]The group suggested that the term, "Digital National Library," be replaced with a better descriptor. Members proposed "World Education Learning and Resources Network" (WE-LEARN).

[16]See "Literature Cited," page 57.

TABLE 1. Things to Put in the Repository/Library

Formal Materials		Informal Materials	
"Traditional" Archival Materials	Other Refereed Materials	Unrefereed Materials	Exploratory/ Experimental
Journals	Conference Proceedings	Technical Reports	Classroom Notes (faculty/students)
Books (Publisher licensing)	Reports	"White Papers" (Industry)	Term Papers
Maps	Documents	Position Papers	Programs & Data
Images/Videos	Refereed Software Applications		

TABLE 2. Tools for Use in a Library

Creation and Authoring	Usage	Resource	Downloading and Packaging
Index Terms Creation	Search/Browse	Locator Services	On CD-Rs (for individual course packages)
Incorporating: Simulations	Index Based: Full Text	Outside Resources: URLs	Classroom/Lab Use: Interactive courseware
Animations	Pattern Recognition		
Visualizations			

posed NL's contents, while "Resource Locator Services" would provide electronic pointers (e.g., URLs) to materials located elsewhere. "Downloading and Packaging" tools would enable people to take materials that are available in an NL and elsewhere and package them for their own use in courses, laboratories, and so on. All of these resources pose their own challenges in terms of hardware and software platforms and operating systems on which to mount an NL, which languages to use, how the different components of an NL would operate seamlessly with other components, and how to serve the needs of users who will have vastly different levels of expertise and comfort with using electronic resources. The system also must have careful oversight through a clearinghouse mechanism to monitor contributions, to measure their value (specific metrics for doing so were not discussed), and to help in decisions about what should and should not go into this resource. Expectations for what would be included in an NL's collection will likely change as the project evolves.

The group suggested that, in its earliest stages, an NL might focus on enabling faculty to learn about effective practices and approaches to enhancing learning. As the system evolved, it could enable a restructuring of learning environments to support the needs of both faculty and students in various SME&T disciplines. Ultimately, the system could serve as a driver of change and the focus of communication for a community of learners in SME&T.

The group concluded that any NL initiative must "improve with age." The collection of materials and tools must continue to grow in ways that add value for its intended users. The tools and resources must keep pace with rapidly advancing technology and research into learning about SME&T. Its overseers must develop self-sustaining and self-funding models for operation that engage support from both the public and private sectors.

Logistics and Technology Issues

Of the two break-out groups that considered these issues, the members of the first decided that they would focus on what the NSF wishes to accomplish through its NL initiative. The agency's goal is not to build a digital library per se but to improve undergraduate education and instruction. Thus, this breakout group decided its question was whether building the proposed NL would enhance or contribute to the NSF's goal of improving undergraduate education. With this premise, the group focused on teachers as the primary users and community for the proposed NL's collections and content. They also explored the question of helping instructors create materials that other instructors can easily use and adapt to their own classroom and institutional situations. Thus, clearly identifying and attending to the needs of the intended users was seen as more important in the beginning of the process than making decisions about the technology and other issues associated with traditional libraries. How can an NL make more effective use of instructors' time and resources as well as leverage investments made already by the NSF and individual instructors?

Clearly defining the intended users should be of paramount concern. The social milieu in which students live, study, and work, and their motivations for using this kind of resource are not the same as for faculty. Therefore, deployment strategies for students could limit usage by faculty. If one says that the primary stakeholders are teaching faculty, many of whom will be in tenure-track positions, then the proposed NL's structure would have to consider faculty rewards and incentives, motivation, other tasks teachers perform that constrain instructional time and effort, and sources of funding for instructional and scholarly productivity. Given the current culture in higher education, the question arose as to why faculty, and especially untenured faculty, should spend time creating and upgrading instructional materials and then sharing them when these activities typically are not recognized as criteria or accomplishments for professional advancement.

Of all teachers, faculty in higher education usually have had the least amount of formal training in pedagogy or learning theory and processes. Most have not been educated in instructional design, how to evaluate instructional models and materials created by others, or how to adapt these materials to their own classrooms. Also, because teaching is not openly discussed with professional colleagues to the same degree as research, individual instructors often are idiosyncratic in their teaching methods. Again the question arose as to why college and university faculty should be expected to seek out someone else's materials and spend time adapting them to their own purposes.

An NL could address lack-of-incentive issues by having as a primary component a registry for pedagogical materials and learning resources. These resources could be evaluated through a peer-reviewed process. The proposed NL also would need to develop a strategy for achieving "buy-in" from faculty who previously have not used these kinds of resources. The developers of such a resource will need to identify early adopters and work closely with them to determine their patterns of usage and the problems they encounter. Prominent individuals in all SME&T disciplines should be recruited to tout the benefits of this kind of resource. In addition, materials would need to be easily transferable and to operate with minimal outside assistance on computer configurations with which faculty were familiar and comfortable. Faculty should be able to pull materials from an NL, modify them to suit their own needs, and then make them available to students to enhance learning. Under this model, students would benefit from an NL, if indirectly, by using downloaded materials locally.

Continuing to build on this model, the group thought that an NL's resources should be distributed across the Internet. This resource would be expected to account for and resolve issues centrally associated with copyright and intellectual property. On the technological side, an NL would still also need to deal with issues such as metadata, description of information, searching, archiving and maintenance, preservation, and access.

The members of the second break-out group on "Logistics and Technology" also considered user and pedagogical issues. They emphasized that, unlike other digital library projects, an NL for undergraduate SME&T education should deliver services and not be a site for conducting additional research about digital libraries. An NL should be expected to keep abreast of research in other digital libraries but primarily for the purpose of improving service to users.

This group also strongly agreed that an NL would need to stay in close contact with its customers, whoever they might be. They stated that any project must incorporate extensive market research and evaluation of customer needs from the beginning so that it can change in concert with the needs of its users. Faculty especially must become engaged in these efforts from the start of any NL project that might emerge.

This break-out group thought that the design, technology, and logistics employed in an NL project also must become integrated with all other digital library efforts under way both domestically and internationally. They saw this NL project as ultimately moving toward one coordinated, distributed system that would be overseen by some high-level governance body. Initially, however, organizations such as scientific societies that have access to materials and can review them for their scholarly content and suitability for inclusion in an NL might serve as overseers of the process. Since these organizations were founded along disciplinary lines, what initially went into an NL for undergraduate SME&T education through their oversight also would likely be disciplinary in nature.

Members of this group thought that the NSF might establish an initiative to decide the best use and applications for an NL for undergraduate SME&T education. In Phase I of this initiative, some group members suggested that NSF issue a Request for Proposal (RFP) in the format of a cooperative agreement to create four or five models of an NL. By testing different models over time, NSF might then be able to decide the best paradigm to support. Other members of the group felt that an RFP in the format of a cooperative agreement to start a single project could be issued. Regardless of the number of contracts issued, the group emphasized that these projects should be structured in such a way that there would be collaboration and cooperation among them. Phase I might last up to two years. Phase II would coordinate best models and practices from Phase I to develop a single NL that is distributed physically but coordinated centrally.

The group proposed that any RFP should contain suggestive rather than prescriptive language to encourage the emergence of new ideas and technologies that otherwise might not be considered in a more restrictive venue. At a minimum, the members of this break-out group said that a successful proposal should demonstrate awareness of other similar projects and include a plan for integrating and coordinating with these projects. The proposed project also should identify users and their needs, deal with customer satisfaction, define a rating system for adding materials into an NL (including which kinds of people or organizations would be responsible for overseeing the system), and demonstrate how such an NL could be economically viable, sustainable, and robust. In addition, successful proposals would detail how to address technological issues such as identification and naming, authentication, classification, and descriptions of metadata.

The discussion that followed this group's report focused on some of the details of how these proposals might be divided, the topics on which each might focus, and the development of appropriate evaluation tools.

Economic and Legal Issues

Like the groups dealing with "Logistics and Technology," this break-out group also struggled with user issues, in this case to give some context to the economic and legal issues they were asked to consider. The role of an NL and its users could be considered on a continuum, the group thought. At one end of the continuum, an NL would provide content and instructional materials that could stand alone and serve as replacements for textbooks. At the other end of the continuum, an NL would be mediated by teachers who would select, adapt, and launch some of these materials into a broader pedagogical context.

The members of the group predicted that an NL ultimately would assume a format where teachers were its primary users, and these teachers would contextualize and personalize the available materials for their students. The development or acquisition of stand-alone materials for students would not be precluded by this model, but an NL might simply point to such resources elsewhere rather than commissioning their production or storing them.

The group next considered the scope of an NL for undergraduate SME&T education. They agreed that an NL primarily would be an index and, to a lesser extent, a repository for materials not available elsewhere (e.g., faculty-authored materials). The proposed NL might accept submissions from elsewhere but would not make commissions nor fund in other ways the creation of content; other organizations, such as the NSF or publishers, would be responsible for supporting such projects, the group thought. Neutral about its specific origins, an NL would index content and assist users in finding, evaluating, and sharing it. Faculty were seen as the primary users, but students also were viewed as being able to extract useful information from an NL. If materials were directed primarily toward faculty, however, the group surmised that most students would not be able to use them directly unless faculty provided additional context within a course.

Conversations continued about what might be included in the index of an NL and also what should not be included. The group thought that classic literature from scholarly publishers that is being digitized does not belong in the proposed NL since this material falls more within the realm of traditional research libraries. However, an NL for undergraduate SME&T education should work with conventional libraries to develop good pointers to these materials. Because the proposed NL also should be viewed as a "working facility for faculty" to improve teaching, long-term preservation of materials would not need to be a high priority and would be a responsibility that fell more to research libraries.

What should be included in an NL according to the members of this break-out group are models and simulations, courseware modules, curricular materials, syllabi, reading lists for courses, and annotated reviews and evaluations of these materials by other users. The group could not agree on whether an NL should point to data sets and sources of data. For example, public domain databases, such as the National Library of Medicine's *Visible Human Project*,[17] could become a part of an NL in the sense that the NL might point readers to such databases and then also provide additional tools and value-added components (e.g., course modules where students could work with the database in a particular context).

As conceptualized by this working group, the indexing service provided by the proposed NL would not require a large physical infrastructure. However, to point effectively to what is likely to be a large and rapidly expanding volume of available materials, infrastructures for technology, networks, compatibility with local computer systems and servers, and coding of materials would need to be developed carefully.

The group also discussed the issue of "critical mass." If an NL does not contain enough material to meet the needs of users, it will fall into disuse. The group was uncertain how much and what kinds of materials collectively constitute critical mass and suggested that librarians be brought into this discussion, as the establishment of any new library raises these same issues.

Quality control also presents an interesting dilemma for a digital library. In a scholarly journal, quality control consists of a decision to publish or not to publish a submitted or commissioned paper. For the kinds of materials being suggested for this proposed NL, different rules probably would apply, especially for materials such as syllabi or course modules.

Economic and legal issues that the group considered centered on the following:

Paying for the proposed NL's services: Several possibilities emerged. If an NL provides resources that replace textbooks and more traditional materials, then perhaps students should bear some of the costs through university user fees, lab fees, or the cost of software or other materials that they use in

---

[17]Information available online at http://www.nlm.nih.gov/research/visible/visible_human.html.

place of textbooks. For indexing services, contributors could be libraries, scholarly societies that are looking to increase their involvement in improving SME&T education,[18] and federal and private sources. The group did not think that directly billing users for services would be a viable option.

Intellectual property rights: Many of the materials likely to be included in or indexed by the proposed NL are composite multimedia works that continually are moved from one institution to another and repeatedly adapted and modified to address users' needs. This kind of use results in problems with derivative works, works in which many institutions may claim property rights, and the rights of multiple authors from different institutions as colleges and universities become more interested in claiming part of the rights to materials that their employees produce.

Liability of authors who produce such materials: In cases of liability claims against multiple authors from different institutions, will the institutions stand behind their employees?

Privacy and confidentiality: The break-out group expressed concern that if materials from an NL were to be used to evaluate programs (e.g., to measure the effectiveness of courses or instructors based on student learning), legal problems could arise with regard to access to student records. Some issues also are ethical; for example, in the case of simulations or self-assessments, would it be appropriate for faculty to know how many hours students have worked with a program or how they are using it?

Any of these issues, if not resolved early in the development of the proposed NL initiative, could become a major barrier to its use.

Following the group's presentation to the workshop-at-large, Edward Fox asked how much such an NL project might cost. Clifford Lynch, facilitator and spokesperson for the break-out group, responded that his colleagues had not considered the actual cost. However, he contended that such an NL, as perceived by this group, would be far less expensive than a system that commissions or licenses content

on behalf of its users. Lee Zia asked the librarians participating in the workshop how much of a student's tuition goes to support the library system at a university. Richard Lucier responded that, in California, university libraries are line items in the state budget. Michael Lesk indicated that 3-4% of a typical university's budget goes to its library system, although there can be considerable variation depending on the type of institution.

Michael Lesk wondered about sources for long-term financial support of an NL. He stated that unless universities paid some of the costs and then charged students additional tuition in exchange for having to purchase fewer textbooks and other materials, an NL could not be financially viable. Additional discussion ensued about the use and importance of various types of student fees, including those for laboratories and information technology being applied to support access to the proposed NL. Tryg Ager worried that financial support for such an enterprise would be in peril if each state had its own method for covering these kinds of costs or for collecting money from students.

With regard to intellectual property rights, Michael Lesk said that if universities were to become more involved with issues of intellectual and other property rights for their employees, such matters would be easier to resolve since far fewer people would be involved in negotiations. Clifford Lynch said that some indication of who holds property rights to an object should accompany that object when it is transmitted to users. Michael Raugh said that one advantage of the registry or catalog model for an NL is that it avoids many of these intellectual property issues because the burden for resolving them is placed on users of the materials, who would most likely enter into negotiations or purchase arrangements with providers.

INTRODUCTORY REMARKS AND DISCUSSION, DAY 2

Jack Wilson opened the second day of deliberations about whether the NSF should support the establishment of an NL for undergraduate SME&T education by reviewing the discussion to date. He pointed out that he had not heard a strongly articulated need for an NL expressed the day before. He also noted that workshop participants had not

---

[18]Some people in this group felt that the NL should promote the crossing of disciplinary lines. By asking disciplinary societies to contribute materials and other resources, this interdisciplinary function might be compromised.

reached agreement on many of the issues. Wilson summarized the sense of the workshop from Day 1 as follows:

Audience—The greatest area of agreement was who the proposed NL's "customers" were. Workshop participants seemed to feel very strongly that faculty were the primary customers. Students, librarians, SME&T professionals, and lifelong learners also might be considered as customers, but agreement could not be reached about this. It was noted once again that potential users who could best articulate who would use this facility and whether it would enhance undergraduate teaching and learning were not well represented at this workshop.

Content—Wilson stated that he sensed no agreement about content. Rather, the following questions consistently recurred in the discussion: Should an NL absorb pre-existing materials and/or point to them? Also, should an NL support the generation of new materials?

Legal issues—Workshop participants appeared to agree that these problems transcend their discussions. Legal issues would be addressed by others and could not be meaningfully resolved in this forum. The directors of an NL would need to stay closely connected to ongoing discussions and legislation in this realm.

Technology issues—Most speakers and breakout groups that considered these issues agreed that the key element was to let the needs of users drive the development and implementation of the technological features of any NL initiative. How this will be achieved is a more difficult question. The rate at which technology advances far outpaces both the development of content of undergraduate SME&T education and the cultural features of higher education that catalyze and reward educational reform.

In closing, Wilson returned to the point that the workshop had not yet strongly articulated a need for an NL despite the outcome of the straw poll on the previous morning. He asked participants to address this point clearly in subsequent deliberations since the Steering Committee was charged with advising the NSF about whether or not to proceed with a project or series of projects to establish an NL for undergraduate SME&T education.

General Discussion

Several participants addressed the conundrum of the previous day's straw vote in favor of establishing an NL, on the one hand, and the apparent lack of clear objectives or raison d'être for it on the other. Francis Miksa saw the problem in the nature of undergraduate education itself. Libraries currently do not play a major role in the education of many undergraduates. To make a strong case for an NL, the culture of SME&T education itself would have to change. Christine Borgmann continued this discussion, saying that before an NL can be implemented, we must ascertain how potential users of the proposed NL actually do their work, what their needs are, and how they work within their organizations. Then a system can be designed that is capable of being embedded in and compatible with its potential users' working environments. This goal must be the first priority in any design for an NL. Further, it is more of an organizational issue than a technology one. Robert Lichter suggested that the proposed NL be developed as commercial products are. Businesses require extensive market research to determine users' needs and desires before deciding how to produce a product that will meet those needs. In the present case, much more input is required from users. Richard Furuta said that if the proposed NL was designed to promote professional development for faculty, it also could catalyze the reform of undergraduate teaching which, in turn, would change the ways and cultures in which students learn.

Tryg Ager said that the Library of Congress, which has a mandate to undertake K-12 outreach, is placing into its digital library a photographic record of American history, primarily for students. Ager suggested that a sheet of paper be passed around so that everyone present could add her or his top priorities for materials that could be included in an NL for undergraduate SME&T education. An assessment of user needs and preferences could go far toward articulating not only what an NL should contain but its importance, as well.

Edward Fox emphasized that, ultimately, this proposed NL has to support students, who are the end users. Faculty create materials for students to use, not just to share among faculty. Thus, rather than being considered a primary resource for faculty, an NL should be set up in ways that millions of students can use it. The proposed NL also should be designed so that faculty can share teaching materials easily. Functionality and interoperability should be of paramount concern in its design and establishment. Francis Miksa stated that the word "student" has too narrow a meaning in this context. The proposed NL actually should be thought of as a science digital library for independent learners—a perspective that would include everyone who needs to use this kind of resource, whether in a school setting or not and regardless of the user's professional status. Let an NL be independent of any formal educational structure and put materials into it that are useful to learn, Miksa advocated.

Margaret Gjertsen felt that the group should not spend so much time on the question of whether or not the need for an NL can be articulated. The group agreed that a specific need had not yet been stated. If that need were well known, some commercial entity already would have begun to undertake this project. Gjertsen emphasized that the real issue is in how the proposed NL is developed so that many people will have access to the materials in it. Precisely because there has been no articulated need that could be met by a commercial enterprise, an NL should be built by non-commercial sources.

REPORTS FROM BREAK-OUT SESSIONS, DAY 2

On Day 2, two break-out sessions focused on "User and Pedagogical Issues." One break-out session focused on "Logistic and Technology Issues." One break-out session concentrated on "Economic and Legal Issues."

Economic and Legal Issues

Because there was general agreement that legal issues would have to be resolved elsewhere, this break-out group concentrated on economic issues. Clifford Lynch, group facilitator for both days, reported that the morning's discussions were almost opposite to those of the day before, which had focused on the proposed NL's mission of supporting teaching. Today's discussions focused on how to help people learn SME&T. The second-day break-out group discussed the facilitation of learning and the level of content in an NL for undergraduate

SME&T education. It was thought that the proper level for content would take into account the experience, skills, and knowledge one would likely encounter in undergraduate students, but that the content need not focus exclusively on the needs of individuals formally enrolled in undergraduate SME&T courses. The group discussed how a primary means for constructing an NL would be to impanel groups of specialists and charge them with identifying and selecting materials for inclusion. Here, professional and scholarly societies and organizations could play a leading role by identifying core subjects and the kinds of materials needed to provide an effective and exciting picture of different disciplines. It was thought that organizations such as the NSF might decide to support a major initiative in some disciplinary area (similar to the chemistry and calculus initiatives). Partial funding for such projects might come from individuals or organizations interested in developing specific content and tools to promote learning in and appreciation of certain subject areas.

Economically, the group thought that any NL initiative should emphasize open access to materials, including those already in the public domain and those for which an NL had negotiated broad distribution rights for educational purposes. For example, professional societies might be encouraged to make available to this NL selected materials to further development of subject matter and educate the public about their particular disciplines. It was noted that the American Chemical Society makes materials available through its Education Division that are already widely distributed elsewhere through other arrangements. Perhaps an NL also could provide or point to other copyrighted items to which users could have open access, either through the NL itself or from other sources. Commercial interests also might be encouraged to become involved as a means of promoting other salable goods. The sense of the group was that an NL should not purchase rights to materials and then try to recover those expenses by charging users or by seeking reimbursement through government or other sources.

This group also agreed that "library" is not a good descriptor for this project. Members suggested that what is envisioned is more an electronic science center or some modification of a science encyclopedia.

Discussion—In response to a workshop participant's question about who would pay for the development of content, Lynch replied that much of the material is already available. Materials commissioned specifically for the proposed NL could be handled outside its operation. For example, some other organization such as a professional society or the NSF might decide that some specific content should be added to an NL and would provide the funds to develop or acquire and insert that information into the system.

Logistic and Technology Issues
This group agreed that any NL initiative should be driven by an overarching vision that this resource should incorporate all kinds of opportunities for improving undergraduate SME&T education into its infrastructure. However, until this grand vision is more fully developed, a set of smaller, tightly defined initiatives should be undertaken. Thus, most of the session was devoted to discussion of how to support undergraduate learning and to defining a set of functional requirements for users that could encourage the most innovative set of responses from the technology experts who would build the proposed NL's infrastructure. This group agreed with other groups that a needs assessment focused on communities of users should precede any actual effort to build an NL.

This group basically agreed that an NL should be a registry of information, although some members felt it also should be a repository. Regardless of how an NL ultimately is constructed, its registry should allow users to understand and interface easily with the system. The proposed NL would include both formal and informal materials (see Figure 2) that would start with input from professional organizations in the SME&T disciplines about what constitutes both core information and "critical mass" (as described on pages 50 and 38) for each discipline. An important key to success in promoting such activities would be to develop an incentive structure that recognizes and rewards these kinds of scholarly activities. Materials might include examples of best practices, information about how to teach, tools to support simulation, visualization, and animation. Indeed, the NSF might require all of its grant recipients who develop curricular materials to place them and evaluations of their efficacy for enhancing stu-

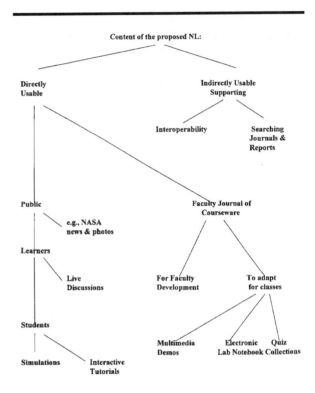

FIGURE 2. Another perspective of the content for an NL.

dent learning in an NL's registry. The system should also support bringing into an NL existing digital materials developed with grant support, for example, from the Division of Undergraduate Education. The group discussed how authentication and accurate, interactive searching features will be important components of an NL, especially if it does not serve as a repository for materials. Extremely important will be data authentication devices, such as algorithms that digitally sign data to make tampering easier to detect. These will help reassure users that the data or other materials they have accessed outside an NL actually correspond to data or other materials in the NL's indices. An NL also should incorporate tracking features that will allow its overseers to determine what and how often users are accessing particular materials in the collection. This information would assist their making informed decisions about future acquisitions and features as well as retention periods for current holdings. An NL also should support features to promote interaction among users such as discussion groups.

Discussion—Lee Zia offered the counter position that an NL should be much more than a registry, even if the material listed has been peer-reviewed. An NL should, at minimum, allow users to at least sample snippets of the materials to which it points. But much more material could be stored and distributed from an NL. This proposed NL project should be seen as being much more dynamic and evolutionary than would be possible if it assumes only a registry function.

User and Pedagogical Issues, Group 1

This group concentrated its efforts on articulating a need for an NL. The members agreed that a sense of urgency to construct this facility cannot be found in the SME&T higher education community. However, by committing funds to its development, the NSF can help drive this community toward desired reforms while simultaneously providing tools to help accomplish change. Another reason for the NSF to support this project is that it is not yet commercially viable. Providing such a service now could provide models to the commercial sector, which is seeking guidance about what needs to be done in this realm. However, the impetus for beginning such a venture must come from a non-commercial source, such as the NSF. In addition, the NSF is the only organization at this point that can provide the guidance, breadth of knowledge, and access to resources for interdisciplinary activities, promote standards across disciplines for materials to be included in an NL, and foster the kinds of professional recognition that is needed for those individuals who undertake this kind of work.

This facility could facilitate SME&T education-related activities that otherwise would be difficult or impossible to accomplish. Professional people who want to begin new projects for improving education could be informed by the materials already listed or provided in an NL. If the proposed NL had high standards for accepting or listing materials, having such materials accepted for inclusion would be considered professionally prestigious and would promote recognition that developing such materials is an important aspect of scholarship.

The group recommended that the NSF support the creation of an index of existing quality courseware materials, including work that has been sponsored by NSF grants. In this case, courseware was broadly defined to include all types of materials to support teaching. The NSF also might consider supporting individuals or organizations to review comments made by users of these items or to create comments about the usefulness of products in the proposed NL. Such comments would be for the benefit of users rather than serving as an "accept/do not accept" decision by a governing body for inclusion of these items in the proposed NL.

Discussion—Lee Zia questioned the assumption that there is no sense of urgency to improve undergraduate SME&T education. Tora Bikson argued that the urgency should be evident from the data on SME&T undergraduate rates in the United States that Michael Lesk had presented. Ronald Stevens responded that, while change is coming, he does not feel that the SME&T community is willing to abandon the present system yet or to design a digital library that will set the standard and direction for undergraduate SME&T education for the next 15 years. By adopting the establishment of this proposed NL as a priority, the NSF could help catalyze such change. Jack Wilson pointed out that a sense of urgency does indeed exist, even if it is not within the SME&T community itself. Many state legislatures and governors are proposing legislation and regulations that could fundamentally restructure higher education.

User and Pedagogical Issues, Group 2

Figure 2 summarizes this group's discussion about the types of content that might be included in an NL for undergraduate SME&T education. This scheme arose from earlier discussions about the purpose of teaching and learning technologies: improving the quality of classroom education vs. increasing the productivity of faculty so that they can teach more students. The latter purpose reflects more of an administrative rather than a learning-oriented perspective. This group agreed that the role of relevant technology should first and foremost be to improve learning. Increasing teaching effectiveness should be a secondary goal.

Toward that end, this group agreed that the NSF should support an initiative to provide worldwide access to resources that improve student learning in SME&T, that are usable in a variety of settings, and that also increase faculty teaching productivity by 1) enhancing existing courses and labs, 2) encouraging development of new courses and labs, and 3) engaging learners in the process of doing science. This group agreed with the definition of digital library provided by Borgmann (1996, see footnote 1). They noted that this definition implies that a digital library is not only for information retrieval. Rather, it also is a place where users can create and deposit their scholarly contributions as well as search for and use materials already there. The proposed NL should contain rich collections of materials with the kinds of choices available that allow users to tap its resources for multiple purposes. Students should be able to learn about SME&T through this resource in ways that would be difficult or impossible through other media, including access to such items and information as NASA's up-to-the-minute accounts and pictures of its missions which also engage the public at large. An NL should engage learners from all walks of life in the thrill and beauty of science via learning opportunities such as live discussions with experts and with each other. While the scheme in Figure 2 separates faculty resources from other components of an NL, it is meant to imply that faculty also are learners and can benefit from these resources in the same ways as all other learners.

Further, this group felt that 1) the proposed NL should be a *national* digital library in the sense that resources should be constructed by and for SME&T instruction in the United States, and that 2) the proposed library also should be a U.S. contribution to international cooperation in education. However, the United States should monitor carefully developments in other countries to take advantage of international advances in technology and/or in available content.

This break-out group also considered the logistics that would be required to implement their model. If the NL project were to go forward, important components for its overseers to consider would be its registry, classification of materials, standards for accepting and posting objects, and interoperability. Although users should have direct access to the content listed in an NL's registry, this access could have important ramifications for the cost of establishing, supporting, and maintaining the enterprise. Searching and indexing features might be tailored to different user communities so that users could access the same information through different search paths. The group noted that training of users and authors will have to be a very important component of this project since the information in an NL and the platforms on which it operates will change frequently.

Discussion—Michael Lesk asked whether people in other parts of the world should have to pay for the materials and services provided by this proposed NL. The group thought that fee structures for users outside the United States should be examined. Lesk also suggested that a way to deal with this issue is to trade with other nations. For example, the United States might provide access to digital libraries dealing with subjects which have been well developed here in exchange for access to information in digital libraries elsewhere in the world that focus on other topics. For example, nations that have developed extensive materials for language education might provide otherwise restricted access to that information in the U.S. and gain similar access to United States digital libraries, such as the one proposed for SME&T education.

Closing Discussion

Ensuing discussion focused on several points raised by the presentations from the break-out groups. Richard Furuta said that members of his break-out group concurred that the NSF should view this project in broad terms initially rather than focus on the specific components that will be needed to develop an NL. Furuta also stressed that this effort should be a long-term one, although he acknowledged that other groups thought that shorter term projects (six months to two years) should be undertaken before the NSF commits to a particular paradigm for developing an NL.

The proposed NL was compared to a zoo, where the "inhabitants" of both constantly change over the course of their "lives" and therefore require changes in nurturing, care, and sustenance. Unlike a traditional book that remains available in a traditional library for many years, an entry in a digital library may not be useful or even readable five to ten years in the future. Tora Bikson said that the NSF is key to the success of the proposed NL because the agency is now the only organization that can imbue the project with both a coherent vision and overarching organization and coordination of its various components. Without this oversight, it is unlikely that the individual pieces of the project will meld into a usable whole.

Bikson underscored the issue of time scale, saying that short-term efforts are likely to be futile because faculty users will not invest the time and effort necessary to locate and evaluate materials in an NL if they cannot be assured that these materials will remain available when they are actually ready to use them in their classrooms or teaching laboratories. She suggested that we need to start now to learn how to construct this entity because it will take a long time both to educate faculty in its use and to learn from efforts by faculty to make the proposed NL even more useful and accessible. Bikson related a sense of urgency to begin this project because it could be important to the national economy. Governors of several states and leaders in business and industry are contemplating the creation of virtual universities on an interstate scale and will be recruiting more and more people who are well versed in science and technology (e.g., Western Governors University). An NL could be one way to increase the number of U.S. undergraduates who enter these fields.

Ronald Stevens explored further the perception of urgency for establishing an NL for undergraduate SME&T education. He argued that while there may be an urgent national need to establish this NL, there is no such sense of urgency to do so among faculty or academic SME&T departments. Faculty are not currently receiving tenure or promotions based on professional activities in this realm. Many faculty do not explore new teaching methods or actively change their courses on a monthly or even yearly basis. Little research is available on which teaching practices are most effective[19] and outcomes of effective teaching practices are not widely disseminated. However, Stevens emphasized that a well-constructed NL could stimulate a sense of urgency among faculty to reexamine their teaching practices. Robert Panoff agreed, saying that it is difficult for faculty to sense urgency or crisis about the state of undergraduate education when most undergraduates with degrees in SME&T are finding jobs. Further, given the *perception* among some faculty that problems with their students originate in the lower grades and the fact that undergraduate SME&T majors find employment or places in postgraduate education after leaving their institutions, some faculty may believe that shortcomings in undergraduate SME&T education are someone else's problem.

Roberta Lamb stated that by encouraging potential users to visit its registry, an NL might help them to understand better what already has been developed and what is usable. By providing this forum, the NSF could advertise and promote good science and science education and showcase attractive environments for learning that also might increase participation in and appreciation of science by the larger community. Thus, an NL should appeal to many potential user constituencies. The NSF is the government agency that can best coordinate the continuing discussion about these diverse and potentially conflicting goals.

Jeanne Narum said that an NL would be the newest tool in an arsenal of SME&T education projects and initiatives that the NSF has promoted during the past ten years to disseminate examples of "what works" to improve undergraduate SME&T education. She stated that the sense of urgency should be to capture the richness of the innovations that are occurring in this realm, many of which have been supported by the NSF. There is a need to articulate a vision and mission that will move the SME&T education community into the next century, utilizing the best tools available to do so.

James Davis then challenged the group by proposing that NSF should *not* construct or support the construction of an NL for three reasons. First, workshop participants had not articulated specific needs or demands for such a resource. If undergraduate SME&T education is indeed in crisis, an NL is not the current solution for this problem. Additional work with curricula, new institutional initiatives, or metrics may be better tools to mitigate these problems at this point. Second, Davis stated that a high percentage of the functionality of an NL as it had been discussed in this workshop would likely emerge from grassroots efforts and the commercial sector without assistance from the NSF. Third, given the likely emergence of these resources from other sectors, the funds that would have to be committed to this project could be better applied elsewhere, especially in efforts to develop better content materials.

Michael Raugh agreed with Davis on most aspects of his statement but added that the current situation for locating materials on the Internet is chaotic

---

[19]Although an extensive body of literature examines effective teaching practices, few college and university SME&T faculty have examined these resources or even realize that they exist.

because reasonable standards for cataloging and indexing materials have not been applied to this medium. Through an NL project, the NSF has the opportunity to bring some order to this chaos by catalyzing the creation of a standardized infrastructure that can serve as the model for the many different approaches to searching for and sharing information on the Internet. Raugh also felt that by placing its imprimatur on faculty and other developers of such materials who agree to participate in rigorous evaluation of their creations, the NSF would provide support for work that too often is not recognized by the academic community as scholarly and promote greater participation and professionalism in the evaluation of content on the Internet. No other agency in the United States has the ability to encourage this kind of activity. Peter Graham added that the humanities and social and behavioral sciences communities also would benefit from work done on an NL for undergraduate SME&T education in resolving issues such as authentication, incorporation of metadata, and engines for searching and retrieving information in their disciplines. Thus, the benefits of the NSF's support of an NL for undergraduate SME&T education potentially could extend well beyond the sciences.

Michael Lesk felt that evidence for the efficacy and success of existing digital library projects should be provided to the NSF so the agency can make a more informed decision as to whether additional support of them is warranted. Several participants offered examples of successful projects.[20] Tora Bikson said that the NSF itself has done a very good job in supporting the development of content for undergraduate SME&T education but that it has fallen short in making sure that this content is developed in such a way that it can be placed into formats and forums where it can be readily located and used by others. She also noted a need on the part of the NSF to relay to potential users of this content the kinds of standards the developers had to meet to receive project funding. If the fruits of these projects simply appear on the Net, their true value is likely to be obscured by the morass of other similar information. Bikson suggested that the NSF should make available in some well-publicized forum the results and products of the projects the agency has supported. This forum should allow additional commentary on and evaluation of these materials by users. In addition, many NSF-sponsored, large-scale research projects are usually undertaken at only a limited number of research universities with large graduate programs. Making the results of such research available to the larger scientific community via an NL could advance inquiry-based teaching and learning at schools that emphasize undergraduate education. Another participant[21] suggested that the NSF might require those who produce educational materials with the agency's financial support to serve as mentors for some period of time or at certain events so that they could interact with and offer their expertise to other potential users of those materials. An NL for undergraduate SME&T education could facilitate a level of dynamic interaction between the creators and users of materials that would be impossible in other types of media.

Gordon Freedman next approached these issues from a public policy perspective. The federal government could have a multiplier effect on reforming education by improving the dissemination of innovative educational materials and activities, many of which have been produced and field tested with public funds. If the government does not support ways to connect these materials and make them available and useful to the widest audience possible, then citizens do not receive the best value for their tax dollars. Whether an NL is the best avenue to accomplish these goals remains open to discussion. However, Freedman contended that next steps must include mechanisms to maximize the effectiveness of programs and materials that are already being supported by the federal government.

Following this discussion, the workshop was adjourned.

---

[20]Examples included the mathematics forum organized by Swarthmore College (http://forum.swarthmore.edu), which attempts to identify, review, evaluate, and recommend materials to the mathematics community that are appropriate for teaching a variety of subjects at many different levels. The National Engineering Education Delivery System (NEEDS) (http://www.needs.org) was offered as a second example. Sponsored by the Engineering Education Coalitions Program and the Engineering Directorate of NSF, NEEDS provides a database of effective and tested engineering courseware. The University of Minnesota's Geometry Center (http://www.geom.umn.edu) has developed a set of searchable examples that users (both students and faculty) can download and then manipulate to improve their understanding and appreciation of concepts and constructs in geometry.

[21]The name of this participant was not identified in the verbatim transcript of the workshop.

SYNTHESIS AND CONCLUSIONS

As the narrative from the workshop proceedings shows, key themes emerged at the workshop, and some level of agreement was achieved on several issues. Most workshop participants agreed that the establishment of some kind of NL could be a useful —possibly critical—addition to the existing arsenal of tools and other resources that have been created by grants from the NSF's Division of Undergraduate Education and other sources to improve undergraduate SME&T education. However, workshop participants expressed a sufficient variety of different views and perspectives about the clients an NL might serve, the materials it should (and should not) contain, and how it might be constructed, organized, maintained, and supported that the Steering Committee urges the NSF to proceed cautiously and judiciously before making a final decision about establishing an NL for undergraduate SME&T education.

Highlighted below are key observations and critical issues that the NSF may wish to consider before deciding whether to issue one or more Requests for Proposals (RFPs) to sponsor the establishment of a digital NL for undergraduate SME&T education. The Steering Committee offers these ideas with the suggestion that the NSF address them either internally or by seeking additional advice from outside experts. Where appropriate, specific recommendations are provided to assist the NSF in deciding how to proceed with this project (see Steering Committee Recommendations beginning on page 53). The Steering Committee notes that both the workshop and the papers provide a breadth of possible strategies for the NSF to pursue if an NL initiative goes forward.

KEY OBSERVATIONS

In synthesizing the workshop proceedings and stating its conclusions and recommendations, Steering Committee members would ask the NSF to give serious consideration to the following key observations:

- **In terms of feasibility, the pedagogical, technical, economic, and legal issues sur-** rounding the establishment of an NL for undergraduate SME&T education are complex, interrelated, and will quickly assume new dimensions as technology improves and litigation proceeds through the courts. However, the challenges posed by these issues are most likely surmountable.

- **In terms of desirability, if the NSF is to commit its financial support to a digital NL project, workshop participants and the Steering Committee agree that the agency also must be satisfied that it can answer the following questions affirmatively before proceeding:**

  1. *Would the establishment of an NL improve undergraduate SME&T education?*
  2. *Would establishing an NL be a more effective alternative for improving undergraduate SME&T education than other initiatives that might compete for the same funds?*

CRITICAL ISSUES

Audience: To whom should an NL be directed?
This issue pervaded the entire workshop. Broad agreement developed that faculty engaged in SME&T education would be among those targeted as primary users of an NL. Specifically, an NL might enable faculty rapidly to locate, download, use, and modify and adapt materials that would assist and improve their teaching in undergraduate classrooms and laboratories.

Workshop participants also concurred that the central focus of an NL should be to improve and enhance learning of SME&T. By providing useful pedagogical tools, an NL would partially realize this mission. However, there was considerable divergence of opinion about the extent to which an NL should provide learning resources for undergraduate students and possibly other users (e.g., advanced high school students, adults engaged in distance learning through a university program, lifelong learners seeking information on some specific topic, or those wishing to increase their understanding and appreciation of SME&T in general). Some workshop participants argued that the proposed NL should provide such materials for use and exploration by students and other users that would enhance and improve self-developed learning goals. Because they too are lifelong learners, faculty also would benefit from the availability of such resources, both by increasing their own disciplinary and interdisciplinary expertise and by having tools readily available to develop and enhance their undergraduate courses.

Again, as also noted in the NSF's vision statement above (page 18), an NL makes the most sense in the context of a broader culture of higher education that provides both strong incentives and the necessary tools to promote continuous improvement in education. Only when the undergraduate SME&T community broadly shares the values of such a culture will an NL achieve its full potential for disseminating and sharing information.

A number of workshop participants made arguments about why such a cultural change was inevitable. For example, they pointed to various reports decrying the state of undergraduate SME&T education (e.g., National Research Council, 1996a; National Science Foundation, 1996b) and to increasing pressures on institutions of higher education to improve undergraduate teaching in general and SME&T education specifically. However, some workshop participants noted that a large part of the SME&T teaching community has not felt a sense of urgency about the need for reform. Indeed, for the most part, workshop participants believed that the case had not been made that an NL would be an essential component of SME&T education reform.

Specifically, many workshop participants thought that further research is needed to address the following:

- **The need for an NL in SME&T education**. At present, the extent to which an NL would actually be used by faculty intending to improve their teaching of SME&T courses is unknown.
- **The leverage for educational reform that would be provided by an NL**. Even if an NL is used by SME&T faculty interested in improving their teaching, whether the numbers of useful innovations and concerned faculty would be sufficiently large to warrant such an investment is unknown.

It is possible that an initiative to support an NL would be an important statement by the NSF that would facilitate cultural changes by underscoring the importance of educational reform in a highly tangible way. On the other hand, funds used to support an NL would not then be available to support other educational initiatives, and there is simply no analysis one way or another that indicates the relative efficacy of an NL compared to alternatives.

Thus, workshop participants emphasized that making specific recommendations about the breadth of users of an NL was very difficult because the community for whom this resource might be created (faculty from SME&T disciplines who routinely teach undergraduate students and undergraduate and graduate students) did not attend the workshop in sufficient numbers to articulate clearly their needs for content and how they might or might not utilize an NL. Workshop participants who submitted additional comments were unanimous in their concern that potential users become much more intimately involved in all aspects of this project.

Despite the Steering Committee's efforts to include teaching faculty from different kinds of undergraduate colleges and universities, insufficient numbers attended to provide a clear vision about how much and under what circumstances the proposed NL would be utilized. Lack of attendance by a broad spectrum of teaching faculty also highlighted the importance of articulating a clear, unambiguous mandate for establishing an NL.

Content: What should an NL for undergraduate SME&T education contain?
Workshop participants expressed many ideas about what types of information an NL might offer. They agreed that, from a technical standpoint, an NL for undergraduate SME&T education could offer materials such as digitized text (e.g., from professional journals, course syllabi, student works-in-progress), videos and still images, instructional software and simulations, and anything else of relevance that could be stored digitally. However, there was little consensus about which classes of these materials an

NL should make available. Part of the disagreement was related to the issue of who an NL's primary users will be. If an NL is designed primarily for the benefit of teaching faculty, then it should focus on making high-quality and easily adapted teaching materials available. If an NL is to satisfy the needs of a broader spectrum of learners, then its content should include many other types of materials and media.

Workshop discussions also focused on whether an NL should store as well as commission content (e.g., an interactive, multimedia-based calculus curriculum), serve primarily as a resource that electronically "points" users to information stored on other computers (e.g., the Web sites on which such calculus curricula are maintained), or do both. A broad consensus developed to support, at a minimum, an NL that points to useful materials. Pointers are much less expensive to create and maintain than what is required to acquire, store, and provide access to stored materials. Pointers also allow input about content from a wider variety of interests and organizations in the SME&T community and enable owners of the materials to update and revise content as disciplines and knowledge advance. Importantly, pointing to materials rather than storing and disseminating them allows an NL to minimize current legal challenges related to intellectual property rights, copyright law, and licensing agreements for commercially produced content or content produced by individuals seeking compensation for their efforts (see additional discussion of this issue beginning on page 51).

However, an NL could face several important constraints if it were to rely exclusively on the use of pointers rather than the storage of existing materials or the commissioning of at least some materials. First, the project would have to await the availability of consistently reliable software and standardized protocols that would enable its registry regularly to update the addresses of materials stored elsewhere on the Internet (these tools are currently under development; see page 27). Second, the proposed NL's ability to catalyze development of or exert control over the quality of materials specifically suited to this electronic medium could be very limited. Finally, if the intellectual content or quality of materials in some disciplines was not sufficient to provide the proposed NL with "critical mass," its development and evolution would have to be accompanied by other, potentially costly programs that create such content and make it widely available to users.

Also discussed was whether an NL should simply make materials available (either directly or by pointing to other Web sites), such as traditional libraries do now, or also allow users to contribute materials. Contributed materials might include items such as new teaching tools and modules or annotations (e.g., reviews, comments by users, supplemental information) of materials already available.

With regard to the selection of materials, workshop participants also asked, on what basis should materials, pointers to material, or annotations be reviewed and evaluated for inclusion in the proposed NL? Strategies for editorial oversight of this resource would differ depending on whether it merely points to other materials and resources or whether it stores and disseminates them. It is more difficult to establish standards for materials outside a library than for materials already owned by that library. The workshop participants agreed that some mechanism for distinguishing formally reviewed from unreviewed material would be necessary, both from the standpoint of users and for the credibility of the resource itself.

At the same time, many participants pointed to the value of an NL's making available "works-in-progress" and informal papers, syllabi, notes, and other similar unrefereed materials that could help inform the community of users about new and interesting ideas. Some workshop participants noted, however, that nonrefereed material now constitutes the bulk of materials and information on the World Wide Web. Including significant amounts of such unvetted material in the NL's holdings or registry could lead to rapid deterioration of the overall quality of materials made available or pointed to by the proposed NL.

Precisely how to review material was the subject of lively discussion. Some of the possibilities discussed included

- *Using approaches currently employed by refereed journals.* There was concern, however, that given the variety of materials that might be included in the proposed NL, current review processes may result in the exclusion of experimental or other innovative materials that embrace new media, formats, or methods.

- *Delegating at least some oversight to professional societies.* There was concern, however, that this approach would compromise recent trends toward interdisciplinarity in undergraduate SME&T education because most professional societies promote knowledge and activities that are primarily within the purview of their specific disciplines.
- *Soliciting and encouraging commentary by users of an NL's materials.* There was concern, however, that this approach might not allow for a representative or informed sampling of opinions from users.

A fourth issue for the workshop was who the creators of content should be. Here there was fairly broad agreement that creators could include faculty, publishers, professional societies, and students.

The issue of "critical mass" arose again in the context of the creation of content. Experience with the management of information resources suggests that if a library does not contain sufficient amounts of information that have been evaluated for quality and value it will fall into disuse due to user disappointment. Such disappointment is subjective, but if the information in an NL is either not sufficient in quantity or quality, it is to be expected and could be devastating. Issues of critical mass have implications for what is entered into an NL and how long those materials are archived.

A final content issue was the need for tools to facilitate browsing and searching by users. For example, experience with the Internet clearly indicates that simple keyword searches, though sometimes useful, are inadequate and too indiscriminate when searching large volumes of information. Interactive, "intelligent" tools that facilitate searching for materials, especially those that have been designed specifically to exploit an NL's electronic capabilities, would be very useful.

Is the proposed NL a library?
Most workshop participants agreed that, as envisioned during this meeting, an NL for undergraduate SME&T education certainly would have many of the characteristics of traditional libraries, such as tools for indexing and searching. This resource also might have other traditional library capacities, such as classifying and archiving content. However, the digital National Library for undergraduate SME&T education was envisioned as being designed with many other features that are not found in traditional libraries, such as the capacity for users to publicly comment about or add new materials and to work interactively with and upgrade materials already available in the proposed NL. Workshop participants suggested that a better set of terms or descriptors be devised to reflect more accurately the proposed NL's broader vision and objectives and to convey better to potential users how the resource might be utilized. Additional discussion of this issue can be found on page 34.

IMPLEMENTATION: ECONOMIC, LEGAL, AND TECHNOLOGY ISSUES
In addition to focusing on the potential value of an NL for undergraduate SME&T education, the workshop also addressed a number of critical issues related to the implementation and deployment of this resource.

Economic Issues
While government agencies and private foundations might provide key start-up funding, workshop participants agreed that, over the long term, the proposed NL will likely need to become self-sustaining. However, there was little consensus about how best to address questions of economic viability and sustainability, as well as equity of access for all people who wish to utilize this resource as a teaching and learning tool.

Economic viability reflects both costs and revenues. In terms of costs, any NL initiative will require a variety of editorial services (similar to those required of journals). Basic technology services also will be required to store materials, to develop and update pointers to materials on other computers, and to oversee the annotation of materials in the collection or list of pointers. Searching and authoring tools will need to be developed and continually updated as technology advances. Decisions will need to be made about how much material should be archived and for how long. The problem of archiving and the costs associated with it will be difficult to determine until the overseers of the proposed NL establish what types of non-traditional materials will be included and from which sources.

Here again, there is a great need to identify potential users and patterns of use of such a resource. Workshop participants noted that an added benefit of investing in an NL is that it will lessen development time and thus lower costs for future projects in other learning communities such as the humanities and social and behavioral sciences.

Revenue is likely to be a continuing problem and must be confronted directly and early in the development process if this NL is to remain viable and able to grow and adapt to changing user needs and advancing technology. Workshop participants discussed the imposition of fees on students, educational institutions, and publishers but came to no agreement about the desirability or feasibility of charging any of these communities for an NL's services. Here again, the feasibility of any given option will depend on the clients an NL is intended to serve. If students utilize this resource extensively, then user fees collected by colleges and universities that subscribe to this NL (possibly in lieu of money that students might otherwise have spent for textbooks or laboratory fees) could be used to support it. Publishers might support an NL if it provided a plausible advertising showcase for their wares. Educational institutions (e.g., through some kind of consortia) and professional societies also might support an NL financially if it provides recognized value to faculty and members, respectively. It also is important to note that an NL is likely to emerge in an era of electronic commerce, which may provide the means for micro-payments that could sustain it in the long term.

While the costs of hardware and software are likely to decrease over time, initial costs for establishing an NL and the certainty of upgrades that will be needed to maintain this NL on the cutting edge of technology[22] must be factored into total costs along with the considerable costs of the personnel that will be required to maintain its infrastructure and oversee its content. Other direct or indirect costs that could affect how extensively the proposed

NL is utilized include those associated with training users. Should those costs be borne by the users themselves or their places of employment? Or, should public or private funds be made available to provide this training, at least initially? Equity of access always must be a high priority in any discussions or decisions about the costs and financing of an NL. Workshop participants discussed but could not provide definitive answers to these difficult questions.

Legal Issues

Workshop participants identified a number of legal issues that would need to be addressed before an NL could become a practical reality. These include

- *Intellectual Property (IP).* IP issues in the context of an NL are very similar to those facing any on line provider of content. However, some types of material may not be as problematic (e.g., course notes) because remuneration to authors of these materials is unlikely to be involved. Some of these issues could be resolved if an NL pointed to rather than provided materials. Users would then incur responsibility for compensating providers through arrangements defined by the providers (although the governing body for the proposed NL may wish to help define some of those financial arrangements as a condition for referring users to the provider's Web site).
- *Liability.* Given that online references are sometimes perceived as more "threatening" than the same information contained in books (e.g., a laboratory experiment that could potentially harm an unwary student), NL materials that involve risk to students may involve liability for the overseers of that NL or for authors and creators of materials to which it points.
- *Privacy.* To the extent that students use materials or information found in an NL (e.g., an online self-diagnostic test that may be packaged with educational materials), well-meaning faculty may be interested in the extent and nature of such usage. Would obtaining such information impinge on students' rights of and expectations for privacy?

The general conclusion of the workshop was that these legal issues will not be resolved in the context

---

[22]While incorporating the latest advances in technology into an NL's arsenal is tempting, this desire must be tempered by the fact that many of the computers that will be used to access the NL may not have the capacity to use new software platforms or programs that require excessive amounts of memory. Here again, it is imperative that any project include a complete discussion of users' and institutions' needs and limitations.

of this project. Rather, a regime of law and practice will gradually evolve as online publishing and dissemination of information becomes more extensive. Any NL that is built for undergraduate SME&T education will need to be flexible enough to accommodate a wide range of possible legal regimes and challenges.

Technology Issues

Workshop participants discussed many technology-related issues. First and foremost, consensus was reached that the primary purpose of the proposed NL should be to satisfy the needs of users rather than to be a vehicle for advancing technology or research about digital libraries. Participants did recognize that, from time to time, new tools will be created that might be used in entirely unexpected ways. Nevertheless, on balance, they expressed a strong sentiment for placing users first and making sure that any technologies employed to operate this resource are developed and deployed to accommodate the needs of NL users.

Associated with their desire to serve the needs of users, some workshop participants questioned the conventional wisdom of making this proposed NL available only via the Internet. Some institutions of higher education do not now enjoy access to the Internet, and others have only limited access through data lines that do not accommodate rapid downloading of large applications or data sets. The problem is exacerbated in other countries; if the proposed NL is designed to serve the needs of users beyond the United States, the Internet may not be the appropriate vehicle for delivering such services to everyone. Rather, it was suggested that other formats, such as CD-ROM sets, might be included as components of any strategy that develops for delivering information to users from this resource. Other participants noted that the development of Internet II also could limit access to the proposed NL, since Internet II may only be available to selected colleges and universities. Here again, equity of access must become a prime issue for consideration.

Workshop participants felt that emerging technologies that are being developed by other digital library projects now under way and should be utilized by this project. But such technologies should be deployed with careful attention to how they improve services to users, life-cycle costs, and long-term usability and sustainability. Workshop participants emphasized that an NL should employ technologies that are adaptive, flexible, and responsive to unforeseen user needs and problems. It is impossible to anticipate every way in which individual users might want to take advantage of this NL's resources, but customizable tools should be available to facilitate its use by as many people as possible. New applications and modules should be designed to operate with software that is widely available for other applications (e.g., commonly used spreadsheets). This design would reduce the time required for users to learn how to work with such materials.

An NL that is sustained over time must plan to accommodate new information technologies as they emerge while dealing with content that was designed to run on older computers and operating systems that are or may become incompatible with newer hardware and software. This will apply to search engines and other tools that might be used in an NL, as well as for pedagogical materials developed by one user or institution and offered to or shared by others.

Finally, the workshop participants reached broad agreement that the technology in an NL must be developed with advice and oversight from professionals who are most knowledgeable about how people organize and use information: librarians and social and behavioral scientists. Librarians grapple continually with technology interface issues as they strive to make electronic information available and complementary to materials in other formats. They also give much consideration to how such information should be stored and archived. Similarly, social and behavioral scientists can help with considerations of how individuals organize and contextualize information. Without the informed perspectives of librarians and social and behavioral scientists, an NL is likely not to optimize opportunities for teaching and learning.

STEERING COMMITTEE RECOMMENDATIONS

Workshop participants generally agreed that the idea of an NL for SME&T education is sufficiently promising that the NSF should pursue it further, and the Steering Committee concurs. Although workshop participants did not agree on specific next steps, the Steering Committee makes the following recommendations to guide the NSF's planning for an NL initiative and its issuance of one or more Request for Proposals (RFPs). The Committee suggests that these recommendations be acted upon sequentially.

1. Clarify the potential customers of an NL for undergraduate SME&T education

1.1 Because workshop participants were unable to delineate the stakeholders or to specify the content for this proposed NL, the NSF should do so. The level of funding that the agency can devote to this project may dictate the breadth of the proposed NL's users, and that, in turn, may help with content decisions. However, the Steering Committee recommends that, *prior to making final decisions about this issue*, the NSF should make a concerted effort to bring together in a series of focus groups representatives from *all* communities that might be an NL's likely users and service providers. Focus groups should be small and should be structured to encourage participants to discuss freely 1) their requirements for resources and tools that would help them improve teaching and learning of undergraduate SME&T, and 2) the ways in which the digital National Library could address those requirements. At a minimum, participants in these focus groups should include

- *College and university SME&T faculty from all types of postsecondary institutions*, including two-year colleges, undergraduate liberal arts colleges, predominantly undergraduate and comprehensive universities, and research universities. Special attention should be paid to including in these discussions people from insti-

tutions that have limited access to information technology so that an NL can be designed to take these limitations into account.
- *College and university SME&T faculty at different stages of their academic careers*. Discussions should be held with pre-tenured faculty as well as those who are at various stages beyond tenure (associate and full rank). Faculty who are not in tenure-track positions (e.g., adjunct and part-time faculty) also should be involved.
- *College and university faculty involved with research and practice in science and mathematics education, including the preparation of future K-12 teachers.* These faculty have knowledge of and familiarity with the research on effective techniques for improving learning and teaching. Their input is essential to inform discussions about content that is appropriate for undergraduate learners and other users of this resource and for the special needs of students who aspire to careers as science and mathematics teachers for Grades K-12.
- *SME&T faculty from middle- and high-schools across the United States.* These faculty may become important users of this proposed NL, and they will greatly influence the motivation of students to study SME&T both in high school and in college. These faculty also are often more well versed in pedagogy than university SME&T faculty and, therefore, can provide critical input about an NL's organization and user interfaces.
- *Undergraduate students* from different types of colleges and universities. This group should include both "traditional" students (i.e., those who enter college immediately after graduating from high school) and "non-traditional" students (e.g., adult learners who are returning to higher education).
- *Graduate and postdoctoral students* who are likely to enter careers in academe also should be consulted since they can help define needs of future faculty users.

- *Librarians.* Librarians already possess the requisite background and knowledge about users' borrowing habits and the tools that they employ to search for information. They can work with all of the other user groups to help define the roles and the services that an NL for undergraduate SME&T education might assume. Librarians also deal routinely with people who have special needs that any NL should accommodate.
- *Social and behavioral scientists* with expertise in organizational constructs and in the ways in which people learn new information can provide valuable insight and perspective to the NSF about how to design an NL's technological platforms and also how best to develop teaching and learning tools that would be widely utilized and educationally effective.
- *Computer and information system specialists* with specific experience with digital libraries. This community will define what is technologically possible for a digital NL for undergraduate SME&T education. Because so many other digital library projects are now in various stages of development and implementation, individuals involved with those projects should be brought into the discussion both to share information about their technological advances and to take back to their communities information about the potential for an NL.
- *Directors of college and university information technology services.* The groups of users listed above will help define the vision and objectives for an NL. However, if an NL is to be widely accessible, then it must be constructed with an appreciation of the current computing capabilities and limitations of potential users. Directors who work daily with computer systems on college and university campuses will help define the user interfaces that are currently available and that might be developed in the future.
- *Representatives from the commercial publishing sector.* Representatives from this community can best inform the NSF and other potential users about the kinds of materials that would likely become available for inclusion in an NL and the costs of procuring those materials. Since commercial publishers are intimately involved with the debates concerning intellectual property, copyright, and fair use of materials, their repre-

sentatives also can update and listen to recommendations from the other players on these legal issues.
- *Representatives from professional SME&T societies.* Professional societies could serve this project both as providers of information and materials and as catalysts for engaging their members. Many professional societies maintain extensive collections of information related to their disciplines and may be very interested in an NL as a vehicle for disseminating that information. Professional societies also are recognizing their obligation to improving science education. Direct involvement with an NL could help focus the educational mission and activities of professional societies and encourage their members to see the improvement of undergraduate SME&T education as an integral component of scholarly activity and productivity.
- *Representatives from the private non-profit sector,* such as foundations. These people will likely provide at least some of the funds to sustain an NL for undergraduate SME&T education in future years. Their input will be critical.

1.2 The Steering Committee suggests that two different types of focus group meetings be held. Some focus groups should concentrate on receiving input from single communities, especially SME&T faculty and students. Others should involve people from many or all of the aforementioned sectors in cross-cutting sessions, with the primary objectives of having convenors listen and respond to the ideas and expressed needs of potential users.

1.3 The Steering Committee recommends that NSF also might employ the services of one or more professional organizations to organize these focus groups, to facilitate discussions within the groups and to prepare an independent assessment of user needs and desires based on the group discussions.

2. Articulate priorities for content, technological considerations, and economic and legal models before committing to the establishment of an NL.
The Steering Committee can offer no specific recommendations about whether the proposed NL should commission the creation and storage of materials vs. developing a sophisticated system of

STEERING COMMITTEE RECOMMENDATIONS

pointers to materials that reside and are maintained elsewhere (see footnote 8, page 29, on archiving and preserving). Differences in cost between the two systems, evolving legal precedents with respect to copyright and fair use of materials, and the emergence of new technologies that may overcome some of the limitations of pointing to information stored elsewhere all must be factored into the final structure of an NL. Moreover, these parameters are likely to change during the development phase of the project. Ongoing advice from appropriate experts in all of these fields is warranted if the project proceeds.

2.1 The Steering Committee recommends that the proposed NL be viewed primarily as a resource for improving and inspiring *learning* of undergraduate SME&T rather than merely as a means to promote more effective *teaching* of these subjects. If an NL is to be a central component of current efforts to reform and improve undergraduate SME&T education, it must offer more than teaching tools alone. The NSF should appoint a Board of Overseers consisting of acknowledged experts in SME&T education, library sciences, and digital libraries that is charged to work with a broad spectrum of intended users and the other stakeholders *before* decisions are made about what kinds of materials should be placed into the proposed NL. If an NL initiative cannot afford to support all areas of SME&T, then the Board should decide on the initial areas of focus and look to expand coverage as the project develops.

2.2 Steering Committee members also agree with many workshop participants and recommend that an NL should strive to focus on collecting or pointing to materials that either are inaccessible through other media formats or are so innovative that they are unlikely to be commercially available or viable in the short term. Because a "critical mass" of materials is vitally important to the success of an NL, the acquisition of such innovative new materials will likely need to be balanced with more traditional materials, at least initially.

2.3 The Steering Committee recommends that the NSF emphasize involvement by professional SME&T societies in developing content that could be appropriate for an NL. Many of these organizations already have produced materials that might be incorporated into an NL at little or no cost. By promoting the development of these kinds of teaching and learning tools and by officially recognizing their members who do so, professional societies could become key catalysts in changing the culture of higher education to embrace as legitimate scholarly activities the promotion and evaluation of teaching and the promotion of effective learning by students.

2.4 The Steering Committee recommends that an NL should provide information about and access to projects in undergraduate SME&T education that the NSF and other agencies have supported financially.

2.5 The Steering Committee recommends that the NSF also seek a new, more encompassing descriptor for this project. Workshop participants recognized, and the Steering Committee concurs, that "Digital National Library" or "National Library"—the terms that have been most commonly used to describe this entity—may be more confusing than enlightening to anyone who envisions the potential stakeholders in this project and the services it may provide. Any NL initiative is likely to transcend the functions of many conventional libraries. A more appropriate descriptor might help to focus the higher education community on the need for such a resource and its importance.

3. Develop and issue one or more RFPs to establish an NL for undergraduate SME&T education

As the NSF receives additional input from stakeholders about the goals of and need for an NL (via Recommendations 1 and 2), the scope and potential cost of the project should become clearer. During the workshop, Steering Committee Chair Jack Wilson charged participants with trying to arrive at answers to the following major cross-cutting questions: 1) Is an NL a good idea for improving undergraduate SME&T education? and 2) Is an NL a better idea than other initiatives that might compete for the same funds? *If the NSF is convinced on the basis of its explorations that it can answer these questions in the affirmative, then the question of how to implement this project should become the central focus.* Options for proceeding at that point would include

Option 1: Undertaking a single, large initiative that would result in an operational NL within several years.

Option 2: Undertaking several smaller initiatives for shorter periods of time (12-24 months). These initiatives might be competitive and operate independently of each other or they might be components of some larger cooperative agreement. These various models for establishing an NL could then be evaluated against each other, with a final coordination of best practices that might lead to a single, integrated project.

3.1 Given the tremendous complexity of this project and the number of communities that must be directly involved if it is to have any chance for success, the Steering Committee recommends that NSF consider adopting _Option 2_. Steering Committee members envision that the smaller initiatives suggested in _Option_ 2 might be incorporated into a program similar to those that the NSF's Division of Undergraduate Education has sponsored in recent years to change the ways in which chemistry and calculus are taught. Optimally, this new initiative would incorporate many similar components, including those delineated in Recommendations 3.2 and 3.3 below.

3.2 The Steering Committee recommends that the NSF, in following through with Recommendation 3.1, should develop an RFP articulating the need for and issues involving the establishment of an NL as outlined in this report. The RFP would encourage diverse groups of stakeholders to focus on some subset of the issues. Collaboration among stakeholders and interdisciplinary approaches to address the questions posed here would be encouraged. Preproposals could be sought, with funds then awarded to successful groups to encourage them to develop full proposals. Depending on the funds available, the NSF might then award larger contracts to one or more groups to tackle specific issues or sets of issues. Each of these final awardees would be expected to inform each other of their progress and problems through routine communications, reports, and through meetings of teams convened on a regular basis (at least annually).

3.3 Because the central concern of workshop participants was to define the users of and the need for an NL for undergraduate SME&T education, the Steering Committee recommends that RFPs for preproposals not be formulated until the NSF sponsors the focus groups described above. Feedback and evaluation of information from these groups of users and providers could then serve as the basis for constructing RFPs that would help eventual awardees to address specifically the established needs and requirements of potential NL users.

LITERATURE CITED

Bishop, A.P. 1995. "Working towards an understanding of digital library use." *D-Lib Magazine*, October. See also http://www.dlib.org/dlib/october95/10bishop.html.

Borgman, C.L., Bates, M.J., Cloonan, M.V., Efthimiadis, E.N., Gilliland-Swetland, A.J., Kafai, Y.B., Leazer, G.H., and Maddox, A.B. 1996. "Social Aspects of Digital Libraries." Proceedings of the University of California Los Angeles-National Science Foundation Social Aspects of Digital Libraries Workshop, February 15-17, 1996. Final report submitted to the National Science Foundation (Award No. 9528808). (Materials from this workshop are available on the Internet at: http://www.gslis.ucla.edu/DL/.)

Boyer, E.L. 1990. *Scholarship Reconsidered: Priorities of the Professoriate*. Princeton, NJ: Carnegie Foundation for the Advancement of Teaching.

Clinton,W.J., and Gore, Jr., A. 1994. *Science in the National Interest*. Washington, DC: Office of Science and Technology Policy.

Daniel, J.S. 1996. *Mega-Universities and Knowledge Media: Technology Strategies for Higher Education*. London: Kogan Page.

Egan, D.E., Lesk, M.E., Ketchum, R.D., Lochbaum, C.C., Remde, J.R., Littman, M., and Landauer, T.K. 1991. "Hypertext for the Electronic Library? CORE Sample Results." Proc. HypertextSan Antonio, 15-18 Dec. 1991. pp. 299-312.

Friedman, E., McClellan, J., and Shapiro, A. 1989. "Student performance in an electronic text environment." *Machine-Mediated Learning*, 3(3):243-58.

Glassick, C., Huber, M.T., and Maeroff, G.I. 1997. *Scholarship Assessed: A Special Report on Faculty Evaluation*. San Franciso: Jossey-Bass, Inc.

Joint Policy Board for Mathematics. 1994. *Recognition and Rewards in the Mathematical Sciences*. Washington, DC: American Mathematical Society.

Laurillard, D. 1993. *Rethinking University Teaching: A Framework for the Effective Use of Educational Technology*. London: Routledge.

Leavitt, M.O. 1997. Testimony before the Senate Committee on Labor and Human Resources on Reauthorization of the Higher Education Act of 1965. April 16, 1997.

Marchionini, G.C. 1994. "Evaluating hypermedia and learning: methods and results from the Perseus Project." *ACM Transactions on Information Systems*, 12(1):5-34.

McArthur, D., Lewis, M., and Bishay, M. 1995. "ESSCOTS for Learning: Transforming Commercial Software into Powerful Educational Tools," *Journal of Artificial Intelligence and Education* 6(1):3-33. Also available at http://www.rand.org/hot/mcarthur/Papers/esscots.html.

National Council of Teachers of Mathematics. 1989. *Professional Standards for Teaching Mathematics,* Volumes I, II, and III. Reston, VA: National Council of Teachers of Mathematics.

National Research Council. 1991. *Moving Beyond Myths: Revitalizing Undergraduate Mathematics*. Washington, DC: National Academy Press.

National Research Council. 1994. *Realizing the Information Future: The Internet and Beyond*. Washington, DC: National Academy Press.

National Research Council. 1995. *Engineering Education: Designing an Adaptive System*. Washington, DC: National Academy Press.

National Research Council. 1996a. *From Analysis to Action: Undergraduate Education in Science, Mathematics, Engineering, and Technology*. Washington, DC: National Academy Press.

National Research Council. 1996b. *National Science Education Standards*. Washington, DC: National Academy Press.

National Science Foundation. 1992. "America's Academic Future: A Report of the Presidential Young Investigator Colloquium on U.S. Engineering, Mathematics, and Science Education for the Year 2010 and Beyond." (NSF 91-150.) Arlington, VA: National Science Foundation.

National Science Foundation. 1996a. "Science and Engineering Degrees: 1966-94. (NSF 96-321.) Arlington, VA: National Science Foundation.

National Science Foundation. 1996b. "Shaping the Future: New Expectations for Undergraduate Education in Science, Mathematics, Engineering, and Technology." (NSF 96-139.) Arlington, VA: National Science Foundation.

National Science Foundation. 1997. "Digital libraries will make information more accessible." *Frontiers: Newsletter of the National Science Foundation.* May. p. 2.

Panel on Educational Technology. 1997. "Report to the President on the Use of Technology to Strengthen K-12 Education in the United States." Washington, DC: President's Committee of Advisors on Science and Technology.

Project Kaleidoscope. 1991. *What Works: Building Natural Sciences Communities. A Plan for Strengthening Undergraduate Science and Mathematics, Vol. I.* Washington, DC: Project Kaleidoscope.

Project Kaleidoscope. 1997. *The Question of Reform.* Washington, DC: Project Kaleidoscope.

Resmer, M. 1997. "Universal Student Access to Information Resources." *Syllabus,* 10(6): 12-14.

Schatz, B., and Chen, H. 1996. "Building large-scale digital libraries." *Computer,* 29(5):22-26.

Smith, E. and Weingarten, W.F. (eds.). 1997. *Research Challenges for the Next Generation Internet,* Washington, DC: Computing Research Association.

U.S. Senate Committee on Labor and Human Resources. 1997. Hearing on "Technology and the Virtual University: Opportunities and Challenges." Washington, DC: U.S. Government Printing Office.

APPENDIX A: COMMISSIONED PAPERS

A National Library for Undergraduate Science, Mathematics, Engineering, and Technology Education: A Learning Laboratory

PRUDENCE S. ADLER
Assistant Executive Director
Association of Research Libraries

MARY M. CASE
Director, Office of Scholarly Communication
Association of Research Libraries

INTRODUCTION AND SUMMARY

Digital technologies are transforming all aspects of education including scholarly communication. These technologies provide an unprecedented opportunity to rethink how the education community including the research library community creates, uses, publishes, accesses, and manages these resources. The greatest impact of these technologies can be seen in the creation of new knowledge and how scholars, researchers, and students are increasingly finding new means of providing education services and collaborating via the networked environment. This transformation or transition to a new mode of scholarly communication and education generally necessitates a rethinking of the concept of a "digital library." One does not want to recreate the current system that predominately reflects the print environment and as presently constructed, does not provide equal benefits to all participants.

Instead, in designing a digital library for undergraduate science, mathematics, engineering, and technology education, a starting point could be identification of the values or ethic of a new scholarly communications medium in support of education and to map these against the potential of the net-worked environment. As Einstein commented, "The significant problems we face cannot be solved at the same level of thinking we were at when we created them." There will be more than ever the need to heed Einstein's advice and think creatively in these discussions.

The development of a digital library for undergraduate science, mathematics, engineering, and technology education (SME&T) presents a unique opportunity to build a "library" which breaks out of the current system and incorporates the unique capabilities of the networked environment into its structure. It also permits the scholarly and research community to recapture and reengineer one facet of the scholarly communication process to meet their needs.

SELECTED ATTRIBUTES OF AN SME&T NATIONAL LIBRARY

The National Library should provide an active learning environment. Using the vast capabilities of the Internet and the Next Generation Internet, the National Library should provide a distributed system of access not only to primary data resources, reference materials, and other resources, but to a variety of interactive components including such features as: computer-aided design, lab simulations, access to research tools such as telescopes, instructional software, virtual reality, multimedia, teleconferencing, among many others. With the emphasis on introducing students to research early in their undergraduate careers, the National Library could provide not only instructional packages for basic undergraduate classes, such as calculus and statistics, but could also provide the opportunity for students even at small institutions to participate in the research of scientists located at major research universities. Simulations, online lab notebooks, shared problem solving would all support the collaborative environment that makes learning so exciting.

Key to this vision of a National Library is the concept of providing the resources, tools, and collaborative environment to support the creation of new knowledge. The promise of the networked environment is not in the pipes or the data alone. The great promise of the network is in the ability for human interaction with vast amounts of data and with numerous other students and researchers from around the globe. The value of many minds exploring the same problem or the serendipitous connection of seemingly unrelated efforts is enhanced by a national network. A National Library system that supports and encourages the creation of new knowledge by undergraduates could serve as a model for reshaping the educational process for other disciplines.

This National Library would need a number of attributes to succeed. First, the user must be able to access the available resources transparently, regardless of his or the information's location. A robust network, and effective and affordable delivery systems (bandwidth, scalable systems, and quality of service) are inherent parts of such transparency. Second, applications to retrieve, access, authenticate, evaluate, and utilize data and information, including detailed metadata and/or object content, will be critical in the effectiveness of the National Library and its adoption and use. Third, applications to perform operations on the data—to make it meaningful to the user—including the provision of links to other providers' sites, commercial or non-commercial, and/or to compile data objects to meet a user's needs, will be an essential component of the system. Fourth, authoring applications that simplify the reporting of research results, the incorporating of data sets or simulations, the building of curricula, will be critical to ensuring timely and active reporting of research results by faculty and students. Finally, communications systems that support interactive real time text, audio, and visual transmission—the key to the student-faculty, student-student, and student-resource interactions—are equally as important to the success of the National Library.

In addition to these technical issues, there are a number of practices and policies that need to be considered to achieve the vision of the National Library. Access to robust content is essential to the education and training of tomorrow's scientists and engineers. Content in the National Library must be provided with the understanding that it will be used in various ways to support the educational mission. These uses may include access through multiple sites by students across the country, printing and downloading for individual student and classroom use, excerpting for inclusion in papers, projects, instructional packages, multimedia presentations, etc. The uses may also include the making of preservation copies by designated library sites to ensure long-term access to the resources and new knowledge created through the system.

Content for the National Library will come from a variety of sources. Several years of backfiles of scholarly journals, varying by discipline, will need to be included. Permissions will need to be obtained and broad use rights as described above negotiated. Indexing and abstracting files will also be needed to support efficient access to the published literature. Primary resource data, such as photographs from Mars, human genome data, astronomical observations, the periodic table, geographic information data, should also be at the student's fingertips.

To be successful, new practices and policies are required, particularly with regard to copyright and intellectual property. The current balance between users of proprietary information and creators of that information must be maintained while at the same time, rethinking how creation of information and access to that information is managed.

The education community is both a creator and user of proprietary information. Thus members of this community participate in the full spectrum of activities regulated by the laws governing copyright and must be sensitive to the balance of interests. As digital technologies revolutionize how information is recorded, disseminated, accessed, and stored, these technologies eliminate the technical limits that have supplemented the legal framework of balance between ownership and public dissemination. Unlimited technological capacity to disseminate by transmission in ways that can violate the rights of copyright holders confronts equally unlimited technological capacity to prevent works from being used in ways contemplated by law. Carried to its logical extreme, either trend would destroy the balance currently enjoyed, with results that would likely undermine core educational functions as well as radically transform the information marketplace.

New practices could extend this balance but ones that would represent a different ethic, namely balance in support of furthering the goals of the education community. For example, a legal regime which ensures that such factual data critical to the progress of science remains in the public domain is essential. It will also be important that current work of faculty and students be a vital part of the library. Participation in the library as an active learning environment will require faculty and students, if they choose to publish their work elsewhere, to retain the rights that would allow full use of the resource within the National Library. Participation in the National Library will also mean that faculty and students accept the responsibility to respect use restrictions where they apply and to respect the principles of attribution and fairness in the use of others' work.

To encourage faculty contribution to and participation in the National Library, implications for promotion and tenure will need to be addressed. If the new knowledge created through the National Library is highly collaborative in nature, with the potential for students and faculty from around the country making contributions, how is the contribution of an individual evaluated? Technology may provide some help, if methods can be found to track unobtrusively the flow of discussion as a group makes its way through a problem, simulation, or experiment. But at what point does such tracking invade the privacy of the participants? In addition, how is the extensive contribution of a faculty member to the development of a national curriculum in undergraduate science to be evaluated within an educational context that emphasizes research and publication?

Finally, the National Library will only be a success if it indeed improves the education of undergraduates in science, mathematics, engineering, and technology. Evaluation methods will need to be designed to measure pre- and post-library use. Not only skills and knowledge could be measured, but also interest in the disciplines, interest in research, and career plans.

SELECTED CONCERNS/ISSUES TO RESOLVE

- The SME&T National Library would be an extremely useful application to test the evolving and proposed infrastructure for the Next Generation Internet, the vBNS, and the I2 project. But to be effective, the SME&T National Library should be accessible and available well beyond those participating in these efforts. It needs to reach a much wider audience (e.g., community colleges and selected K-12 institutions) who generally do not have the necessary connectivity nor the resources to gain such connectivity. This represents a significant hurdle for the success of the proposal. Collaboration with the networking division of NSF would be essential to design strategies to promote needed connectivity to these other institutions. It will be important to view this as a multi-phased initiative; one that acknowledges the shortcomings and limitations of the current environment yet continues to promote a broader vision.

- As noted above, there will be a need to refocus the expectations and in many instances, practices, of faculty and students regarding publication, education, and access to resources beyond an individual institution.

- To be successful, the National Library must meet the timing and access needs of community, reflect how the materials are used, and in the settings that are most productive. This again may be particularly problematic with regard to connectivity issues.

- The availability of trained and committed staff able to build, navigate, and to translate the needs of users in this complex environment is another key factor in the success of this initiative.

If we think broadly and imaginatively, the digital National Library has the potential to create an exciting new learning environment for undergraduates that may result in better education and an increased interest in pursuing careers in science, mathematics, engineering, and technology.

The Digital Library as "Road and Load": Partnerships in Carrier and Content for a National Library for Undergraduate Science, Mathematics, Engineering, and Technology Education

HAROLD BILLINGS
Director of General Libraries
The University of Texas at Austin

INTRODUCTION

The "digital library" is still being defined very much with respect to how it is perceived in the mind of the beholder. A librarian, a computer scientist, an educator, a journal publisher, or a Web master will each have a different perception of what a digital library is from their point of view. For the majority of participants in the technical construction of the infrastructure that provides access to information on the Internet or within the World Wide Web, and for most of the users of that world, a digital library is simply a collection of information stored in electronic format.

Defined in this fashion, cyberspace is a virtual wilderness of digital information of frequently dubious content, utility, authority or longevity. The rapid growth of information sources that are of more obvious benefit to the business, governmental, educational, and technical communities—and to the prospectively larger benefit of the social weal—has led to an intensified examination of the infrastructure that supports the provision of and access to such resources. In several ways, there has been much more attention paid to the "road" to distribute and reach digital resources than there has been paid to the "load" it carries.

The digital library is much more than the definition above assumes it to be. Its roots lie much more deeply in the traditional library than is generally assumed, and its users are likely to be more typical, in need and habit, of traditional library customers than might be imagined. But road and load are dramatically different within the traditional and the digital library. This difference, built around the new information technologies, represents both the opportunity and the challenge for the establishment of a National Library of Science, Mathematics, Engineering, and Technology Education, because such a library must incorporate the best of each.

ROAD AND LOAD

Road as carrier, and load as content are the most basic elements of a digital library. Carrier is defined by computing and telecommunications—information technology. Content is defined by the boundaries of several digital library spatial concepts. These concepts include those of information stored "somespace" in electronic format. It includes information in physical format stored somewhere, usually within the traditional library, capable of being transmuted into digital form and delivered through electronic transmission. And it includes the interactive distribution and receipt of purposeful scholarly communication, teaching, and distance learning content—all deliverable through the information technologies that provide the road.

Digital content may consist of textual information, sound, video, animation, raw data, response-invoking semiotics such as art or music, streaming communication, electronic curricula or teleconferenced course content, and so on—all of it hypertextually linked. Its sources may be commercial Web sites, "publications" by amateurs on the Web, interactive courseware developed at a faculty member's home page, databases at national laboratories, traditional library Web sites which supply information stored in local servers including bibliographic, textual and multimedia content, and a plethora of other information providers with a presence on the Internet.

The fact is that the information available via the Internet is dwarfed by the holdings of most academic libraries. The problem is that the road to the content of most libraries continues to be a manual circulation or interlibrary lending system that reaches print-on-paper resources. Comparatively little useful information is yet available through the Internet digital road and load, and as suggested above this information is a complex mix of digital library contributions.

The manager of the digital library selects and organizes this content, supplies access to it, and may provide new types of digital library assistance: e.g., routinely staffed interactive help-desks, electronic messaging between user and library, the sharing among institutions of human expertise to provide specialized subject assistance, and information-gathering tools that use every hour of the day to identify and deliver to the scholar information of interest that has gathered in its space.

The best of traditional libraries are now identifying and providing the Internet address on their Web home pages of the most useful digital content providers. These libraries are providing access to electronic journals and other information mounted on local or remote servers, and are encouraging the reformatting and delivery of information from library print collections into a load suitable for the national information highway. This is the same plan that is most likely to serve as the architecture for the National Library, a library of selective digital library and distance learning linkages.

Question. The selection of resources to be "held" in the National Library will certainly be a major issue. Is the concept of distributed selection the best model, or should there be a central "collection development" office? (It should certainly be assumed that a "collection development policy" similar to those used in contemporary traditional libraries would need to be constructed if determinations of the content of the National Library were to be made at the top, rather than built up through the accretionary development of choices made at the local SME&T participant level by faculty and library collection development experts.)

The growth of information available over the Internet has started to attract more attention by the federal, state, educational, and scientific sectors for its potential to enhance learning and research. The recent submersion of the Internet by commercial and personal interests has led to consideration of a means to establish an Internet dedicated to education and research. It is apparent, however, that there will have to be gates between these roads since a digital library will require access to loads on each. A number of projects at institutional, state, and library association levels have been established to promote a higher-quality information infrastructure and to foster the development of a more useful national structure of digital libraries.

Question. How is it possible to relate federal government and state activities in the changing model of distance learning and distance information? There is a growing federalism of library programs—that is, a distinct urging through funding and legislative mechanisms at the state level to push libraries into information management organizations or networks to leverage their resources. Will this conflict with the concept of a National Library for SME&T Education?

In my view, the traditional library that in the past has supported the informational needs of the K-12, higher education, and the general public communities has not been as closely involved in the digital library movement as it should have been. This is a result of both lethargy on the part of the traditional library community and of a misapprehension by the information technology and instructional communities that there will be as important a role for the traditional library in the information future as there has been in the information past.

As I see them, traditional research libraries are being rapidly enhanced and extended electronically. In the most accurate sense of the word, these libraries are becoming increasingly "bionic"—organic, evolving bodies whose collections are growing rapidly in both traditional paper and in digital format, and that are increasingly responsive interactively with their users.

It is from the grass-roots growth of information resources into the contemporary "bionic library," and from the creation of pockets of digital information created by multiple agencies and authors and distributed throughout the Web, that the hypertextual fullness of a National Library for Undergraduate Science, Mathematics, Engineering and Technology Education can be realized. To some extent, just as the definition of a digital library poses uncertainties in a discussion of issues relating to it, the metaphor of the "web" may confuse the necessary definition of the National Library and the prospective role of the National Science Foundation in that enterprise.

Given the organic nature of libraries and knowledge, a superior metaphor in these circumstances might be that of a hypertextual Knowledge Tree, with its roots in undergraduate scholarship and research and its limbs and twigs the result of the growth triggered at these grass-root levels. The information resources that abound today on the World Wide Web are not the results of a top-down effort, but rather that of a libertarian attitude that lets the many roots and trees and flowers grow. It is almost ironic that much of the current digital library environment was designed by students who had the foresight to seize and exploit information technology opportunities. It is likely that this will be the same group that will continue to use the Web in unique and uncontrollable ways, helping create new mechanisms from which digital libraries and distance learning can grow. It may be that it is this group, also—students active in SME&T—who can tell us how a National Library might be constructed and how it might best meet the needs of the undergraduate student.

In terms of the information content of digital libraries and the services required of them, there is basically little evidence available today to differentiate between the methodologies of the users of science, mathematics, engineering and technology library materials and those of other disciplines. Content is the point. A major problem at the moment is the difficulty in attracting the attention of either faculty or students to the richness of the resources available to them through the Internet or the World Wide Web. But, ultimately, it will be this audience who will determine which information resources, which faculty, whose courses, what kind of learning techniques, flourish on the Web and which are assigned to the digital dust heap.

Question. How can the National Library and the National Science Foundation make the best use of the experience of institutions that have established digital library models and have provided both general content and learning resources to accompany the information they provide? An example is the Library of Congress's American Memory Project, and its accompanying Learning Page. How to adapt such programs for SME&T?

DISTANCE EDUCATION AND DISTANCE INFORMATION

The location of information is of little importance until it is needed. Every hypertext location on the World Wide Web is immediately present to any other location, and every visitor on the Web is in virtual assemblage with other visitors. Time presents fewer constraints on access to information than it has in the past. Through the use of new information technologies it is increasingly possible for libraries to provide information to the user wherever, whenever,

and in whatever format it is needed. The availability of the technology, however, does not ensure access to the needed information.

The barriers of cost, copyright, licensing, an absence of economic models, a deficiency of skilled knowledge workers and teachers versed in the capabilities of the new technologies, and a lack of understanding at policy-making levels of the advantages to be gained from the new information opportunities, have all restricted the level of progress that should have been made in this arena.

Perhaps the most serious impediment to progress has been the difficulty of gaining the attention, or maintaining the attention, or providing a sufficiency of attention by the groups that should gather in partnership to encourage a rapid and orderly progress towards a richer digital library model and, in this instance, to develop the National Library. Michael Goldhaber certainly has a point when he contends that the new natural economy is not information but attention. Whatever catches and commands attention becomes a major currency, although the target of that attention is only worth the informational substance imbedded in it.

The economy of digital libraries is a major concern. Digital reference works, electronic journals, and scholarly databases are already here, already on the Web, and already delivered to millions of undergraduates, and the number of these products grow by the minute. But these products do not come cheaply.

The enormous costs of information products in SME&T can be illustrated by the recent deal that Elsevier made with OhioLINK, the digital library alliance of Ohio. Elsevier has licensed its journals to members of OhioLINK, some 40 libraries, for three years, for $23 million—quite a load of another kind. Given this arrangement in one state, from one publisher, for three years, it is possible to gain some perspective regarding what the costs might be for the digital products of several publishers for just a few states for just a few years. Can a National Library offer a lower-cost model?

Question. NSF must ask itself what its most appropriate role would be in helping develop a National Library. Should it place its resources and effort at the top? or at the grass roots? Could it develop cost models, collect background materials, provide expert testimony, underwrite the preparation of electronic curricula, support an organizational partnership to design the National Library? Or, might not its best role be as facilitator and enabler, not just of the National Library as a "collection," but as an agent to help direct scholarly communication towards a new model of SME&T information creation and delivery exemplified by the National Library?

It is very much the case that many funding bodies for educational institutions have seen the digital future and believe it holds the answer to reducing costs and achieving efficiencies in the learning process. The elevation of cost in the educational process has certainly captured the attention of those who provide its funding. Many examples of the implementation of distance education are appearing quickly on the national educational scene.

This rapid emergence of a demand for distance education and learning among institutions of higher learning—even though most teachers do not appear ready to embrace the concept—is leading also to the required availability of information to support these programs. Any learning process must include an information source. "Distance information" is just as relevant in this new paradigm as are new pedagogical considerations, as are issues that relate to teaching methodologies and learning skills, as are new environments for this process.

The traditional teacher-centered environment that has been a characteristic of the university as place is beginning to be replaced by learner-centered environments, where the requirements for distance education enterprises and for distance information are unlike those for the classrooms and the libraries of the past. There are new road and load issues implicit in this new model that require thoughtful consideration.

Any successful transportation or delivery system must pay attention to both road and load, to carrier and content, and to how each of these elements relate to one another. One must consider as a part of this entire system the technological, fiscal, legal, political and social issues, as well as telecommunications, content selection, content organization, indexing, human and machine interfaces, instructional tools, and, yes, even "sand boxes" to try the systems out in.

New alliances must be formed and focused on these issues since there is no single entity that can address them all. The National Library project can provide a venue for such a partnership.

DIMINISHING THE BOUNDARIES BETWEEN EDUCATIONAL INSTITUTIONS

The development of distance education and learning programs, with its attendant integration of digital libraries, of computing, information technology, and telecommunications, may very well shake apart the fundamental distinctions between the very institutions that have previously provided the educational experience. A more placeless role for educational institutions could lead to a diminishment of the boundaries between the K-12, the higher education, and the lifelong learning processes and the institutions in which they have traditionally been located. It might also more easily provide for a binding of the teaching, learning, and research processes into a more seamless model that could help reduce the presumed fracture that too many persons believe exists between these tightly related educational activities.

The dissolution of the university as we have known it is a topic that appears frequently in the literature. The establishment of the "virtual university" is already occurring on at least a limited basis. As suggested above, it is undoubtedly the case that the same information content, pedagogical and learning processes, and similar interactive exchanges between teachers and learners—and their "libraries"—could very well be shared among the K-12 community and the undergraduate population of institutions of higher education. Lifelong learners, who will become an increasingly active component of the distance education population, as well as information users and learners in the research and business sectors, can very well make use of many of the same resources. The prospective far-reach of the National Library is probably far greater than can be immediately imagined.

More meaningful partnerships need to be established to extract the full advantage of what the digital library opportunity holds to improve the level of knowledge skills required for competition in a new world commerce of goods, services, and ideas where information resources and a command of attention are the chief currencies.

Information technologists, Internet engineers, computer scientists, human and machine interface designers, information service providers and publishers, experts in intellectual property rights, classroom teachers, and librarians, who know the audience and the content—*and including especially students themselves*—who can articulate and resolve the complexities of the vision of the National Library, will be important to the success of any project that emanates from distance learning plans and digital library concepts.

Question. What is the best structure in which to incorporate the participation of those parties identified above to establish and maintain the National Library? Would the concept of a single centralized national center of responsibility be the best choice, or would cooperative, distributed centers of digital library excellence, centrally coordinated—a Virtual National Library—be a better model?

Whatever our preconceptions are of a digital library and the behavior of its users, the actual determination of those points will be made by the use that people make of the library. That will be determined by the marketplace of learning. That is the chief reason why the National Science Foundation must have as clear an understanding as possible of the road and load digital library issues that will confront the effective creation of an as potentially important learning and research resource as a National Library for Undergraduate Science, Mathematics, Engineering, and Technology Education.

REFERENCES

Billings, H. 1996 [i.e. 1997] Library Collections and Distance Information: New Models of Collection Development for the 21st Century. *Journal of Library Administration* 24 (1/2): 3-17.

Billings, H. 1991. The Bionic Library. *Library Journal* 116 (17): 38-42.

Bothun, G. 1997. Seven Points to Overcome to Make the Virtual University Viable. *Cause/Effect* 20 (2): 55-57.

Goldhaber, M.H. 1997. The Attention Economy and the Net. *First Monday* (http://www.first monday.dk/issues/issue2_4/goldhaber/index.html)

Library of Congress *American Memory* (http://llcweb2.loc.gov/ammem/)

Wulf, W. 1995. Warning: Information Technology Will Transform the University. *Issues in Science and Technology* 11 (Summer): 46-52.

A National Library for Undergraduate Science, Mathematics, Engineering, and Technology Education: Needs, Options, and Feasibility (Technical Considerations)

WILLIAM Y. ARMS
Corporation for National Research Initiatives

DIGITAL LIBRARIES AND UNDERGRADUATE EDUCATION

Introduction

This is a discussion paper for the National Research Council workshop on August 7-8, 1997. The paper is arranged as a series of key topics that fall within the theme of the workshop. Although the paper emphasizes technical aspects of a digital library, it is impossible to introduce technical considerations without discussion of the overall goals and form of the library.

> "Please can I use the Web. I don't do libraries."
>
> ANONYMOUS CORNELL STUDENT,
> REPORTED BY CARL LAGOZE.

The fundamental question for the workshop is how can a national digital library enhance undergraduate science education. My basic assumption is that there is little utility in taking existing education materials, designed for other media, and simply placing them on a computer network. The greatest benefits will be gained by modification of curricula and creation of different forms of materials, in parallel with the deployment of the digital library.

Some Personal Examples

Each of us brings to this workshop pre-conceptions based on our own experiences. Here are two examples of my own.

During the 1980s, as part of the Andrew project at Carnegie Mellon University, we invested heavily in the creation of educational materials. They were delivered over the campus network, through a networked file system—a campus digital library for edu-cation. The computing initiatives that grew out of the Andrew project have had an impressive impact on education at Carnegie Mellon. Our regular surveys of faculty showed more than half the faculty regularly using computing as an integral part of their courses, but the surveys also showed that most of this impact came from materials that were not developed explicitly for education. The surveys showed that the dominant educational uses were as follows:

1. *Professional computing tools.* Many of the enhancements in education came from providing students with the same tools that the faculty use in their research and professional activities. These include applications programs (e.g., statistical packages such as SAS, symbolic mathematics such as Maple and Mathematica, graphical programs such as AutoCad or Quark), and mainstream computing applications (e.g., electronic mail, databases, and compilers). They also include data sets such as census data, NASA's images from space, and the genome data base. Although some of these tools began as non-commercial materials, by the time that they became widely used in science education, they were of a scale and complexity that required a commercial framework of support.

2. *Communication.* For many years, the dominant applications over the campus network were electronic mail and bulletin boards. In addition, from 1986, extensive reference materials were provided by the university libraries over the network. These materials were widely used by both faculty and students. They also appear to have helped stimulate the steady increase in the use of traditional library materials that occurred during the same period, though it must be admitted that the use of libraries by engineering and computer science students (and faculty) never reached the level that one would hope. As soon as the Mosaic browser was released, the World Wide Web was adopted by the Carnegie Mellon community as a very important source of communication, both for finding and for publishing information.

The second example comes from my time as a faculty member at the British Open University in the early 1970s. This was the first large-scale university organized completely around home-based learning. Although Britain has good public libraries, many students do not have easy access to a library.

Therefore, we were forced to construct courses on the assumption that students had access to no materials other than those provided by the course team. The university provided each student with a set of educational materials. These materials included printed texts, reprints of articles, and home experimental kits. Television and radio were used to augment these materials; they were an important part of some courses, but less important in my areas of mathematics and computer science.

The academic achievements of the Open University have shown that good undergraduate education is possible without providing the students access to a library. However, it places serious limitations on course design. In particular the options for independent work are severely limited. As distance learning becomes more common, the workshop might ask the question how can modern technology help a home-based university, or any university, improve on the Open University's approach thirty years ago.

Both these examples show the importance of creating services where the teaching faculty have a large measure of control over how the services are used in education.

Potential Benefits

To begin to answer the question how can a national digital library enhance undergraduate science education, here is a list of the potential benefits that might be hoped from a digital library aimed at undergraduate science education.

1. *Provide faculty and students with access to original scientific materials.* Studying science from original papers, research reports, data sets, etc. is fundamentally different from learning based on distilled materials, such as textbooks. As the volume of scientific information that is crammed into undergraduate courses has grown, universities have moved from the ideal of a liberal education in which students explore a subject through reading original materials to heavily structured curricula. Recently we have seen a trend, at least in some universities, that is partially reversing this direction by encouraging students to carry out independent work, which requires easy access to the source materials of science. Independent work requires good libraries and a digital library has much to offer.

2. *Provide faculty with materials used in preparing courses.* Preparation of a good course is extremely labor intensive. Faculty need ways to discover and evaluate educational materials and scientific source materials. They also need access to curricula, course notes, problem sets, etc. The better the services that are provided to faculty, the more they are able to build on the successes of others, and the less likely to use inappropriate materials or to re-create materials.

3. *Provide communication among faculty and students.* Communication can be within a university or college, or across organizations. Many faculty, particularly in small colleges, are quite isolated. Networked services, such as bulletin boards and the World Wide Web, develop a community where they can cooperate in both education and research. In a similar manner, students can interact with others from around the world. There is continuing development in collaborative tools that allow faculty and students to distribute their work to others, including annotations and comments.

4. *Deliver specific educational materials.* An increasing variety of educational materials are intrinsically digital. They include computer programs, data sets, various categories of multimedia items, etc. Computer networks and digital libraries provide a cost-effective way to store, retrieve, and deliver these materials.

One topic has been deliberately left out of this list, reflecting a personal bias. Because of a combination of technical and economic issues, my instinct is not to focus on using the digital library as a substitute for traditional textbooks. Computer networks have long proved to be an effective way to deliver course notes and other supplementary materials, but textbooks and courses built on textbooks are so closely tied to the strengths of printed volumes that they are difficult to migrate to digital libraries.

The Technology of Digital Libraries

Assumptions

The following are my basic assumptions about the proposed library.

1. *This is a digital library.* Although materials will sometimes be printed by the user, and some materials may be available on CD-ROM, the focus is

on materials that are created and stored in digital formats, and transmitted to the user over the Internet.

2. *It will be a virtual library*. This will not be a conventional library in that it will not acquire and store all its materials. The digital library collections will be managed by many organizations, with materials stored on many different computers. Three models of delivery of information to faculty and students are possible: (a) directly from the originator of the materials (e.g., a publisher), (b) from a service center at the educational establishment (e.g., a library or media center), (c) from collections maintained by the national digital library.

3. *The library will contain both proprietary and public materials*. Many of the best educational materials are created by companies or individuals who wish to be paid for their efforts. However, as the World Wide Web has shown, there is also an enormous quantity of high quality material that is made publicly available at no cost. In some areas of science, large amounts of scientific source material are available online with no restrictions on access.

4. *Faculty and students will be able to interact with the collections*. In a traditional library, it is a serious misdemeanor to write on the books or otherwise alter the collections. In a digital library the collections can be dynamic. People can annotate the materials, or link them to others; some materials are programs that students can execute or interact with; others can carry out computations, simulations, searches, or other actions on behalf of the user.

A Possible Technical Framework

Today's remarkable growth in digital libraries results from the maturing of several technologies: personal computers, the Internet, the World Wide Web, and protocols for searching online databases. Major areas where technical barriers remain include: interoperability among disparate systems, user interfaces, authentication and security, archiving, real time and other non-static media, copyright management, payment for services, and searching vast amounts of information.

In each of these areas, there are adequate short-term solutions, supported by extensive research and development. Hardware costs and performance continue to improve rapidly. There are no fundamental, technical barriers to the development of digital libraries for scientific education.

A rough technical outline might be as follows:

1. *The digital library will be built on the Internet*. Almost every university and college now has a good connection to the Internet. Faculty and students working at home can dial-up to their university or connect through an Internet service provider. All protocols will be based on the TCP/IP suite.

2. *Users will have a standard personal computer (PC or Macintosh) running widely available software*. For the foreseeable future, the user interface will be a Web browser, such as Netscape Navigator or Microsoft's Internet Explorer. The library will select a specific set of standard formats and protocols. The aim will be to follow the technical mainstream as it evolves with time, but the library will probably need to provide some additional software to handle special formats, authentication and payment, and identification of materials. These will be provided as applets, plug-ins, or other extensions that can be installed over the network.

3. *Materials in the digital library will be stored on a variety of servers*. The collections will be managed by a variety of organizations including universities, publishers, and libraries. With a large-scale library, where collections are maintained by many organizations, it is naive to believe that all the computers will be equally up-to-date or run the same protocols and formats. The library must accommodate the problems that are associated with heterogeneity. Today, many of the servers will be HTTP Web servers, but there will also be servers based on other protocols, such as relational databases (SQL), and Z39.50. Object-oriented systems using IIOP may be the next important development. Interoperation among such systems is not easy but can be achieved by adopting suitable formats and protocols. (The Stanford University Infobus project has done good work in this area.)

4. *Materials in the digital library will be entered into a registry*. The registry is a centrally managed list of materials that have been selected for the library. The registry contains information about each item, but not the item itself. The information includes an identifier, a digital signature, the location of the material, and perhaps indexing information and annotations. (CNRI has developed a registry for the U.S. Copyright Office and is planning to deploy a modified version in other library applications.)

5. *There will be a central index to materials in all the collections.* The indexing information will include cataloging and classification information, organized for distributed retrieval using modern methods of information retrieval. (Several good commercial systems are available today.)

6. *The library will permit annotation of materials.* When an item is selected for the collections, an annotation is entered into the registry evaluating the material. Subsequently, users of the library can add annotations that comment on the effectiveness of the materials. (A fascinating approach to annotation is the Multi-Valent Document protocol developed by the Berkeley Digital Library Initiative. This is still a research project that has not yet resulted in any products.)

7. *Key parts of the library will be replicated.* The registry and the indexing information will be replicated at several locations for performance and reliability.

Technically, all these components already exist, at least in preliminary form. Assembling and integrating them is, however, a significant undertaking. One challenge for the workshop is to set a framework that balances long-term ambition against short-term implementation difficulties.

Student Access

Student access is a problem. Students will use the digital library routinely only if it is convenient. Although student ownership of computers is increasing steadily, it is far from universal. The capabilities of their computers vary considerably and network access is still patchy.

Currently universities follow several different approaches to providing student access; none is ideal. Most universities provide some computers in student labs or computing clusters, connected to a campus network. This forces the students to go to the computer, thus wasting some of the potential of a digital library. Supply and demand are always a problem at peak times.

Another approach is for students to own their own laptop computers and to connect to the campus network on an ad hoc basis. This is increasingly common with law school students, whose computing needs are very simple, but in science education there are problems of cost, access to soft-

ware, and hardware limitations. Many scientific applications require substantial computational power or network bandwidth. A variant to this approach, which is followed by some of the best undergraduate colleges, is to urge students to buy their own computers with their own money. The institution supports them by providing software, training, and network connections in the dormitories. This approach is usually supplemented by public computers in labs or clusters.

Each of these approaches is more convenient for a student or faculty member than being restricted to a traditional library. None is as convenient as owning a physical copy of each book. As a result, we are seeing a broad movement to provide digital copies of lightly used scientific information, such as journals, but limited enthusiasm for replacing core education materials with online materials, except for those education materials that are intrinsically computer applications.

Information Discovery and Guidance for Students and Instructors

The organization of materials in the library collections is central to its success. Faculty and students must be able to find relevant material quickly; they must have confidence in its accuracy and its suitability for their purpose.

Recently, the NSF sponsored a workshop in Santa Fe to discuss what should follow the current Digital Libraries Initiative. One clear theme emerged from the discussions. The Digital Libraries Initiative emphasized the creation of online library collections. Now, four years later, enormous amounts of material are online. Some of it is excellent, some is junk. Information overload is emerging as a fundamental issue in digital libraries. The undergraduate science library faces this problem. Instructors need help in identifying materials and evaluating their potential for specific courses. Students need help in exploring beyond the required materials. Because of their inexperience, students are often unable to evaluate the quality of materials. Therefore, evaluation and systematic description of material are vital parts of the library. How best to do this is a research topic, but there are some basic approaches that can be used today. Here is a possible framework.

1. *All materials in the library will be selected by members of the library staff.* Sometimes, selection will be at an item level, at other times by groups of material. The method of selection and the selection criteria will be stored with all material, so that users will know why each item is in the library.

2. *Reviews and other annotations will be added to the materials.* The library will systematically assemble reviews of materials and feedback of educational usage, from both faculty and students.

3. *External annotations will be welcomed.* The library will encourage unsolicited annotations and recommendations from third parties. (As described below, some editorial control will probably be needed.)

4. *There will be a central index.* Descriptive metadata about all materials will be consolidated in a central index to the library. It is anticipated that the process of creating this metadata will combine automatic indexing, with selective human cataloging and quality control.

5. *There may be other indexes to parts of the collection.* Many of the individual collections that constitute the library will have their own indexes, catalogs, or finding aids.

This strategy does not expect the central library staff to be responsible for all aspects of information discovery. The Internet has shown us the power of private initiatives in organizing and presenting information in novel ways. The digital library needs to harness this utility and creativeness.

Policy Questions

Economic and Licensing Issues

Some materials in the library will be openly available. Others will be commercial products. Most core educational materials are created commercially as business ventures. The budget for each new edition of a major textbook approaches a million dollars; publishers of research papers are large and profitable; software packages and multimedia materials are equally expensive to produce.

Copyright has been used as the mechanism by which materials are controlled. At present there is intensive debate about the form that copyright should take in digital libraries. One opinion (which I share) is that this is fundamentally an economic debate. Whatever legal framework develops will enable the owners of educational materials to control their use, set terms and conditions, and price them as the market will bear.

Materials are paid for in three different ways. The first is by the student directly, by purchasing books, photocopies, computer software, lab fees, etc. The second is by the educational establishment, through its library, computing, and media budgets. The third is by the producer of the materials, such as by creating Web sites.

1. *Controls on access to materials.* We are currently seeing a change in the balance between these three methods of payment, particularly with the growth of open-access publication of scientific research and other resources over the Internet. Thus we can expect that large amounts of good material will not require payment, but the library must be built around a framework that permits control of access to materials if required by the owner. (Currently the tools to do this are rather limited, except where a university or college has installed a comprehensive authentication system, such as Kerberos. Because progress has been disappointingly slow, systems have to rely on crude authentication, such as IP address or ID and password.)

2. *Controls on accuracy.* The principal reason that authors and publishers wish to control educational materials is the desire to make money. A secondary reason is the wish to control the content, in particular to ensure accurate representation of the ideas and concepts, with appropriate attribution. One approach to this issue is to register each item as it is added to the collection with a unique identifier and a digital signature, which can be used to verify that an item has not changed. (This technology is becoming widely available from several sources.)

Good Science versus Bad Science

A tough policy decision is how much the library will be an arbiter of good science. The library must anticipate pressures from those whose political, economic, or religious agendas are antagonistic to good science and good education. With considerable reluctance, I suggest that, from the start, the library will need an editorial board of scientists committed to defending the library from these pressures. For example, unsolicited annotations are highly desirable, but the library must be prepared to exercise editorial control if necessary. The aim is to find a balance between openness to new or controversial ideas, while weeding out the cranks and the bigots.

Conclusion

To build a large-scale distributed library for undergraduate science education is technically difficult. It faces no fundamental barriers, but to do it well requires a skilled and motivated team. It is vitally important that this team be driven by the wish to build a practical, high-quality service for education.

Even more importantly, the creators of the library must focus on the underlying challenge, how to have a major impact on science education. The challenge is to create a framework that will allow the teaching faculty flexibility to use the library in ways that were not envisaged by its creators. In this manner, it can indeed become the premier focus of materials for undergraduate science education.

A Digital Library of Undergraduate SME Education Materials: The Need and Technical Issues

SU-SHING CHEN
Department of Computer Science & Engineering
University of Missouri-Columbia

INTRODUCTION

In the 1945 *Atlantic Monthly* article, Vannevar Bush provided a vision for an information system to disseminate and manage the vast amount of information accumulated about science, mathematics, and engineering. After 50 years, we are realizing his vision in information highways, information services, digital libraries, and many other information infrastructures, all made possible through the advances in computer science and engineering, information technology, and communications networks.

Since the NSF/DARPA/NASA Initiative of Research on Digital Libraries was started in 1993, many digital library projects have flourished around the world. In this article we discuss the need and technical issues of a digital library of undergraduate SME (Science, Mathematics, and Engineering) education materials. Such a library not only covers a wide variety of backgrounds and disciplines but also connects well the digital library content developers and technology innovators. In undergraduate SME education, content developers and technology innovators may be the same instructors and their student assistants. This is most evident in the fields of computer science, information science, library science, information technology, and computer engineering. This article provides some arguments for the need and a list of technical issues about a digital library of SME Education Materials.

THE NEED

Let us examine how traditional libraries were institutionalized. A library is a body of collected information brought together for the purpose of knowledge dissemination and utilization by users. Library collection evolves throughout the ages. The ancient library structure of handwritten books changed significantly by the introduction of the printing process in the mid-15th century. The printing process was capable of producing multiple copies of the same text. The proliferation of printed books for use in universities and learning centers drove the development of these institutions in which books were collected and stored.

This time a similar revolution stimulated by the advent of digital information is reshaping the library structure. Today's libraries contain materials in many different media and formats. In addition to printed materials, libraries collect films, videos, filmstrips, computer disks, sound recordings, digitized files, and various kinds of media records. Despite the many changes in library operations and structures, the basic functions of the library remain the same: acquisition, collection, indexing, organization, dissemination, and utilization. We call this process the life cycle of information.

In the Information Age, technologies have the capabilities to potentially expand the life cycle of information into many new dimensions, and change the operations and structures of existing libraries as one of the oldest social institutions. In a digital library, information can be read, communicated, and utilized over subjects, spaces, and times by many library users. Fundamental but only intuitively understood is that knowledge may be disseminated and utilized in a digital library. Through knowledge discovery and visualization tools, information becomes knowledge of users. A digital library has more collaboration, explanation, interpretation, and presentation capabilities than traditional libraries. Information content can be processed and synthesized by computers into knowledge of users.

Throughout the recent years, SME education materials have been developed in a very large scale. There is a significant amount of digital courseware for SME education purposes. The digital courseware is mostly in the form of online and CD-ROM materials provided by publishers, information technology vendors, and not-for-profit organizations. There is also federal funding for SME education. A notable example is the NSF Engineering Education Coalition Program. It was founded in 1990 with the purpose to change the paradigm of engineering education to an integrated experience focusing on the development of human potential and resources. The results of these efforts can be captured, organized, and utilized in a digital library.

A digital library containing SME education materials serves students and faculty in colleges and universities. The collection and services of this library should be designed to match the need of their users that range from basic support of the curriculum to the research requirements of students and faculty. As the book, journal, and courseware production expands and spreads, worldwide information output has increased to the point where it is now impossible for a traditional library to acquire all the items produced in any but the narrowest of subject fields. As a result, a national digital library should identify and register the holdings of SME education materials around the country.

The following questions should be discussed:

- Who will be the potential user group?
- What will be the scope of faculty and students utilization?
- What will be the impact for improving undergraduate SME education?

TECHNICAL ISSUES

This article will describe several technical issues about a digital library of SME education materials. At present, digital libraries still seem to be different things to different people. A key observation is that digital libraries should not be simply networked information services. Digital libraries should be more organized and structured as traditional libraries.

As digital libraries are organizations involving humans and collections of information content, they are not just information retrieval and database management tools, nor they are object-orientation environments. A balanced overview of organization, users, information content, and hardware/software system shells is important.

There has been significant progress in the direction of hardware/software system shells. The increasing research funding, thriving information services and Internet related business activities are responsible. However the development of hardware/software system shells—e.g., information retrieval, database management, and object-oriented environment—alone will not guarantee the success of a digital library. A digital library of SME education materials must become a dynamic learning organization involving humans and collections of information content. Some technical issues to be discussed include:

- Organizational structure
- Content collection
- Authoring and creation
- Formats and standards
- User interaction
- User needs
- Copyright

The organizational structure and content collection of a digital library are its defining forces. For SME education, the learning process should be carefully defined, evaluated, and formulated. The organizational structure and content collection of a SME digital library must be compatible with the learning process.

The learning process of SME may be considered as a constructive theory of information seeking and utilization. The constructive theory of information seeking and utilization could be traced back to John Dewey. Recent researchers have addressed the limitation of the traditional system-centered approach to libraries. In that approach, library services, as the intermediary between information resources and information users, define all functions and operations without much considerations of usability and user needs as the primary purposes. The alternative is a new user-centered approach. Will digital technology realize the user-centered approach? At least it increases the usability and satisfies user needs in terms of the user/system/information interaction of digital libraries. To name a few capabilities, it supports information seeking planning, task analysis, and information utilization evaluation.

The organizational and technical aspects of digital libraries are mutually dependent. Digital libraries provide potential paradigms for the user-centered approach. New technologies enable users do information seeking, knowledge dissemination, collaborative learning, and other organizational activities. The linear life cycle of information seeking is thus extended to a spiral life cycle—a self-organizing process. In it, users are involved directly with the life cycle. A digital library impacts the tasks and activities of users and user groups. The design and implementation of a national digital library of undergraduate SME education materials should take the user needs, usability, and learning requirements into consideration. Several relevant questions naturally arise:

- What will be the learning process of SME education?
- What will be the organizational structure of a national digital library for undergraduate SME education?
- What will be the SME education content?
- What will be the types of SME education materials?
- What will be the scope and nature of curricular content vs. pedagogic materials?
- What will be the adaptive process of change in curriculum and pedagogy?
- What will be the mechanism of integrating library materials and course materials in curriculum?
- Who will be responsible for the implementation, maintenance, and management of the library?

- Who will be responsible for the editorship of SME education materials?
- What will be the cost of establishing a national library of undergraduate SME education materials?
- What will be the long-term technical implications for hardware and software to support advances both in content and pedagogy?

CONCLUSION

A digital library of SME education materials will be different from a digital library of culture and history. SME education materials are not rote and mechanical. They are interactive and pedagogical. There are new challenges and opportunities in this effort. The user-centered approach to information seeking and utilization leads to the organizational structure of users and the knowledge dissemination of collaborative learning. The spiral life cycle of information seeking and utilization is a self-organizing process. In it, users are involved directly with the life cycle. This is our perspective of the learning process of SME education.

Digital National Library for Undergraduate Science, Mathematics, and Engineering Education: Comments and Another Option

STEPHEN C. EHRMANN, PH.D.
The American Association for Higher Education

WHAT IS "THE LIBRARY"?

We have been asked to posit the nature of a digital library for undergraduate science, mathematics and engineering education, and then to critique what we have invented. My initial assumptions about its character:

- The library would maintain a refereed and indexed collection of curricular elements such as interactive exercises, heavily annotated syllabi, assessment tools and the like. Otherwise it would rapidly silt up and be abandoned. The collection would need to be reviewed and filtered frequently, especially since digital materials are likely to continue to have a short half life.

- There would be no presumption that NSF-funded materials would, or would not, be included; they would need to pass the refereeing process.

- The refereeing process would seek materials that would not be published by other means, typically because the costs of finding, editorial, indexing, and support would not produce returns worth a publisher's investments. (This intention is easy to defend in the beginning but may produce objections from publishers or the Congress later on.)

- Such a library would require significant funds to create and maintain.

NEED FOR SUCH A LIBRARY?

- There's too much reinventing of round and square wheels in MSET teaching. There are a number of reasons for that, only a few of which would be dealt with by a library alone, however.

- Will enough faculty take the time to search the library? There are limits on faculty time available for screening and selecting materials, published or unpublished, once found; textbooks are relatively easy for veteran faculty to screen, as are short assignments; videos and nontraditional texts require a greater investment of time by potential users; interactive software on disk or Web can require most time. Good (expensive) screening can help this problem but only to a degree. For this and other reasons faculty seem to do little such searching. Is that changing?

- Would enough good material be available for the collection? For example, preparation for publication, and perhaps publication, of curricular materials would be the author's responsibility (?). Such editorial reengineering is a time-consuming business. Curricular materials that work for one's own students are rarely bullet proof enough, or documented enough, to work for others who have no special training or orientation.

- Other reasons to worry about the supply of good materials: free sharing of the library materials might mean no monetary incentives for the author or anyone else. Nor does such publication of curricular freeware usually earn professional rewards.

ISSUES TO CONSIDER IF NSF DECIDES TO CREATE THE LIBRARY

- NSF, I'm sure, does not want to subsidize such an expensive endeavor forever. But where would continuing revenue come from? Who would continually pay, or donate, and why? Can you suggest a business plan that relates a user base, frequency of use, fees and costs?

ADDITIONAL COMMENTS

- This idea reminds me a little of a CD-ROM called "Mathfinder" that was funded by NSF and developed by the Education Development Center, composed of K-12 math materials, organized using the NCTM Standards. It would be worthwhile to see how influential that product was. One of my former colleagues at the Annenberg/CPB Project commented recently that Mathfinder was "a solution in search of a problem. How big a need is there for easier access to a comprehensive collection of aging curricular materials?" That's just one person's view, of course, but I suggest you study its character, full costs, benefits, and fate.

REFERENCES AND A SUGGESTION FOR WHAT NSF MIGHT DO INSTEAD OF A LIBRARY

We tackled similar problems of reinvented wheels a few years ago at the Annenberg/CPB Project. We used a rather different design: the "Rethinking Courses" funding program that focused on selected content areas. Our six projects were intended to:

a. seek out hard-won experience (negative and positive) in applying technology to educational needs in a particular content area of high priority (finding good instructional materials was only a small part of this inquiry),

b. analyze and synthesize the resulting findings in order to create outreach materials and opportunities that could help large numbers of faculty improve their teaching in these content areas,

c. market and offer that outreach widely, especially using the Internet (libraries, directories, online seminars, train the trainer, etc.), CD-ROM, video tape, and print.

I'm proud of what those projects have accomplished so far. However in retrospect they were badly underfunded, averaging $150,000 each for a two-year project.

Two examples drawn from the six projects:

1. Central Michigan University's awards program for rethinking service courses in math (co-funded with NSF, about $150,000 over two years) <http://www.cmich.edu/~mthaward/> and

2. the American Studies Association's Crossroads Project, co-funded with FIPSE (total funding of $400,000 over three years). <http://www.george-town.edu/crossroads/> The latter project demonstrates a mix of scholarship and outreach that might be one good model for NSF.

Given Annenberg/CPB's experience with "Rethinking Courses" and my subsequent experience with AAHE's Teaching, Learning and Technology Roundtable Program, I would suggest the following not-really-a-library strategy:

a. *Identify key, focused instructional problems* —Moderately Grand Instructional Challenges (MGICs) such as learning bottlenecks and other reform priorities in specific fields.

b. Fund a *continuing inquiry* for existing wisdom about each of these MGICs (including but not limited to curricular materials)—a process of continual searching, gathering, editorial work, and publication. This search for wisdom would include a search for problems encountered when adopting new approaches, for staff development strategies needed to implement approaches, and so on.

c. Support extensive *scholarly analysis* of the findings.[1] Cross-indexing would help spotlight the inevitable relationships between the responses to the various MGICs. When the Initiative finds important gaps in what's available, even after rigorous searching, it would publicize them to academics, to NSF, and to other funders.

d. *Active outreach*: Sort these MGICs not only by content and educational level but also by whether the problem can be dealt with by an individual faculty member (e.g., adopting a new assignment or reading) or whether it requires departmental or institutional action (e.g., studio courses). Use different outreach strategies for each of those two categories, e.g., problem-specific e-mailed periodicals to alert individuals to new "holdings"; team-oriented workshops and seminars online and in regional meetings to help teams utilize "library" resources in developing local attacks on more complex problems (e.g., reforming math sequences and the facilities supporting such teaching).

e. *Economics*: seminars and workshops would be fee based. For access to the collection, institutions would pay a fee to give their own staff free access, similar to the way colleges provide free access for their communities to journals or the Internet. My guess is that revenues could never pay the full price of the enterprise, but the enterprise *would* be required by NSF to recoup a fixed and substantial fraction of its operating costs. So long as the enterprise could find and keep a sufficient market, it would be subsidized by NSF. I think this market discipline would help attract a more aggressive and creative staff.

---

[1] I mean "scholarly" in Ernest Boyer's sense of the term, the kind of scholarship characteristic of widely influential master teachers rather than a scientific or scientistic kind of experimental research.

Digital Libraries for Educational Reform: Instantiation, Ignorance, and Information

JOHN R. JUNGCK
Mead Chair of the Sciences
Department of Biology
Beloit College

Education for the future must be based on a more profound appreciation for actual professional practice in science, mathematics, engineering, and technology (SMET) than current classroom and laboratory practice. Students are screened off both from the power and potential of contemporary technology. Why is it that when powerful research software operational on microcomputers, that can do the work of main frames affordable only to major research universities, is easily affordable, if not free, that few students are even exposed to learning how to use these powerful design, analysis, computation, and visualization tools? Why is it that when databases exist on the World Wide Web which students could use to perform original research that they have to continue doing cookbook exercises or simple demonstrations? Why is it that when the World Wide Web can serve to connect millions of learners that we persist in an individualistic orientation to education rather engaging students in collaboration, communication, and peer review of their finest ideas and projects? Is this not an enormous waste of intellectual power, a misuse of human effort, and an antidemocratic view of education?

If these four questions serve as a preliminary introduction to NRC's questions about the role of digital libraries of SMET educational materials, then what alternative metaphors can we explore for instantiating a radical alternative to outmoded views of education that focus on one-way transmissions between teachers and students, that depend upon the acquisition of information rather than the evaluation and utilization acquisition of information, and that isolate, individuate, and alienate rather than connect learners.

Recent reports have suggested that scientists and engineers have access to "collaboratories" which enable them to remotely operate expensive and sophisticated scientific equipment. Science studies

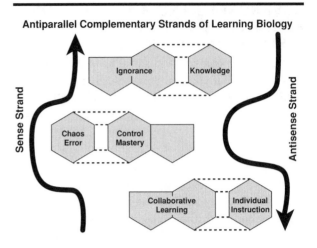

FIGURE 1. A BioQUESTian learning paradigm: Ignorance, Error, and Chaos.

have reported upon the enormous sociological shift in SMET work where international teams of teams work on projects. For example, consider the recent sequencing of the entire genome of *Bacillus subtilis* (*Science* July 1997) that involved seventeen teams from Europe and Japan or the MIR space station that has teams from both Russia and the United States as well as scientists from other countries and projects of global interest or biodiversity studies in the Amazon that involve the development of data bases based upon data collected over many years by participants from numerous countries. Scientists publish papers as multi-author teams. These practices are distinctly different from those currently seen in schools. As evolutionary biologist Michael Wade, of the University of Chicago, has said: "It takes a whole village to educate a graduate student in systematics and evolutionary biology." What other subjects reflect this concern? In this particular context, how do we organize, collect, access, share, and query a digital library for SMET education if we are to base its instantiation upon these contemporary SMET practices?

Let us consider an antiparallel model to much of contemporary education (see Figure 1):

Please note that we (members of the Bio-QUEST Curriculum Consortium) have used the sense strand of this antiparallel double helical representation of learning biology as containing three bases or cornerstones of this alternative mode: (1) ignorance, (2) error and chaos; and (3) collaborative learning. Since the latter is so much a part of most American higher education reforms in science education (e.g., Priscilla Laws' and Ron Thorton's "Workshop Physics," David Smith's and Lang Moore's "Project CALC" {a calculus reform project}, and Brock Spencer's and George Lisensky's "ChemLinks"), we simply refer readers to them (links describing their projects are connected to the BioQUEST Curriculum Consortium homepage). One critical element of the collaborative learning approach where BioQUEST differs from some of the other reforms is that we distinguish between simple cooperation in the acquisition of already known scientific principles and the collaborative construction of meaning in the world promoted by educational constructivists (Bruffee, Driver, Stewart, von Glaserfeld), by "strong programme social studies of science" theorists (Latour, Woolgar, Barnes, Knorr-Cetina, Shapin), and many feminists (notably Longino).

In order to instantiate science education with a more robust possibility of preparing students (all future citizens, some future scientists) to comprehend and/or participate in scientific decision making or investigations, several aspects of ignorance, error, and chaos that might lay a better philosophical foundation for such enabling possibilities. Also, scientists may better appreciate why "the public" frequently misunderstands them if they see that usual measures of education based on knowledge, mastery, control, and individual competition misconstrue much of their own motivation for pursuing science based on curiosity, love of puzzle solving, desire to collaborate with their peers and respond responsibly to criticism, and ability to persevere with enormous frustration in their pursuits. How does this "sense strand" influence: Individual student learning? Collaborative student learning? Interest, confidence, and competence in scientific problem solving? Ability to cope with frustrations in pursuing unsolved problems and to deal with resistance to change? An ability to do scientific research and draw warranted inferences from research? The context of scientific research whether by a student or a professional? An appreciation for history of science? Roles of science in society? Professional responsibilities?

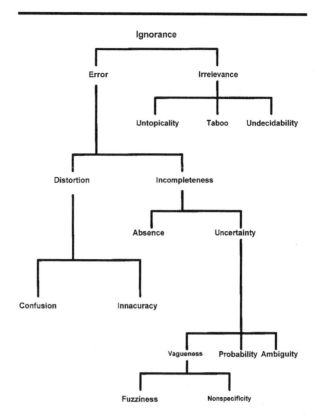

FIGURE 2. Michael Smithson's "Taxonomy of Ignorance" (1989). From *Ignorance and Uncertainty: Emerging Paradigms* © Springer-Verlag, 1989. Reprinted with permission.

IGNORANCE

Why ignorance? We assert that the purpose of science education is to help citizens understand scientific values of humility about the current state of our knowledge, the limits of our practice, social responsibilities of scientists, and respect for the processes of investigation and communal peer review as well as the education of future scientists who are able to explore new and difficult problems creatively, rigorously, and responsibly. Michael Smithson, a fuzzy set theorist in the social sciences who is concerned with public decision making about environmental risks, has laid out a decision tree for ignorance (Figure 2).

Why ignorance as a value for informing science education?

First, while ignorance is socially constructed, it is usually less commodified or reified than "knowledge" (usually with an inferred capital K). Smithson (1989) elaborates this thusly: "Ignorance is a social creation, like knowledge. Indeed, we cannot even talk about instances of ignorance without referring to the standpoint of some group or individual. Ignorance, like knowledge, is socially constructed and negotiated (p. 6). " One of the widely shared values of scientists that is usually difficult for students to understand is widespread skepticism. The poet Kenneth L. Patton asserts this positively in his poem, "The Faith of Doubt" of which I only share a few verses:

> Doubting is but the forefront of faith,
> a faith in the inexhaustibility
> of growth and the illimitable
> extent and wonder of the universe.

> A doubting age is an age in the restlessness
> and discontent of growth; a doubt is an
> idea that is still alive.

> To doubt that the past has uncovered
> all things is to express faith
> that many things are still to
> be uncovered.

Thus, the wonder, awe, and mystery that drives many scientists throughout full and long careers can be more easily shared with students. Science can be a search for deeper questions rather than a quest for eternal, absolute truth. The fallibility of science can help to differentiate our practice from aspects of religious conversion. In *The Encyclopedia of Ignorance*, the editors Ronald Duncan and Miranda Weston-Smith (1977) introduced the volume by stressing these values: "Compared to the pond of knowledge, our ignorance remains atlantic. Indeed the horizon of the unknown recedes as we approach it. The usual encyclopaedia states what we know. This one contains papers on what we do not know, on matters which lie on the edge of knowledge. In editing this work we have invited scientists to state what it is that they would most like to know, that is, where their curiosity is presently focused. We found that this approach appealed to them. The more eminent they were, the more ready to run to us with their ignorance." One such famous scientist, Charles Darwin, notes that being: "Deeply stirred by the excitement of hard scientific thought, he succumbed to the full force of ambition. To chase a theory through the mind like this was marvelous: an intoxicating combination of effort, skill, caution, and bravery - and in this case too, a healthy dose of ignorance which encouraged imaginative leaps in the geological dark... (Browne, 1995, pp. 185-186)." Note that this approach flies directly in the face of Jeremiads such as most recently John Horgan (1996) who proclaims in his book, *The Ends of Science,* that "further research may not yield much." Today's students have infinite possibilities for problem-solving opportunities that are as likely to radically transform science as in the past: with an explosion of knowledge, there is a parallel development of associated questions that have never arisen before.

I. Considerations about the potential nature and impact of a National Library:

- **Who and how large is the potential audience? What is the evidence that faculty and students would utilize this resource?**
- **What impact can be expected for improving undergraduate science, mathematics, engineering and technology (SME&T) education community?**

Several of the greatest problems in transforming collegiate science curricula relate directly to people's knowledge of resources. If there is no "library" that focuses upon collecting, classifying, indexing, querying, sharing, and making accessible technological curricular resources and reviews of those materials, then there are enormous costs in the initiation, instantiation, maintenance, and extension of curricular reform:

a. because a democratic view of SMET education should support the ability of students to pose problems, solve problems based upon in-depth searches and analyses of complex, multidimensional, multivariate data sets, and persuade their peer reviewers of the quality of their hypotheses, a digital library should serve students in each of these phases of their work. Collaboration among students is as critical as the need for national collaboratories, international genomic data bases, and massive biodiversity analyses that include GIS, GPS, geographic, geologic, meteorologic, cartographic, hydrologic, and biotic data sets;

b. because there is no equivalent to *Science Citation Index* for the many curricular initiatives that are funded, or are local to one campus, or even those which have articles on them in journals, newsletters, and magazines, there is enormous wastage due to the "not-invented-here" syndrome. In particular, NSF does not get the full benefit of their critical investment. Many marvelous innovations of the post-Sputnik era have simply been lost because few others than the innovators themselves have any knowledge at all about these NSF-funded innovations;

c. because many technological changes have come "top down" on campuses by adoption of hardware, across campus wiring programs, and commitments to use of the World Wide Web in the absence of consulting faculty about what software has been most transformative in the teaching, learning, and research in their discipline, professors frequently have inadequate exposure to what exists out there because of limitations imposed by these top down decisions;

d. because the diffusion of technological innovations has been "owned" by developers and "early adopters," there has been enormous discussion about how to make what has been created much more accessible to the vast majority of professors who may only be using "worldware" such as e-mail, WWW searching, word processing, spreadsheets, graphics, mathematical and statistical packages, or presentation packages. Even if they have physical access to curricular materials to review, they may not have learned about how to evaluate the diversity and quality of many discipline-specific software applications for learning and research. Evaluation should not only be based on the SMET content, but also on the GUI interface, the quality of the algorithms implemented and how they have been implemented, and perhaps most importantly, upon the pedagogy involved. Most professors have no experience in evaluating software that are incompatible or incommensurable for cooperative versus collaborative learning, for formative evaluation versus outcomes-based education, or for active learning in a student-centered approach versus teacher-centered instruction. Frequently, professors eclectically treat the potentials as a Chinese menu and fail in their initial attempts because they have combined mutually exclusive approaches that are based on diametrically opposed educational philosophies;

e. because the professional costs to individuals have been enormous without such a "library" due to the difficulty in documenting the impact of their work on transforming college curricula through the development of curricular materials. Many professors who have taken the risk of being innovators, particularly of those innovations that extensively employ technology, have suffered because of the lack of understanding for the professional quality of good technological innovations. If the new, primary, and extremely productive contributors have been raised in a new generation that is computer literate, used to enormous computer power and wide access and democratic practices associated with expression on the World Wide Web, then how do we build a library that helps document their contributions and their impacts?

II. Considerations about content of a National Library for undergraduate SME&T education:

- **What types of materials should be included? Should materials be removed from the library as curriculum and pedagogy evolve? Who should make these decisions?**

Thus, the National Library for SMET Education must store, classify, and make available *"every"* funded SMET educational innovation in a highly democratic fashion that provides both access and equity. Since philosophy and history are critical to informing a deep view of educational reform, it is necessary to not only seek out "best practices" but to extensively collect, evaluate, and make more available an exceptionally wide diversity of materials: books, journals, magazines, software, syllabi, grant proposals and reports, equipment, and gadgetry. Thus, it is hoped that the National Library for SMET Education will develop and maintain archives, rare collections, and other antiquaria rather than falling to the whims that anything five years old is obviously irrelevant.

- **How can the library respond to changes in curriculum and pedagogy? How might the scope and nature of the content of curricular and pedagogic materials for inclusion in the National Library be made? Who should be involved in making such decisions? What**

standards are needed for inclusion of materials in the library? How would those standards be implemented?

Bruce A. Shuman (author of *The Library of the Future: Alternative Scenarios for the Information Profession*) suggests a list of tools for futurists involved in such planning:

- an open mind
- pooled intuitive judgment
- thoughtful reading, especially of science fiction and fantasy
- computer simulation and modeling
- gaming and role-playing
- scenario writing and discussion

Note that this list is heuristic rather than algorithmic. The exploration of needs for the National Library for SMET Education should not be based upon the technology that is currently available to construct such a library, but instead upon the diversity of materials already produced and an openness to the sorts of materials that are likely to be immediately on the horizon. As an evolutionary biologist and computer educator, I will risk that the National Library for SMET Education should model itself on those aspects of living systems that enhance potential for adaptation to rapidly changing fitness landscapes. Some of the current technology that has been used to develop (note: not design) such systems have employed genetic algorithms, evolutionary programming, neural networks, and multivalue or "fuzzy" logic. While I would not prescribe any one of these with great confidence, I do believe that these investigators are seriously addressing the problems of building (evolving) open, flexible, robust approaches to problem solving. I therefore believe that these investigators as well as many curriculum innovators and library reformers should be involved in the planning conversations. In that way, it is hoped that any arbitrary notion of "standard" be visciated in favor of a dynamic, adaptive approach that will constantly be re-evaluating the "state of the art."

- **What other kinds of support would users need to integrate materials from the library into their courses and curricula and use them effectively?**

The establishment of the National Library for SMET Education should be coordinated to a variety of workshops, listserves, chat rooms, national meetings, dissemination, information bulletins, and collaboratories. Fundamental to change is taking risks. Asking people to take risks should be coordinated with the development of sustained support for people while they make forays into unexplored territories. Thus, long-term commitment is one of the most important aspects of providing support for change.

There should also be an appreciation for the diversity of institutions in which SMET educational reform is occurring. Community colleges in large urban areas face different problems from geographically widely dispersed institutions in rural regions. Small liberal arts colleges have a long historical set of expectations than engineering universities. Teaching is differentially valued in state universities that serve a local populous from internationally famous research universities. Students from various backgrounds socioeconomically, racially, ethnically, and geographically may come to new curricula with widely divergent expectations and prior experiences. Visually and manually challenged individual needs should be met.

Disciplinary differences also should be recognized. One size does not fit all. Engineers assume that contemporary technology should be rapidly assimilated into curricula. Mathematicians may value thinking per se over the introduction of extensive software and hardware into their curricula. Field geologists and biologists may have very different values from experimental bench scientists. Curricula need to be sensitive to the professional practices of these different communities to meet the criteria expressed in the introduction.

CONCLUSION

The National Library for SMET Education should enable the instantiation of curricular reform that is fundamentally democratic, open, flexible, and dynamically evolving. But a word of caution is necessary. In 1971, Thomas Childers ("Community and Library: Some Possible Futures," *Library Journal* 96: 2727-2730) stated: "How generously will a constituency support an institution that is unused by the majority of adult residents, an institution that may be more of a monument than a resource actively responding to the dynamics of society?" Shuman (*The Library of the Future: Alternative Scenarios for the Information Profession*, 1989, page 49) responded: "So what can the library do to prevent its own murder, suicide, or enfeeblement? Childers provides some alternative futures for the library, any of which could happen but each of which would require consensus, goal-shifting, planning, cooperation, and effective carry-over into a new, usually unfamiliar realm of what we do. Childers's list was a promising start and a commendable job of trying to carve out a societal niche for the public library before society metaphorically shelves the library in a rundown warehouse on the outskirts of town. But the authors contends that the list deserves fleshing out and expansion..."

Herein I have argued that a metaphor based upon open questions from students and unsolved scientific and societal problems and a pedagogy based upon ignorance, error, chaos, and collaborative learning will be more appropriate metaphors for the establishment of a library which will continue to serve curricular reform.

Issues in Developing a National Digital Library for Undergraduate Math, Science, and Engineering Education

JAMES H. KELLER
Information Infrastructure Project
Harvard University

Developing a national digital library presents a breakthrough opportunity for redefining the role of the library in supporting undergraduate SMET education, and potentially in reshaping the overall paradigm for undergraduate learning. The creation of such a resource requires an understanding of the unique enabling characteristics of the supporting infrastructure—both those that exist today and those that can be fostered. A national digital library for undergraduate math, science, and engineering education is, of course, not a stand-alone resource. It is one element of the larger, general-purpose information infrastructure. This paper will include attention to issues related to information and digital library infrastructure for other domains and disciplines as they relate to this community.

The digital library and its development will involve not only integration with the larger information infrastructure, but will also require a careful evaluation of the manner in which it will integrate with the larger organizational process for undergraduate education, including peer review, certification, and the system of professional reward necessary to engage participation in content development and evaluation. This latter set of requirements represents perhaps the greatest barrier to the success of the library. Technical development is not trivial, but is largely achievable with existing commercial capabilities. On the other hand, the institutional and organizational requirements of the library are daunting—only achievable with strong endorsement and participation extending well beyond the library community. The goal should not be merely to transfer the traditional library function to the networked environment, but to maximize the learning and

research opportunities that can be enhanced through this new medium. This will require linkages beyond the higher education community to the larger technical and standards development efforts of which the library will be a part. It will also require participation in the ongoing public policy debates about the treatment of copyrighted work in the networked environment and about telecommunications policy, including universal access.

THE VISION

What will the digital library be? The word library conveys the idea of a resource providing access to information, but in the digital realm a library is much more than this. It is an interactive vehicle for instructional learning, providing access to course materials, such as syllabi, and other instructional materials. It will run over a general purpose, most likely web-based, communications infrastructure, and will be accessed through general purpose client machines. The content will likely exist on distributed machines (an issue that will be explored later). Therefore, the question of what is and isn't the library becomes fuzzy. In practical terms, it may be described as a broadly agreed upon and deployed set of conventions for presenting, locating, authenticating, accessing, and using information for purposes of supporting undergraduate education within the worldwide Internet. Some parts of this space will be private, some public. It will support fair use access and market-based exchange. In many ways, this decentralized set of heterogeneous and autonomous networks and servers is, in an organizational sense, very much like the larger Internet. The Internet has evolved based on a set of voluntary agreements about standards for network interconnection and the presentation of information. The success of this system has been attributed to what has been called "the tinkerbell principle," a simple and powerful concept.[1] In other words, it works because everyone believes it will. In the case of the Internet, faith was reinforced through participation in the Internet

---

[1]Mitch Kapor and Sharon Gillette in *Coordinating the Internet*, Kahin and Keller, ed., MIT Press, 1997.

Engineering Task Force, a de facto standards body, whose legitimacy was strengthened by the ongoing participation of the U.S. government. Such an institutional focus will provide essential glue in the development of a national digital library.

The digital library will not replace the physical library. In fact, it is not a substitute for access to text-based materials, which are typically converted to print for use. The digital medium excels in browsing and in providing access to information, rather than text. The organizing paradigm for the digital library should be information, rather than documents, and the structure must support quality and context as search criteria.

A digital library to support undergraduate SMET will be both more than and less than the traditional library. If properly conceived and implemented, it will be more in that it will extend broadly and deeply into the whole set of functions related to undergraduate education. It will be less in the sense that the digital library itself may not house digital works, rather it may just help the user locate them within the larger Internet. The defining element of the library will be its search and indexing functions, and the digital library itself may be purely an index or registry and not a repository.

WHY DEVELOP A DIGITAL LIBRARY?

A digital library can provide a repository and distribution mechanism for multimedia learning resources, but the true opportunity is far more profound. Historically, the links between undergraduate education and library use have been quite tenuous.[2] If a national digital library is to be considered as a resource to support learning, it must go beyond providing access to static resources. The digital library presents an opportunity to overcome physical and geographical barriers and become integrated more closely with other functions of undergraduate education. The library may be brought into the classroom and study session and may also be seamlessly linked to web-based syllabi and computer-

based learning modules. These opportunities require an assessment that looks beyond issues in development of a digital resource and addresses the larger questions of improvement of and expanded access to the undergraduate learning process.

Technical development of the key functional elements of a national digital library to support undergraduate SMET education can largely be fulfilled with existing web-capabilities. It can be built with existing knowledge and tools, but successful use of this resource will require a fundamental rethinking of the larger learning process in which it is intended to operate. This would affect some of the defining elements of the university, including peer review, standards for professional achievement, and undergraduate teaching. Any plan for a digital library which does not recognize and adequately address these organizational requirements should not proceed.

WHAT IS DIFFERENT ABOUT DIGITAL?

The most fundamental breakthrough presented by the move to digital infrastructure is the destruction of traditional notions of time and space as they relate to library access. This phenomenon presents important questions about the functional role of the library. For example, should the digital library be defined by education level and discipline, or be leveraged across a larger community? In other words, how much should it be different from the library that serves high school or graduate education, in math, science, and engineering, and in other curriculum areas? The undergraduate experience with the library could be an introduction to a life-long resource. Similarly, the library would provide infrastructure (software, systems, processes, rules) which could serve many disciplines and communities. The opportunities for institutional and functional convergence are nearly boundless, and, in many cases, create significant and compelling economic effects. For example, the infrastructural requirements of the digital library are very close, and in some ways identical, to those of electronic commerce. These criteria include locating, evaluating, retrieving, and paying for information. In terms of institutional convergence, the library capabilities may be built into distance learning, adult education

---

[2]Branscomb, Bennett Harvie, "Teaching with books; a study of college libraries," Chicago, Association of American Colleges, American Library Association, 1940.

programs, or industry research. The difficulty lies in coordination of systems and processes, and the problem shifts in part from one of invention to one of partnership and leveraging.

As thinking about the library enters the world of intelligent infrastructure, it quickly encroaches on other functions. Just as the digital library is a vehicle for access to information, it also presents a means for publishing and broadcast. It will be a medium not just for text, but also for new data and research results, digital models, and other multimedia objects. The creation of a system that seeks to extend these opportunities, while ensuring quality control and authentication, may promote rapid dissemination of new knowledge. This will rely on a system which recognizes the intellectual property interests of publishers (commercial, individual, and non-profit) and users. A key to minimizing intellectual property concerns is leaving them in the hands of the publisher. This will allow each to rely on policies which serve their respective professional and economic interests, and will reduce central administrative costs by pushing them out to the edges of the system. Such a decentralized, user-driven model minimizes the issues in ensuring continuity for the library beyond the period of its initial funding support.

The ability of the digital library to recast the learning process by extending across traditionally distinct institutions and processes raises the question of whether the word "library" remains an appropriate moniker. The so-called "digital library" will, if properly designed, quickly become a part of most, if not all, scholarly aspects of the university and the larger research community. Creative thinking about the opportunity presented by the digital library may be better served by the use of another name, such as the national digital university, or electronic learning resource. One benefit of the continued use of the term "library" is conformance to traditional funding criteria and guidelines in institutions such as NSF. These institutions must also adapt, however, to shift to a new paradigm for learning.

INTELLECTUAL PROPERTY PROTECTION AND USE

The success of the digital library will rely on meeting the intellectual property requirements of con-

tent developers, owners, and users. Currently, the legal framework for intellectual property rights is being reevaluated.[3] At the same time, new technological approaches to protecting intellectual property are being developed. These technological approaches present potential opportunities and threats to fair use of copyrighted material. While it is currently just about impossible to control copying and distribution of digital works once they leave the immediate control of the owner, it is possible that the pendulum of control will swing dramatically in the other direction. It is possible that technological approaches to intellectual property management will emerge that are so robust as to preclude any access or use that is not explicitly authorized. Such a scenario would effectively obviate the fair use provisions of copyright law relied upon by libraries and other educational and research users. This is of particular concern, as the current leanings of policymakers appear to place the importance of copyright protection over fair use and the public interest. The ongoing development of law and technology related to copyright control should be an area of ongoing concern and attention for the digital library community. The library community is already active through organizations such as the Association of Research Libraries and the American Library Association. Communities of interest in the development of a national digital library for math, science, and engineering education must participate in this effort to ensure that their unique interests are maintained.

The evolution of legal protection of intellectual property can not be anticipated. Change initiatives are under way in the United States and internationally, where efforts are under way to rationalize the heterogeneity among national systems. Beyond this uncertainty, different information providers will continue to have varying needs and values related to what is proprietary and under what conditions they are willing to share material. These factors speak to the development of a decentralized system, which will allow information providers to manage their

---

[3] With regard to fair use of copyrighted materials, these efforts are currently at an impasse. In April 1997, the U.S. Commissioner of Patents and Trademarks announced that a two-year effort, the Conference on Fair Use, had failed to reach agreement and would conclude prematurely.

own intellectual property in a manner that best meets their own objectives. The virtual nature of the medium means that users may be indifferent to or even unaware of the distributed nature of the resource and allows content developers and owners to control the presentation and use of their material. The World Wide Web is a powerful enabler of this type of self-publishing. It provides a common interoperable platform for sharing information objects. The web is a highly functional tool for providing access, but does not yet include widely available tools to support robust control of information access and use. Mechanisms for authentication, authorization, payment, and control of copying are critical to expanding the availability of high quality content online. Market pressures for electronic commerce are pushing the development of these capabilities. Rather than pursue independent solutions to these problems, NSF should encourage participation in ongoing efforts to ensure that they address the needs of the digital library community. Such an approach offers a higher likelihood of success than an independent solution, as it brings larger market forces to bear on accelerating the development and adoption of the tools. Tool developers will be encouraged by the larger market prospects, and users will potentially be able to apply their tools and skills across more functions. A danger in the development of a digital library system closely linked to the world of electronic commerce is highlighted by early case law which questions the applicability of fair use provisions in an environment which supports reasonable mechanisms for payment.[4]

CONTENT DEVELOPMENT

Success of the digital library will rely on creating a system that provides sufficient incentives to foster the development of high quality material and to gain sufficient participation from members of the disciplines to review material as part of the quality process. Incentives are both financial, in part related to legal and technological mechanisms for managing intellectual property, and professional, including benefits that enhance career and reputation.

These type of incentives are more difficult to create in the digital environment, due to the reduced barriers to publishing and participation. Key questions in addressing this issue are who will pay for quality control and access, and what will be the roles of the disciplinary societies. A successful incentive system, as with other aspects of the digital library, must recognize and be linked to core values and institutional processes of academic professional life.

Market elements necessary to support content development and availability include standards to support modularity and systems for protecting and accounting for use of the learning modules.[5] Modularity refers to the ability to move objects—lesson plans, training programs, simulations—across different technical platforms and learning environments. Modularity is relatively easy and established for text and images. It is more difficult for more complex objects, such as simulations and training modules.

PRICING

Information infrastructure and the digital library as part of this larger phenomena, poses a serious challenge to traditional pricing models for information goods. In the physical library, multiple copies of journals and other resources are required to support multiple users in many different locations. In the digital world, one copy can be costlessly reproduced to serve infinite users in infinite locations. As in the print world, a tension exists between making resources as accessible as possible and providing incentives (not always financial) to knowledge providers to generate and make information available. One approach to lessening the tension is to develop and promote means of price discrimination to allow the capture of high rents from those that value early or otherwise differentiated access and low or no price for those with less urgent needs. Economic modeling has demonstrated that such schemes may capture both higher aggregate rents for information providers and higher total utility for users, depending on the demand and supply characteristics of the market.[6]

---

[4]American Geophysical Union v. Texaco Inc., 802 F. Supp. 1 (S.D.N.Y. 1992), and American Geophysical Union v. Texaco Inc., No. 92-9341, 1994 WL 590563 (2nd Cir. Oct. 28, 1994).

[5]See Brian Kahin, *Making a Market for Advanced Distributed Learning,* unpublished working paper.

[6]See Hal Varian, Versioning Information Goods, <http://ksg-www.harvard.edu/iip/econ/varian.html>.

EVALUATION AND FEEDBACK

Evaluation includes two elements—evaluation of the infrastructural elements of the library and of the content to which the library provides access. As a new medium for learning and communication, there is a great deal that is not known or understood about the use of digital libraries. Like all new media, it is impossible to anticipate the uses that may evolve for the library. An ongoing process of evaluation and user feedback will be essential to capturing the potential benefits presented by the library. This process should include assessment of the user interface, usefulness of content, utilization, and impact on the learning process. It should also contain an element of flexibility to capture unanticipated areas of concern or opportunity.

A standard search of the World Wide Web demonstrates that identifying useful material in a large distributed network may be difficult. For example, an Internet search for "molecular biology" currently yields 51,562 sources, including links to a German telephone book and the "McCoy family" home page. Systems for content evaluation must not only ensure the availability of high quality content, but must also be linked to searchable structures that respond to context specific requests. Users must be able to request materials based on the level of knowledge, the teaching model, the budget constraints, and the type of tool. As described above, evaluation relies heavily on the participation of recognized members of the disciplines and success will require a system that includes incentives to satisfy their professional objectives.

Evaluation of digital content will be required to categorize and identify works based on criteria such as quality and targeted educational level. It is also necessary to provide a broadly acceptable means of bringing professional recognition and reward to the development of high quality digital work. If publication in digital form is not linked to opportunities for professional achievement, it will only evolve as a secondary medium. Such evaluation must be conducted by or at least recognized by the traditional disciplinary societies. Conducting this evaluation on an ongoing basis is a highly intensive effort. To encourage participation by leading luminaries who can shine distinction upon contributors of seminal work that occurs in digital form, NSF and the Academy should consider developing a fellowship (or similar) program that brings recognition to participants in the evaluation process.

RELATED INITIATIVES

Many of the issues raised in this paper are currently being explored in a variety of research and policy settings. These include the 6 NSF/ARPA/NASA funded consortia focused primarily on technical issues;[7] the Benton Foundation, the Council on Library and Information Resources, and Libraries for the Future among others. Though these activities are not explored explicitly here, they represent potentially important linkages for NSF and others in the development of digital library infrastructure.

THE ROLE OF NSF

As an element of the larger information infrastructure, digital libraries will rely on tools, systems, laws, and regimes developed for a wide array of applications, including but not limited to digital libraries. Ensuring that the particular requirements of digital libraries are addressed in the development of these supporting structures is critical to fostering a robust sub-infrastructure for libraries. As such, NSF should support the digital library research community in the development of the unique technical features that the library will require and in participation in related technical standards bodies and public policy debates. NSF support includes fostering public policy research in the implications of various legal and technical approaches to intellectual property rights management and their impact on publishing and fair use. The Foundation should also ensure that the library is developed in a manner that recognizes opportunities to improve the overall learning and research processes and embraces the necessary institutional mechanisms to affect these larger functions.

College teaching will not drive the development of the standards, technology, and products that will support digital libraries and electronic commerce. Any effort to develop a national digital library for undergraduate education as a unique and isolated resource will fail. The changes required in the larger undergraduate environment to realize the full

[7]See <http://www.cise.nsf.gov/iris/DLHome.html>.

benefits of the digital library may be beyond what can now be achieved through an NSF initiative. In light of this, NSF should consider a modest program, which would be intended both to stimulate development of library functions and build the institutional awareness necessary to allow eventual change in the learning process. One model for such an initiative would focus on the development of a web-based index or registry of materials to support undergraduate learning. The primary audience for this resource would be teachers. It would include links to both formal (approved) and informal (self-selected for inclusion) materials. Since the site would not be a repository, it should employ a method of authentication, probably through the use of simple encryption (similar to PGP software), to ensure that users locate the exact item they are referred to by the library. Potentially the largest problem posed by such an initiative is evaluation to ensure that there is a critical mass of approved quality material available. As described earlier, this evaluation process should initially be linked closely to the disciplinary societies to instill confidence among users.

The registry is an identifiable and understandable resource that can serve as a defining centerpiece for the initiative. Other supporting elements to which NSF funding could be applied include: bringing existing federally funded resources online; development of new content, such as pedagogical tools; new technological development to support functions such as expanded search features, platform portability, and intellectual property protection; and, needs assessment to determine how the digital library can best improve undergraduate SMET.

Some Technical and Economic Issues in the Design of a National Library for Undergraduate Science, Mathematics, Engineering, and Technology Education

CLIFFORD LYNCH
Executive Director
Coalition for Networked Information

INTRODUCTION

This paper briefly summarizes my view of some of the key issues that would be involved in designing a national digital library to serve undergraduate education in science, mathematics, engineering and related fields. It also tries to emphasize unique characteristics of such an undergraduate-focused library which differentiate it from many existing digital library research efforts, such as those being carried out under the auspices of the ARPA/NASA/NSF Digital Library program. The paper ranges widely over technical, economic, content, and user issues: at this early stage in the conceptualization of such an undergraduate library it is very difficult to separate the issues cleanly or to understand how choices in one area will dictate requirements and approaches in others.

A LIBRARY IN SUPPORT OF EDUCATION

A library targeted to serve undergraduates in science, engineering, mathematics and related subjects (and their teachers) is primarily an engine for enhanced teaching and learning rather than an opportunity to transform the broad system of scholarly communication and publishing. In these disciplines, textbooks have traditionally been the primary materials used by the majority of undergraduate students, rather than the general body of scholarly literature. There is a great deal of emphasis on problem sets and the techniques of problem solving; in some disciplines laboratory work and the analysis of experimental data is also important. In my view, much of the challenge here is how to supplement, extend, and enhance traditional textbooks and related educational materials (such as problem sets or experimental exercises) in the digital environment. Other than reserve materials, undergraduates in mathematics, many sciences and many engineering disciplines are not typically heavy users of library collections—at least when compared to their peers in the humanities and social sciences.

The economics for investing in sophisticated multimedia content are unusually favorable in this environment. Nationally, a huge number of students take undergraduate courses in mathematics, science, and engineering every year (in comparison to advanced graduate courses focused on the disciplinary research frontiers and based closely on an ever evolving research literature). Further, the syllabus for a course like introductory calculus, physics, or biology simply doesn't change a great deal from year to year. This means that investments in content can be amortized over large numbers of students and relatively long periods of time. There is a tradition of passing the costs of most instructional materials—textbooks and lab fees—directly back to the student, so to the extent that a digital library can replace expensive textbooks or the ever more expensive use of laboratory facilities, a funding source to help with ongoing operations already exists.

It would be very useful, in examining the case for an undergraduate digital library, to compile data about the number of students per year that take various undergraduate science, engineering, and mathematics courses, and also to gather some data about the distribution of textbook use in these courses—for example, how many of the students taking first year calculus use one of the five most popular textbooks? How often are new editions of these textbooks issued? Correlating this information, particularly in conjunction with an identification of courses that many students find particularly difficult, might help to identify high-priority targets for content in the undergraduate digital library.

Because of the large number of students involved and the relative stability of many of the courses, this also seems like an excellent context to try to assess and document the extent to which the digital library and its content actually improve the processes of teaching and learning. An interesting issue with an undergraduate-oriented digital library in the sciences and engineering is its need to justify its value early in its lifecycle: when one considers a digital library of esoteric scholarly materials, there are many institutions that will immediately derive value from the availability of such materials, because they do not have them in print (as has been the case with some of the Journal Storage Project [JSTOR] subscribers, for example). An undergraduate digital library primarily focused on instruction is going to be clearly positioned as a substitute—or at best a supplement—for currently available textbooks and related materials almost everywhere it will be used, and must quickly convince its user community that it offers real added value.

CONTENT AND FUNCTION

Content for such a digital library would include not only electronic versions of textbooks, but also solved and unsolved problem sets, courseware modules (drills, simulations, models, virtual lab benches, and class presentation materials), focused educational literature covering optional topics that extend syllabi, and some limited amount of carefully selected scholarly literature. It should be possible to rather quickly establish a critical mass of materials for the users of such a library, which is all important for achieving acceptance of the service. The nature of an undergraduate library of science, engineering, mathematics, and technology is that is should be highly focused and there should be broad consensus on at least its core content. Further, it need not, and is not intended, to replace existing print or digital research libraries but rather to complement them, and it is perfectly reasonable to assume that a relatively small number of requests for primary scholarly literature will have to be passed beyond the boundaries of the undergraduate library to the broader existing research library system.

Clearly, there will be a need for some type of editorial quality control process to manage submissions to such a library. There will be other problems that are unique, however: for example, how to organize material such as problem sets and courseware modules that can be repurposed at a very fine level of granularity in order to facilitate such reuse. Projects such as the National Engineering Education Delivery System (NEEDS) within the NSF-funded Synthesis Coalition have been struggling with these problems for almost a decade, and it is clear that they are difficult.

Standards to ensure wide usability of the electronic content and to permit the management of this content across time will be a critical issue. While there has been a considerable amount of convergence to a very limited number of standards for electronic print journals (Portable Document Format, and SGML, in particular) the kinds of supplementary multimedia and courseware materials in such an undergraduate digital library are likely to continue to push the state of the art for some time, and to be particularly vulnerable to problems of competing standards and closed software solutions. Obtaining consensus about standards and best practices among the contributors to this system on an ongoing basis will be vital to its success.

Another issue is whether the primary user community will be teachers or students. I believe that it properly should be, and will be, students. To the extent that students are the primary users, not only will a much larger-scale system be required, but the system will also need to address questions about who can see what materials—for example, can students review answers to problem sets as well as the problem sets themselves? If the primary users of the system are students rather than teachers, we must also consider whether only students within recognized institutions of higher education will be allowed access, or whether use of the system will be extended to gifted high school students, independent adult learners, and other groups. There are some central questions here about system architecture, and the roles and responsibilities of various parties in the operation and use of the undergraduate digital library. One can clearly imagine some sort of national repository that is coherently managed as forming the core of the library; but will institutions load and tailor materials locally for use by their student populations or simply prepare user profiles that allow their students to make direct use of the one national system. (Note here that the term national need not imply centralized; the computing facilities may be distributed but the point is that they are managed in an organized, coherent fashion for the benefit of a national user community.)

We will need to understand how students and teachers interact through the undergraduate digital library. For example, as electronic "textbooks" are freed from the tyranny of page limitations and become even larger and richer than they are at present (note that it is very common today for a teacher to chart a path selectively through a textbook for his or her class rather than using the entire text cover to cover) teachers will want to tailor selections of materials—perhaps not just from one huge text but from a selection of texts—for students in a particular class. How such views of the digital library's content are tailored and managed, and the extent to which users of the library are kept within the boundaries of these views are important design questions.

An issue that requires careful, discipline-based analysis is the extent to which instructional material needs to be supplemented by professional literature and reference materials. Some work has already been done in this area for engineering in the work a few years ago on the design of the National Engineering Library (NENGIS), where materials such as patents and standards were identified as important materials that might be used alongside textbooks and the professional literature in engineering education.

Simply digitizing printed textbooks will not be very useful; rather textbooks need to be reconceptualized and redesigned for the digital environment. Facilities that permit students to compare expositions of a topic from multiple textbooks, or to explore optional topics in more depth than current textbooks can offer, are likely to be particularly valuable. The ability to integrate access to remedial as well as more advanced material will also be very important; this would allow a student with gaps in his or her preparation to learn the required material in a more integrated fashion. It will also be important to establish and clearly articulate some operating assumptions of this digital library very early in the planning cycle. For example: Is the digital library intended to supplement or replace printed textbooks? Is most of the material in the digital library going to be printed prior to use (in other words, will it act largely as a materials identification and distributed printing system)? Is the system primarily to deliver content, or is it actually an interactive educational system where students can, for example, complete homework assignments or tests and submit them for grading (either by computer or by the human instructor)? To what extent would an undergraduate digital library incorporate specific communication and collaboration tools, as opposed to sharing a common network technology and infrastructure with them? (Note that the broader the functionality of the digital library, the more likely that technologies embodied within it will be at odds with other institutional information technology choices and strategies.)

Economic and intellectual property issues surrounding content in an undergraduate digital library are likely to be very different that those arising in research digital libraries. Articles (or even monographs) that are part of the research literature almost never generate any meaningful revenue for authors. Authors publish in these venues to communicate with colleagues, and to obtain recognition for tenure and promotion. Textbooks, on the other hand, represent real revenue sources not just for publishers but also for authors. The economic structures for developing content in an undergraduate digital library need to recognize this difference. If we are ever to develop models for managing digital intellectual property in the academic context which reward authors financially, an undergraduate library for instruction is one of the few environments where there is actually existing precedent.

INFRASTRUCTURE REQUIREMENTS

The majority of use for a research-oriented digital library is likely to be concentrated in at most a few hundred institutions; for many disciplines the numbers will be considerably smaller. A digital library designed to support undergraduate education in the sciences, mathematics, and engineering will likely be relevant to thousands of institutions in the United States (even excluding the widely scattered gifted high school students who might well gain great benefit from access to such a system).

Full benefit from the investment in an undergraduate digital library requires that all of the user institutions have adequate network connectivity—and, equally important, adequate local information technology infrastructure and competence—in order to make use of the resource. Because it is likely that much of the content of the undergraduate library will involve interactive multimedia, high bandwidth connectivity will be required even to relatively small institutions. Current programs such as the EDUCOM-led Internet 2 effort or the federal government's Next Generation Internet (NGI) program will ensure that the major research universities have sufficient network connectivity to exploit such a resource, but don't do much for the rest of the institutions that might make use of the system, such as the huge number of community colleges.

Large numbers of workstations will also be required at the institutions that use the system, since many students will need to interact frequently with the digital library on a regular and perhaps extended basis. As computer ownership, and the trend to expect individual students to own their own computer, continue to grow, this will be less of a problem—it will not be necessary to massively expand library public access workstation facilities or computer labs to accommodate all of the added use, for example. Certainly the demand for "wired" classrooms of various types will grow substantially.

Non-residential colleges and universities will face a particularly serious access problem: if students at these institutions are trying to use machines at home, it is unlikely that they will be able to obtain network connectivity sufficient to support use of sophisticated multimedia content. The issue is infrastructure to support not just institutions as specific sites, but all members of the institutional communities wherever they learn, and it seems clear that access to high-capacity network access services is going to lag access to computers at least for the next few years.

A sober assessment of the ability of the intended user community to actually exploit the potential of an undergraduate digital library in the sciences, engineering and mathematics is a critical factor in evaluating the viability of the enterprise. It may also shape the design criteria: in the past few years, many of the research efforts to develop advanced content to support learning in the networked information environment have been focused on exploring the leading edge, under the assumption that at least a few well-equipped institutions would be able to utilize the new content immediately, and that experience gained from these institutions would inform the design of the next generation while connectivity caught up for the broader community. These are the wrong assumptions for a broadly-based undergraduate digital library. If a production-oriented undergraduate digital library enterprise (as opposed to a research program in identifying and developing content that may be helpful for undergraduate education) is to be launched, the infrastructure expectations and their design implications for content need to be carefully, and clearly, articulated, and periodically revisited in light of developments in the networking industries.

CONCLUSIONS

An undergraduate digital library to support science, engineering, mathematics, and technology educa-

tion seems to be an extraordinarily attractive environment to explore ways in which sophisticated digital multimedia and networked information can enhance the processes of teaching and learning. It is important to recognize that terming it a "library" is somewhat misleading, however: rather than competing with or potentially supplanting the profoundly endangered system of scholarly communication which is the provenance of research libraries, it will complement or supplant the relatively healthy industry of textbooks and instructional materials. In scholarly communication, the introduction of technologies such as multimedia further stress the economics of an already deeply stressed system; in support of undergraduate instruction, to the extent that it can be demonstrated that multimedia improves the educational experience, the economics are more favorable.

Recognizing that an undergraduate digital library for science, mathematics, engineering, and technology will be a new complement to, rather than competing with, existing research libraries (which manage, and will continue to manage, both print and electronic content) also underscores the need to explore and understand the relationships with the existing library base, and how linkages can be established between the undergraduate digital library and the evolving research library system both at the intellectual and technical levels. It also seems clear that the team needed to develop such an undergraduate digital library will be somewhat different in composition from those leading the development of more research-oriented digital libraries; while it will certainly require librarians, information technologists, and faculty to work in partnership, the focus on education will mean that author-educators will need to take a leadership role.

Readiness factors on the part of the user community need to be carefully considered. Given the broad-based constituency for undergraduate education, the market failure to date in broadband network services to homes and small businesses is of critical importance. Until this market failure is corrected—either through the widespread availability of cable television-based Internet access or through product offerings from the traditional common carriers or other sources—such a digital library in support of education will only be able to reach a relatively small part of its constituency.

Basic Issues Regarding the Establishment of a National SME&T Digital Library

FRANCIS MIKSA
Professor
Graduate School of Library and Information Science
The University of Texas at Austin

Establishing a national SME&T digital library as outlined in Jay Labov's Project Summary appears at first glance to be a worthwhile and feasible prospect. We generally associate the ideas of education and libraries closely and, therefore with respect to undergraduate education in science, mathematics, engineering, and technology, it would appear natural not only to conclude that the proposed library would be a welcome resource but that an electronic digital library would be an especially useful innovation. However, upon examining the prospect of such a library more closely, trenchant issues arise in all four of the areas of concern that Labov has listed. The purpose of this paper is to raise questions related to the first three of the areas, and particularly with respect to how the idea of a library intersects with them. The first sections below are related loosely to his first area of concern—education and pedagogy. The middle sections below are related generally to the intersection between second and third areas of concern—content and technical issues. And the last sections below are related more specifically to his third area of concern—technical aspects of the proposed library.

EDUCATIONAL OBJECTIVES

Labov states in his "Project Summary" that the purpose of the national SME&T digital library will be "to provide a comprehensive, dynamic, and readily accessible and searchable collection of high-quality educational material in undergraduate science, mathematics, and engineering that is intended to facilitate and enhance the NSF's programs to improve and evaluate undergraduate teaching and learning." (p. 1) This conclusion is based in turn on several observations about the growing impact of

digital libraries, not only in the realm of research in various fields, but also in terms of how education is changing at all levels because of information technology and the availability of electronic information resources. As a result he is able to offer the hope that "Digital libraries also might benefit the scientific, mathematics, and engineering communities that are engaged in higher education." (p. 4)

It strikes me, however, that this kind of hopefulness must contend with the formidable reality that undergraduates in the sciences appear to use only a relatively limited range of library resources in their educational work. They are much more dependent instead on textbooks and manuals which they purchase, laboratory work and information resources, and classroom demonstrations and explanations from instructors. There are good reasons why this appears to be so, mainly related to the need in the sciences to learn basic routines, methods, algorithms, and the like, and to demonstrate having learned such things through laboratory work and testing. What does not seem of as much significance is the independent exploration of information resources of the kind usually associated with a library collection. This conclusion was given expression for me in an unpublished study pursued by one of my doctoral students on library use related to the area of mathematics. The student found little evidence that the sizable and comprehensive mathematics collection at the University of Texas at Austin was needed by the general population of undergraduates in mathematics. Rather, it was used mainly by professors and graduate students in mathematics who were engaged in research. A very small number of the most advanced undergraduates did do some independent exploration in the collection. And there was some use of the mathematics collections by undergraduates, graduate students, and faculty from areas other than mathematics, and even many from the sciences. But, all things being equal, their use amounted to a small part of the whole.[1] In sum, an extensive collection of

---

[1] This study remained unpublished, having been pursued as a possible dissertation project. It should be pointed out that studying the use of a library collection of information resources is difficult to the extent that the classificatory system used distributes materials which focus on applications of a scientific discipline or method (e.g., applications of mathematics or computers in particular subject areas) throughout the system—that is, with the subject areas to which the discipline or method is applied.

materials in mathematics was valuable for various populations on campus, but least of all for undergraduates in mathematics.

The foregoing conclusion is bolstered in an offhanded way by research on the rise of modern research over the past century. Generally, over the past several decades scientific and technological researchers have tended to use a relatively narrow range of information resources associated with library collections. This is especially true in cases of highly active and vibrant research fronts. Rather, such researchers are much more likely to use materials generated apart from library storage (for example, data archives or data generated from programs working on such data archives) and information gained through informal channels. When library resources are used, there is a strong tendency to limit materials to only those that are very recent and to those that are very specific to their particular projects.[2] To sum up, there would seem to be significant data that show that extensive library collections in the areas covered by the proposed library do not have a very close correlation with undergraduate education. Rather, the correlation is with graduate education and established research although even there library collection use has certain limitations and constrictions. If this is so, of course, then the idea of the proposed library might seem to be questionable.

Now, one may take issue with the foregoing conclusions in three general ways. First, we could simply question the observations of low undergraduate use of library materials until better data has been compiled. Second, we might assume that the proposed library will collect those kinds of materials that simply haven't been associated with traditional libraries—for example, special data collections, data archives, or data generated from active research, and so on. Third, we might simply pursue a different approach altogether, justifying the proposed library as a necessity to what is hoped and planned to be a basically new and different approach to undergraduate education in the sciences in the near future.

The latter approach appears to be implied in Labov's association of the proposed library with "innovative, research-based educational practices and materials" (p. 5). He, and one supposes others as well, appear to imply that a new and different approach to education in the sciences will be helped in its evolution by the sheer availability of electronic information resources, regardless of whether text and paper-based as associated with traditional libraries or of some new variety. Given the evolution of such a new educational process, the proposed library will be not only of inestimable worth but also extensively used.

This new approach to undergraduate education in science, mathematics, engineering, and technology would join with all other areas of education that are currently developing educational processes that include extensive individual exploration and discovery by undergraduates and extensive use of interactive multimedia. In these processes, not only would information resources of all kinds be used extensively and interactively, but undergraduates would learn to creatively prepare and publish their own findings.

Given the latter, not only could a case be made for the proposed library, but some guidance is offered as to what the library might contain. In the latter respect, one important point to be made is that regardless of how undergraduate use of information resources change, it may well be that the chief users of the proposed library will not be undergraduates themselves or at least not undergraduates in large numbers, but rather will be the teachers of the undergraduates. In this case, the library might major on making teaching materials available, especially those in interactive multimedia format, or materials and interactive instructions on how to prepare such materials.[3] Or, as an alternative, it may be that such interactive teaching materials will exist much like presently published textbooks, methods and materials

---

[2]My own research in this area can be found in Miksa (1987, 1989). But, the main body of research, carried on especially during the 1960s and 1970s, is well summarized in the Annual Review of Information Science and Technology for the years 1966 to 1972 under the section label, "Information Use."

---

[3]There is an enormous and growing body of resources for creating a new approach to education available on the World Wide Web at a variety of websites. One unusually useful such site, with links to many other resources is *Instructional Technology Connections*. An interesting and useful report related to the introduction to multimedia to an entire campus is found in "Development of Technology Integrated Learning Environments: A Report of the Multimedia Instruction Committee, Spring 1995." One also will find scores of new instructional technology materials in the *Chronicle of Higher Education's* weekly column entitled "Information Technology Resources."

available for those teachers who wish to use them or for those people, undergraduate or not, who wish to use them in order to explore topics in the SME & T areas independently of formal educational processes.

Given the foregoing considerations, it would seem imperative that at a minimum answers to the following questions be sought.

1. What kinds of information resources are presently used by undergraduates in their educational work in science, mathematics, engineering, and technology, and how are such information resources used?

2. What kinds of information resources are presently used by teachers of undergraduates working in the areas of science, mathematics, engineering, and technology, and how are such information resources used?

3. To what extent and in what manner will a new approach to undergraduate education in the sciences engage students in independent discovery, analysis, and creation of knowledge which will be dependent on information resources collected in a digital library?

4. If a new educational process is envisioned for undergraduate education in the sciences, what kinds of educational materials will it require for both students and teachers?

LIBRARIES AND THE EDUCATIONAL PROCESS

Libraries have typically been thought of by those outside of their care as something akin to an inert mass of information-bearing entities. This is most likely the case because the obvious physical and structural characteristics of libraries make it difficult to see much else. This view of a library is further exacerbated by a view of information which treats it as inert "stuff," rather like series of encapsulated character strings or byte-sequences that are ready for plundering in some useful way. But, the fact is that a library at its core is a part of a complex communication process involving creators of information-bearing entities on one end and users of such entities on the other end (not to mention an entire range of other persons distributed between these two ends of the continuum who add value to the informational collections in order to help make

them usable or who function in an interpretative and instructional way in relationship to the content of the entities found in the library).

Ultimately, a very useful view of a library is that it occupies a point in time and space not simply where people "retrieve packages of information" but where they interact with it and its creators as "reorganizers" of the content of what the library contains. The process of reorganization is a complex social process that ultimately lies at the basis of the growth of social knowledge. The social process of reorganization, described in provocative detail in two works by Patrick Wilson (Wilson 1977; 1983) applies to all who use the library, although not all will contribute to the process in the same way or with the same intensity. The point to be made here is that what occurs makes the idea of a library into something of a "living" structure rather than merely an inert mass of information-bearing entities.

Those who have the most effect on the collections ultimately are those who contribute their own knowledge to it. We ordinarily think of that activity occurring at the end of an involved publishing process, carried on by people who have become accredited in some particular discipline or field of knowledge, and whose work is submitted to critical evaluation by some sort of refereeing process. However, a digital library by its very nature participates in a radically revised realm of publishing, one that often circumvents the kinds of processes that have been fundamental to higher education and libraries associated with higher education in the past. Doubtless, were a revised approach to education of undergraduates in the sciences to be pursued, one that is interactive and involves independent exploration and creativity on the part of undergraduates, it would be highly likely that undergraduates would be both interested in and able to contribute to the body of knowledge that the library contains. It may even be that they should have this goal set for them as part of their education. This would obviously make the national SME&T digital library into something very different from a traditional library. Certainly, it would make the library proposed here an even more dynamic and "living" entity than is usually associated with the idea of a library. Were the proposed library to be viewed in this way, the following question might need to be considered.

1. What provisions will the national SME&T digital library provide for the interaction and contribution of students to the library as both a passive knowledge base and a "live" publishing venture?

EDUCATION, LIBRARIES, AND INFORMATION LITERACY

One of the most interesting developments in the information age has been the discovery that the delivery of information is often hindered not because of any reasonable fault of document retrieval systems or any fault in the selection of what is in a library, nor even because the users of a library are not conversant with some particular method of retrieval. Rather, information delivery is hindered because of the much more fundamental problem that users often do not know either that they have information needs or how they might satisfy such information needs once they have become recognized. And even were they aware that they have such needs and even that a given information source exists for a need, not all such persons have the capacity to use such information sources. The issues of how people recognize information needs and, given that recognition, how they handle the information-seeking process, is generally the province of people who investigate "information literacy."[4]

With respect to the need by undergraduates for aid in the use of a library and the use of its materials, none of which is automatic, a successful library of the kind proposed here might well consider the use of information ombudsmen who act as facilitators of "information literacy" (not simply computer literacy) in an electronic context (Miksa 1989). Aid in achieving information literacy may also well have to be done as a "remote" facility of the library.

1. What provisions, if any, will the proposed national SME&T digital library have for dealing with information illiteracy?
2. What provisions, if any, will the proposed national SME&T digital library have for what traditionally has been called "reference work" in libraries?

---

[4]Breivik and Gee (1989) and, especially, Farmer and Mech (eds.) (1992) provide useful perspectives on information literacy at the university level. However, the topic has actually had a long history. For example, Dervin (1976) spoke of it in terms of the typical citizen two decades ago.

LIBRARY CONTENT—CONFLICTING DEMANDS

Academic libraries, along with all libraries which serve heterogeneous communities of information users, commonly face conflicting demands with respect to what they are to "acquire" in the way of information resources (i.e., "link to," possibly, in the context of a digital library). One such need is that of supporting research with the very latest texts and other informational materials in a wide range of languages. (Of course, this supposes that the library will be a research support collection at least in part.)

Another need is to provide essential materials for those academic institutions that cannot by themselves afford them—for example in the same manner that the "Texshare" program in Texas supplies electronic information resources for schools in South Texas. In reality, the idea that a library exists in part to supply materials that some users or user communities cannot afford has been a basic part of the "modern library" since its beginnings late in the nineteenth century. In this respect, in fact, the modern library has always represented a kind of economy of scale, where a single library suffices more or less for a large number of persons who individually could not afford what that library collects (Miksa 1996).

A third need is to support the needs of individuals apart from the needs of a larger group—that is, in modern terms to engage in "demand-driven acquisitions," where some resource is gotten for an individual client of the library regardless if any other client needs it. A final need is for a library of the type proposed here to include to an extent well beyond what has been the practice in the print library realm the instructional materials needed by the SME&T faculty—that is, that huge variety of interactive multimedia instructional materials that promise to attend SME&T education in the coming years.

Any close examination will quickly reveal that these four goals often operate at cross-purposes. For example, acquiring material for a group will regularly be in conflict with demand-driven acquisitions, any collecting of research materials will be in conflict with collecting basic materials for elementary curricular needs, and any collecting of instructional materials will often conflict with both research and elementary curricular needs, especially when funding is limited. If this aspect of a proposed SME&T library is to be adequately broached, the following questions might well need to be raised.

1. Who will set the goals of what the national SME&T digital library should contain?

2. What information user groups needs will be served, and in what order of priority?

THE IDEA OF A LIBRARY— VALUE-ADDING ROLES

It seems incumbent that the library proposed here be invested with a viable administrative and operational infrastructure as well as a viable technological infrastructure. As already implied, a library (any library, including one that is "digital") is more than a warehouse or dumpsite of information that is merely delivered. It is more than simply a collection of inert packages of information represented by bits and bytes that are merely shuffled about. It is more than a publishing venture at the head of which is an editorial staff that can decide what to publish or send off merely by market studies. In short, it is not merely a disinterested operational structure with some sort of a simple delivery system for the people who come to it. It is instead a complex operation of selecting, acquiring, organizing, delivering, advising about, etc., information which adds value to the information included in it at every possible point.

The foregoing is the experience learned from approximately 130 years of the "modern" library of print information-bearing entities, the only kind of library that virtually anyone now working on digital libraries of any kind have ever experienced but of which most are not much aware. Were the library being created for undergraduate SME&T education to observe this normative, "enriched" idea of a modern library, the following questions will need to be addressed.

1. What value-adding activities must be provided for in the proposed national SME&T digital library?

2. Given the answer to question 1 above, what sort of an administrative infrastructure needs to be provided for the library?

TECHNICAL ISSUES—INTERFACING WITH INFORMATION USE STYLES

It seems obvious that the national SME&T digital library proposed here will encounter a wide range of information use styles, some of which depend on finding bits and pieces of information-bearing entities useful for one's current information need often in some practical or utilitarian way, but others of which focus on identifying and "reading" whole information-bearing entities so as to interact with entire idea-sets of the creators of those entities. In short, sometimes one needs little more than a character string from a text, or from a database, or simply an illustrative photograph, and so on, and that is quite enough. It would appear that this kind of information use is particularly amenable to quick and dirty (or even cleaner, more structured) indexing devices. And it would seem to be served well by some of the more recent ideas for the creation of intelligent agents.

However, others kinds of information seeking do not simply assemble bits and pieces of information, but need and even revel in the retrieval of and interaction with "whole" information bearing entities. Such objects are sought not simply to solve some immediate problem but rather to augment and even to reconstruct one's own thoughts and emotions in some creative way. This kind of need requires more than an Alta Vista type search engine. It needs, in fact, the plodding, labor-intensive results of cataloging, where information-bearing entities are not simply categorized for searchers to find potentially useful groups of items, but also carefully described so as to identify them uniquely and thus to promote efficient "known-item" searches. It needs, in fact, the capacity for a person to look for and precisely find individually created "works" even when they are buried in other collections of information-bearing entities. Should this wide expanse in information use be recognized in the proposed library, then some attention must be paid to the following questions.

1. What provisions will be made in the proposed national SME&T digital library for listing information-bearing entities "included" in the library (as well as the "works" they contain) in such a way that such entities and works can be specifically found?

2. Given the answer to question 1 above, what attempts should be made to adhere to nationally adopted standards of cataloging and indexing?

THE LIBRARY AS AN INTELLECTUALLY-STRUCTURED SPACE

One mark of a library, regardless of whether it is of the traditional kind or digital form is that the materials that it includes are organized in terms of an intellectually cohesive and structured "space" (Miksa and Doty 1994). Much is made these days of "intelligent agents" and automatic indexing and retrieval devices that will somehow remove the bottleneck of human intervention in the information storage and retrieval process. The quest for this kind of automatic approach to human information organization and retrieval began with the beginning of the computer revolution and has tended to be kept alive especially by the aforementioned "inert stuff" view of information.

But, if the history of the West has any lesson it is that information organization needs an intellectual framework (knowledge structure) to achieve its greatest impact in a given cultural context. Further, applying such a structure to massive collections of information-bearing entities is a labor-intensive human endeavor that has not yet been successfully made into an automatic routine. (It may someday be accomplished and therefore attempts to solve this trenchant problem should not cease. However, it has not yet been accomplished and that places a particular burden on anyone planning a library of any kind.)

Over the centuries a variety of knowledge structures have been imported into information organization so as to make them into a rational realm for searching and discovery. Although it might be difficult to make a case for applying any given current knowledge structure to the library envisioned here, a case can be made that some such structure is needed. Such a structure need not be rigid, at least from the standpoint of an individual's own home-page base for collecting information links. But, one must have a point of departure for retrieving information from a library for many kinds of information searches and that point of departure will ultimately incorporate knowledge structures. Were the library

proposed here to pay attention to this most basic social and cultural need of information organization, the following questions might well be considered.

1. What kinds of information retrieval search engines should be employed in the proposed national SME&T digital library.

2. What recognition should be given to controlled vocabulary, structured searching environments, if any?

REFERENCES

Breivik, Patricia S. and E. Gordon Gee. 1989. *Information Literacy: Revolution in the Library.* New York: American Council on Education.

Dervin, Brenda. 1976. "The Everyday Information Needs of the Average Citizen: A Taxonomy for Analysis." In *Information for the Community,* ed. By M. Kochen and J. C. Donohue, 19-38. Chicago: American Library Association.

"Development of Technology Integrated Learning Environments: A Report of the Multimedia Instruction Committee, Spring 1995." The University of Texas at Austin. Available at: <http://www.utexas.edu/computer/mic/>.

Farmer, D. W. and Terrence F. Mech, editors. 1992. *Information Literacy: Developing Students as Independent Learners.* San Francisco: Jossey-Bass.

Instructional Technology Connections. (Website) University of Colorado at Denver, School of Education. <http://www.cudenver.edu/~mryder/itcon.html>.

Miksa, Francis. 1987. *Research Patterns and Research Libraries.* Dublin, Ohio: OCLC.

Miksa, Francis. 1989. "The Future of Reference II: A Paradigm of Academic Library Organization." *College and Research Library News* 50 (no. 9, October): 780-90.

Miksa, Francis. 1996. "The Cultural Legacy of the 'Modern Library' for the Future." *Journal of Education for Library and Information Science* 37 (no. 2, Spring): 100-119. Also available at: <http://www.gslis.utexas.edu/faculty/Miksa/modlib.htm>.

Miksa, Francis and Philip Doty. 1994. "Intellectual Realities and the Digital Library." *Proceedings of Digital Libraries '94: The First Annual Conference on the Theory and Practice of Digital*

Libraries. Eds. J. L. Schnase . . . [et. al], pp. 1-5. College Station, Texas: Hypermedia Research Laboratory, Department of Computer Science, Texas A&M University. Also available at: <http://abgen.cvm.tamu.edu/DL94/paper/miksa.html>.

Wilson, Patrick. 1977. *Public Knowledge, Private Ignorance: Toward a Library and Information Policy.* Contributions in Librarianship and Information Science, no. 10. Westport, Conn.: Greenwood Press.

Wilson, Patrick. 1983. *Second-hand Knowledge: An Inquiry into Cognitive Authority.* Contributions in Librarianship and Information Science, no. 14. Westport, Conn.: Greenwood Press.

The Case for Creating a Systematic Indexing System for the National SME&T Digital Library

FRANCIS MIKSA

Professor

Graduate School of Library and Information Science

The University of Texas at Austin

JOAN MITCHELL

Editor

Dewey Decimal Classification

OCLC/Forest Press

DIANE VIZINE-GOETZ

Senior Researcher

Office of Research

On line Computer Library Center (OCLC)

Dublin, Ohio

ABSTRACT

A case is presented for creating a systematic indexing system for the proposed national SME&T digital library. Two sets of assumptions are provided as background, the first having to do with what is "included" in the library's collections, the second with typical factors related to indexing in general. Indexing is defined operationally in a very general way, as making available and using for information searches in the library the attributes of information-bearing entities which the library identifies as members of its collections. The main features of a systematic indexing system include a controlled vocabulary for topical and formal attributes of information-bearing entities, a taxonomic and faceted structure (with notation) of the concept terms that shows relationships among terms, and an alphabetical index to the structure. The idea of the system is illustrated by reference to the Dewey Decimal Classification. A rationale is provided. Its two major foci are how the system supports the undergraduate educational process, and how the system supports searches for materials in topical areas. Finally, after problems are presented for implementing this system are given, questions pertinent to the issues are listed.

BACKGROUND

For the sake of presenting our approach to indexing the national SME&T digital library we will begin with two sets of assumptions—one that concerns the nature of the library's collection, the other with factors related to indexing in general. First, we assume that the proposed national SME&T digital library will "include" graphic and textual information-bearing entities such as texts, audio and graphic files (or combinations of such entities in the form of multimedia files), databases, websites (which contain still other collections of information-bearing entities), etc., in its "collections." Here, "include" means that such entities are purposefully and intellectually included in what the library considers its realm; and "collections" refers to the sum of such entities included in its realm. It is understood, of course, that in the context of a digital library, "includes" essentially means available in electronic format through telecommunications links.

Second, we assume certain things about indexing itself. Operationally speaking, indexing the national SME&T digital library simply means making available and using for information searches in the library the attributes of the information-bearing entities that the library identifies as members of its collections. This is a very broad interpretation of indexing which includes the widest possible range of systems. Thus, a library catalog is considered an index to a library collection just as a more specifically named indexing service constitutes an index of the periodicals and other items which it includes in its purview.

When this operational goal is implemented, the form that indexing takes is controlled by various basic factors. Some of the most important of these are shown in Table 1.

The implementation of each of the factors listed should be viewed as ranging along a continuum that begins with the statement in column A and proceeds in the same row to column B. For example, an indexing system might include only carefully assigned attributes as found in 1A, or it might include all naturally occurring attributes identified in the entities by some automatic algorithm as designated in 1B; but likely as not a typical system will include some combination of attributes from the two sources. Likewise, an indexing system might carefully segregate kinds of attributes according to

TABLE 1. Controlling Factors in Indexing

Individual Factors	A. One end of a continuum	B. The opposite end of a continuum
1. Source of the Attributes	Attributes are devised conceptually and assigned to the entities	Attributes are naturally occurring, such as terms, or audio or visual features found in entities, and are used in the form found
2. Relationship of Attributes to the Entities They Represent	Attributes represent the entity as a whole, or totally (Exact, specific match)	Attributes represent part of the entity in extent or only in terms of some measure of frequency of appearance
3. How Kinds of Attributes Are Handled	Kinds are commonly segregated according to function in relationship to an entity—e.g., subject, form, authorial, producer/publisher, etc.	Kinds are not always distinguished but are rather treated as key terms or key features, mixed and matched.
4. How Relationships Among Attributes Are Handled	Relationships are handled formally according to a conceptual schema.	Relationships are handled automatically by clustering, set-theoretic routines, etc.
5. How the Number of Attributes Per Entity Are Determined	Number of attributes used are often predetermined by kind and restricted	Number of attributes used are usually determined by algorithm
6. The Point at Which Attributes Are Compiled or Used for a Search	Attributes compiled prior to any given search and without specific reference to a given search	Attributes are compiled upon a request being initiated by searching through the entities in a file

(Note: The list of controlling factors can doubtless be augmented and some of the individual factors might be appropriately subdivided into parts. However, for the purposes of the argument, the ones listed seem sufficient. Shaded boxes represent factors basic to the kind of system advocated in this paper.)

some tradition as when traditional library cataloging carefully segregates a name functioning as an author of a document from a name that functions as a subject of a document. Or, again, an indexing system may simply intermix all such functions as in searches made by AltaVista on the Internet. Likely as not, however, a planned indexing system will segregate some attributes from others in order to make the system function more efficiently.

We include this table first of all in order to provide a general framework for considering various important aspects of indexing when considering how the national SME&T digital library might be indexed, and also to offer a way to distinguish existing indexing approaches. With respect to the latter, for example, traditional library catalogs as they evolved from the late nineteenth century to about

the 1950s can most readily be associated with column A of the table. However, as library catalogs have migrated to a computerized context, they have tended to move in some respects toward column B. This is especially evident in various efforts to enhance controlled vocabulary subject heading systems in online public access catalogs by automatically incorporating natural language keyword searching on terminology used in the bibliographic records for individual entities listed in such catalogs. One thing is certainly true with respect to indexing that follows many of the provisions of column A, that is, that it tends to be labor-intensive and, therefore, costly.

In contrast to the foregoing, much of the research done in the realm of information storage and retrieval systems over the past four decades has tended to be identified with column B in the table (cf. Belkin and

Croft 1987). One reason for this is that the provisions of column B are strongly related to tapping the computer's capacity to engage in automatic routines. This has generally been viewed as a necessity in order to break through what has been considered the labor-intensive and costly "bottleneck" of indexing under the provisions of column A. Recent efforts to combine derived indexing methods and the information ordering capabilities provided by established classification schemes are being reported with increasing frequency (Programming Systems Research Group, 1996; Koch and Day, 1997; Thompson, Shafer, and Vizine-Goetz, 1997; Weiss et al., 1996).

The second reason for including the foregoing table of indexing factors is to provide a framework for identifying what this paper advocates—*that is, that regardless of any other indexing approaches which might be taken for the national SME&T digital library, one that should be seriously considered is indexing the library according to a systematic, logically related structure of controlled vocabulary index terms for the topical and other relevant aspects of the information-bearing entities included in the library.* This kind of a system will adhere at a minimum to 1A in the table (controlled vocabulary), 3A (for topic, form, etc., attributes), 4A (a systematic taxonomic structure of term relationships), and 6A (a predetermined structure), with extensions into column B on factors 2 and 5. (See shaded areas in the table.) *In short, we advocate the creation of a multiple entry classified index for the library. What remains here is to briefly describe such a system and to provide a rationale and other considerations regarding it.*

A SYSTEMATIC INDEXING SYSTEM

A systematic indexing system of the kind envisioned here will adhere to the following provisions.

1. It will contain a set of controlled vocabulary concept terms which are assigned to each of the information-bearing entities in the national SME&T digital library—as many for each item as are necessary to highlight useful aspects of each entity—and which are expanded as needed for new entities added to the library. Such concept terms should feature the following attributes of the information-bearing entities when appropriate:

- topicality of the entities (i.e., "aboutness" attributes)
- formal aspects of the entities (i.e., such attributes as "genre," medium, arrangement, formal digital characteristics, etc.)
- other formal aspects of the entities (i.e., those related to "of-ness" of items such as saying what a graphic is "of" rather than "about," or those related to the "for-ness" of items such as saying that an entity has been created "for" such and such an audience or purpose, etc.)

2. The concepts so assigned are then arranged in a taxonomic order with heavy emphasis on "faceted" structures such that both indexers and those searching for information-bearing entities with particular attributes of these kinds may be able to use the system as an aid—for indexers in assigning concepts to new items, and for information seekers when constructing search algorithms. Faceting here means grouping like attributes in "families" (not unlike the particular values in any given field in a database) that are highly adaptable for multiple use in different sections of the structure. For the purposes of ease of use, a notation of the system should be attached to the concepts that will "express" the relationships of the concepts and be available as a shorthand way of referring to parts of the system.

3. An alphabetical arrangement of the concept terms (i.e., an index to the systematic structure) should be maintained in order for indexers and information searchers to gain access to starting points in the systematic map of concept relationships, but also for searching independent of that structure.

A moment's reflection will show that what is actually proposed is similar to what in the past has been called a "classified catalog." Classified catalogs consisted of three parts: 1) a listing (numerically by notation from the system) of entries representing items in the system in their classified order (any item being represented by as many different notations as necessary), 2) an alphabetical listing of terms used in the system, sometimes with inverted index references to the entries, and 3) an alphabetical listing of items in the system by author, title, etc. Classified catalogs were almost always made as manual systems. More recently, as online public access catalogs (OPACs) have begun to provide access to items by their library classification numbers, some semblance of classified catalog arrangement has been achieved. It is limited, however, because it generally does not provide multiple representations of any particular item in the system under different class numbers.

The foregoing brief sketch for indexing can be illustrated by envisioning the use of a system such as the Dewey Decimal Classification (DDC) for indexing the national SME&T digital library but with certain variations of the system as now constructed and typically used. The DDC in its present form is a systematic, logical structure of concepts that are assigned to items in a library by attaching the notation representing each concept or combination of concepts to the items. Its structure of concept terms is highly developed, having been modified constantly by including new concepts, modifying old ones, and restructuring concepts over many years by means of a strong, centralized editorial process. It has adopted faceted structures in various places in the system, has a reasonably thorough index of its concepts, and has many other features that cause it to be one of the best such systems for information retrieval available.

What is envisioned here for the national SME&T digital library is using a system like the DDC to index the information-bearing entities that the library includes in its collections. Multiple index terms or term combinations (represented by classification numbers) would be assigned to each entity for each of the various categories of terms noted above. As a result, those who need to search the library will have both the structured system and the alphabetical arrangement of terms available as a way to search the system. In addition, the structured system will also serve as a map of the categories in the system quite apart from specific search needs (cf. Cochrane and Johnson, 1996; Bendig, 1997; and more generally, Iyer and Giguere, 1995).

The purpose for invoking the DDC is not to champion that system in particular, as excellent as it has become, but rather simply to use it as an example of what is meant here. All things being equal, even the DDC in its present state does not yet have all the requirements for fulfilling the goals outlined here, although it has great potential for being able to do so ultimately. For example, the DDC does not have a fully controlled vocabulary of concept terms and does not always differentiate completely between the various formal and other attributes of entities which were described above. It also does not yet use faceted concept structures to the fullest extent possible although these are being incorporated at an increasing rate under the present editorial direction of the system (Mitchell, forthcoming). Finally, the typical application of the DDC in libraries generally follows a "single-entry" approach, where each information-bearing entity in a collection is generally assigned a single concept statement from the system. This follows the common use of the system as a device physically to arrange library items rather than to index them thoroughly. One Internet-based exception is OCLC's NetFirst database which provides access to Internet and Web-accessible information-bearing entities through multiple classification numbers assigned to an entity. (Vizine-Goetz 1997a)

Nevertheless, the DDC is especially adaptable for the present case, and it especially is adaptable for use in an indexing environment with a layered approach to access. For example, keyword access to information-bearing entities in the national SME&T digital library will be one way to approach its indexing needs. However, most people are doubtless aware of the weaknesses of the straight keyword approach. One question this raises is how to blend the keyword approach with the context and relationships provided by the structured approach to improve retrieval.

In the SME&T library, we assume an increasing number of items may be available in digital form. This offers an opportunity to present a layered approach to information retrieval that in many ways represents previous approaches, but in a more efficient manner. Say we have a textbook on machine learning. A general textbook on machine learning is summarized in Dewey under the number 006.31, and in the Library of Congress subject headings by the phrases Machine learning and Computer algorithms. In the index to the book, there is no mention of computer algorithms, but many examples of specific algorithms which may or may not be known to undergraduates. "Machine learning" has just a few entries in the index, but it is the central "aboutness" of the book. An undergraduate may be looking for algorithms for machine learning, with or without knowing the specific name of one. The summarizing function of the DDC number and sub-ject headings brings one to a promising initial set of documents, the general texts on machine learning. Once in this set, the browse could then move to a keyword search of indexes (back-of-the-book) and browse within those indexes to find a particular algorithm (e.g., backpropagation algorithm).

A bottom-up approach would also work within the same structure—a large keyword retrieval could be sorted and summarized by category using the structure and relationships provided by the DDC and controlled vocabulary. A look at the OCLC NetFirst database will help to illustrate this possibility. Using the hierarchical structure of the Dewey Decimal Classification, a NetFirst user can select from subject categories (such as health, home, technology), topics (such as health and medicine) and subtopics (such as diseases, preventive medicine, and public health) to reduce a results set numbering nearly 14,000 to a more manageable set of 249 records. Further refinements in searching can be achieved by combining one or more terms with DDC topic categories. For instance, a NetFirst user interested in finding electronic resources containing information about health concerns for travelers can browse to the second level topic health and medicine under the category health, home, technology and then search for items in this topic area about travel and tourism. Browsing and filtering the database records in this way (using the structure of DDC but not its class numbers) enables users to retrieve relevant items that may not be as easily discovered using traditional keyword searching capabilities. In this case, a keyword search for health and (travel or tourism) retrieves 143 items; a similar search filtered by DDC topic area retrieves 25 items, with several potentially relevant items included on the first page of the results display (Vizine-Goetz, 1997b).

RATIONALE

The rationale for indexing the national SME&T digital library with the kind of systematic indexing approach outlined here resides chiefly in two assumptions about how such a library might be used, the first assumption having to do with the educational support the library is intended to provide, the second, having to do with efficiency in searches which focus on surveying an area of knowledge.

Educational support

We assume that the focus of the national SME&T digital library, being supportive of undergraduate education in science, mathematics, engineering, and technology, will need a capability for searching that enhances the ability of undergraduates to engage in the personal exploration of ideas, and that given this need, the indexing system of the library will therefore need to include a broad range of information search types.

We illustrate this broad range of search types by referring to two parts of the taxonomy of kinds of knowledge-information "uses" found in Fritz Machlup's work. He outlined five kinds of knowledge-information uses, of which the first two kinds have special relevance here—the "instrumental" or "practical" use of information on the one hand, and the "intellectual" use of information on the other hand (Machlup, 1980, 107-9; cf. Miksa, 1985).

The first of these two types focuses on the need for (and, therefore, the search for) very specific information found as a result of very specifically defined information searches. This information is often needed quickly, and it is generally needed in order to complete some task, make some decision, etc. This kind of information use and search is predicated in turn on one knowing exactly what is needed and the capacity to generate an information search that precisely meets the information need. It is certainly basic to known-item searching for library items about which one knows some clue about its attributes and which one pursues because of the expectation that the item will fulfill one's information need in some fashion. This kind of information use is also basic to searches on topical terms for very specific topics differentiated from other closely related topics. This approach to searching is basic to many of the information storage and retrieval systems created over the past four decades and especially to systems created to serve scientists and other educated researchers who one supposes know when they have information needs and have some skill in stating precisely what they want or need in the way of information.

We assume that while the undergraduate education supported by the national SME&T digital library will necessitate this kind of searching on the part of undergraduates some of the time, the second important type of knowledge-information use designated by Machlup and its corresponding kind of search type will play an equally if not even more important role. Machlup's second kind of information use, which he called the "intellectual" use of information and which he associated with information gained in some repose for more general educational purposes rather than for specific instrumental ends, is a much less specific approach to information need and searching. It actually amounts to a kind of exploratory approach to information where information is surveyed by categories in a manner that has great likeness to mapping knowledge, often for little more than one's personal satisfaction. Its main emphasis is the mental exploration of ideas and is characteristically associated with the browsing done by students in the stacks of a library where books on various topics are surveyed according to the progression of topics they represent on the shelves, books being pulled and examined often sequentially, with topical hints and ideas coming in a flood from the books themselves, from their association with other books along side them in the same category, and from differences with books in nearby categories.

We assume that this kind of information use and, by extension, information searching, is especially relevant to the national SME&T digital library as a support for undergraduate education insofar as that education will emphasize the exploration of ideas in the form of personal research and exploration rather than the directed research of seasoned researchers in creating new social knowledge. It is precisely this kind of intellectual activity, in fact, that produces the kind of thinking that appears to be fundamental to the national SME&T digital library idea.

If our assumptions about information use are accurate, and we believe they are, then an indexing system is needed for the library that will support this kind of information use and searching as well as the instrumentally precise kind of information use and searching described above. In this respect we conclude that a systematic approach to indexing the national SME&T digital library of the kind we propose will support this need very directly in a way that no other indexing approach can. Our proposed system will do so because it "maps" knowledge categories into a logical structure, and given a system in which such a knowledge structure is available, will promote this kind of information searching to the undergraduates who use it. It will promote and

facilitate, in other words, the kind of browsing or exploratory searching described here.

As a caveat, it should be noted that the "mapping" of knowledge relationships in the sense meant here is not designed to be some ultimate and absolute set of knowledge categories and their relationships, but rather merely a beginning point for an information seeker's own personal mapping of knowledge. In short, any such structure constitutes no more nor less than a starting point, concluding that it is in the nature of this kind of mental activity to use such a structure to build one's own personal knowledge structure, redefining and extending the relationships one begins with and which are found in such a structure as needed and not simply absorbing the given structure as absolute. The basis for doing so, however, is that some such knowledge structure is available as a beginning point and that one has the capability of browsing through such a structure with both guidance in its use but also with a good deal of freedom (Miksa, 1997).

Efficiency in Surveying Information

The second reason why a systematic indexing system of the kind proposed here will be useful for the national SME&T digital library has to do with a certain kind of usefulness in searching that is sometimes, but not always, needed in information retrieval but which is hard to come by in other kinds of systems—that is, searching for all aspects of a topic where the aspects are indexed under a variety of names. For example, given a search for various aspects of, say, the realm of Bryophyta, unless one were a seasoned researcher who already knew the classes of plants included in Bryophyta (for example, different kinds of mosses, hornworts, and liverworts) or such various aspects of the study of Bryophyta or any of its subclasses as anatomy, physiology, morphology, ecology, molecular and cellular issues, and so on, it would be much easier to find what a library of any kind had on the area were these all gathered systematically in one place in an indexing system. In short, it would be more efficient for one to see a concept map of the area than simply diving in without a clue about what is included trying to survey it.

Searching for related topics such as these can be done by controlled vocabulary systems such as subject headings if a strong structure of narrower and related term cross-references are available, but such cross-references ultimately must be derived from a systematic structure of the kind the system proposed here would supply as a matter of course. Not all searches are conducted with this goal in mind, of course, but where they are the system proposed here would expedite them with some efficiency.

OTHER CONSIDERATIONS

Having hopefully made a case for the need of the kind of systematic indexing system proposed here, we close by pointing out several difficult issues that must be considered in implementing such a system.

1. The system proposed here is labor-intensive and, therefore, relatively costly to implement, as is any controlled vocabulary and concept-assigned system. However, there seems at the present time no alternative to it that would yield this kind of a system. Further, in order to implement such a system an organized, managed, and funded approach to the indexing process will be needed.

2. Creating any systematic system will bog down if its goal becomes to create what could be called the "one best system" or knowledge taxonomy—a system considered to be "more correct" than any other system. We assume that all knowledge structures are ultimately artificial and capable of growth and evolution. Thus, what is needed is an emphasis on adaptability in such a system where the official version of the system can not only be easily modified, but can be used in whatever modified or "non-official" form one wants for the system without losing contact with the form in which the official version of the system is found.

3. Some will claim that a systematic structure of knowledge categories arranged in someone's logical manner will be evidence of little more than what post-modernists such as Michel Foucault and others would consider the blatant exercise of power and authority in the intellectual realm so as to squelch intellectual dissent. We conclude that to the extent that any classification of knowledge categories is at base an information-losing process (i.e., by excluding alternative arrangements, at least in any "official" or basic version of the system), and that the purpose is to provide only one approach to knowledge structure, this objection has some merit. We also conclude, however, that the solution to the problem is not to avoid making taxonomic structures in the first place, or to argue incessantly about what is right or wrong about them, but rather to create a system with malleability sufficient to allow it to be arranged and searched in alternative arrangements, much like one can rearrange the reporting structures of databases.

QUESTIONS

We conclude with a list of questions for discussion that arise from the foregoing remarks.

1. What indexing implications arise from the meaning of the assertion that *information-bearing entities are "included" in the national SME&T digital library* and, in fact, from how that process will function?

2. What do the educational objectives underlying the national SME&T digital library yield in terms of the information search needs and patterns of the undergraduate users of the library?

3. What other users of the national SME&T digital library are expected besides undergraduates in the areas of science, mathematics, engineering, and technology, and how does the expectation of the information use needs of these other information users impact on the indexing of the library?

4. What combination of typical indexing factors are necessary and sufficient for the users of the national SME&T digital library?

5. If the answer to question 4 consists of a layered approach to indexing, of what should the layers consist?

6. What combination of typical indexing factors for the library is both practical and affordable?

7. What alternatives to a systematic indexing system of the kind envisioned here are presently available for meeting the information use needs described in the "rationale" above?

8. If a presently available system such as the DDC were used for creating a systematic indexing system for the national SME&T digital library, what changes might be recommended with respect to the system and how it is typically applied?

9. Which persons or bodies would be given responsibility for indexing the national SME&T digital library?

10. To what extent should the indexing needs of the national SME&T digital library provide a testbed for indexing experimentation?

REFERENCES

Belkin, Nicholas J., and W. Bruce Croft. 1987. "Retrieval Techniques." *Annual Review of Information Science and Technology* 22: 109-45.

Bendig, Mark. 1997. "Mr. Dui's Topic Finder," *Annual Review of OCLC Research 1996*. Dublin, Ohio: OCLC. Also available at: <http://www.purl.org/oclc/review1996>.

Cochrane, Pauline, and Eric Johnson. 1996. "Visual Dewey: DDC in a Hypertextual Browser for the Library User." In *Knowledge Organization and Change: Proceedings of the 4th International ISKO Conference, 15-18 July 1996, Washington, D.C.*, ed. by Rebecca Green. Frankfurt/Main: INDEKS Verlag, 95-106.

Iyer, Hemalata, and Mark Giguere. 1995. "Towards Designing an Expert System to Map Mathematics Classificatory Structures," *Knowledge Organization* 25 (no. 3/4): 141-47.

Koch, T., and Michael Day. 1997. The role of classification schemes in Internet resource description and discovery. [Development of a European Service for Information on Research and Education (DESIRE) project report posted on the World Wide Web.] Retrieved July 29, 1997 from the World Wide Web: <http://www.ukoln.ac.uk/metadata/DESIRE/classification/class_ti.htm>.

Machlup, Fritz. 1980. *Knowledge and Knowledge Production.* Vol. 1 of *Knowledge: Its Creation, Distribution, and Economic Significance.* Princeton, N.J.: Princeton University Press.

Miksa, Francis. 1985. "Machlup's Categories of Knowledge as a Framework for Viewing Library and Information Science History." *Journal of Library History* 20 (Spring): 157-92.

Miksa, Francis. 1997. *The DDC, the Universe of Knowledge, and the Post-Modern Library.* Albany, N.Y.: Forest Press, a division of OCLC Online Computer Library Center, Inc.

Mitchell, Joan S. "Challenges Facing Classification Systems: A Dewey Case Study." In *Knowledge Organization for Information Retrieval: Proceedings of the 6th International Study Conference on Classification Research, 16-18 June 1997.* London. (Forthcoming.)

Programming Systems Research Group, MIT Laboratory for Computer Science. HyPursuit Homepage. [Document posted on the World Wide Web.] Retrieved July 29, 1997 from the World Wide Web: <http://paris.LCS.MIT.EDU:80/Projects/CRS/HyPursuit/>.

Thompson, Roger, Shafer, Keith, and Diane Vizine-Goetz. 1997. "Evaluating Dewey Concepts as a Knowledge Base for Automatic Subject Assignment." Paper presented at 2nd ACM International Conference on Digital Libraries, Philadelphia, Pa., July 23-26, 1997. Also available at: <http://purl.oclc.org/scorpion/eval_dc.html>.

Vizine-Goetz, Diane. 1997a. "Classification Research," *Annual Review of OCLC Research 1996.* Dublin, Ohio: OCLC. Also available at: <http://www.purl.org/oclc/review1996>.

Vizine-Goetz, Diane. 1997b. "OCLC Investigates Using Classification Tools to Organize Internet Data," *OCLC Newsletter* (March/April 1997): 14-18. Also available as: <http://www.oclc.org/oclc/new/n226/frames_man.htm>.

Weiss, R., et al. 1996. HyPursuit: A Hierarchical Network Search Engine that Exploits Content-Link Hypertext Clustering. [Compressed file posted on the World Wide Web.] Retrieved July 29, 1997 from the World Wide Web: <http://www.psrg.lcs.mit.edu/ftpdir/papers/hypertext96.ps.gz>.

APPENDIX B:
WORKSHOP AGENDA

NATIONAL RESEARCH COUNCIL WORKSHOP ON A DIGITAL NATIONAL LIBRARY FOR SME&T EDUCATION

National Academy of Sciences Building
Meeting Room—NAS Lecture Room (unless otherwise noted)
August 7-8, 1997

AGENDA

August 7, 1997: Pedagogical and Logistical Opportunities and Challenges in Establishing a National Library for Undergraduate SME&T Education

8:00 AM   **Continental Breakfast**

8:30 AM   **Announcements, Welcome, Overview and Objectives of Workshop**
- *Jay Labov and Herb Lin, National Research Council*
- *Jack Wilson, Rensselaer Polytechnic Institute (Workshop Chair)*
- *Hal Richtol, Division of Undergraduate Education, National Science Foundation*

9:00 AM   **Plenary Session I and Discussion**
Presentations and Panel Discussion: The Role and Value of a Digital National Library for Undergraduate SME&T Education. What are the Opportunities and Challenges?

Panelists:
- *William Arms, Corporation for National Research Initiatives*
- *Miriam Masullo, Watson Research Center, IBM*
- *Michael Raugh, Interconnect Technologies Corp.*
- *Lee Zia, University of New Hampshire*

Questions and comments from the audience to members of the panel and the workshop audience.

10:20 AM   **Break**

10:40 AM   **Plenary Session II and Discussion**
Presentations and Panel Discussion: The Role and Value of a Digital National Library for Undergraduate SME&T Education. What are the Opportunities and Challenges?

Panelists:
- *Mary Case, Association of Research Libraries*
- *Michael Lesk, Bellcore*
- *Francis Miksa, University of Texas*
- *Nisha Vora, Association of American Publishers*

Questions and comments from the audience to members of the panel and the workshop audience.

12:00 PM	**Description of afternoon break-out sessions and charges to participants**
12:15 PM	**Lunch**
1:30 PM	**Break-out Sessions**

Break-out sessions that deal with specific curricular, pedagogical, logistical, and economic and legal issues in establishing a Digital National Library for Undergraduate SME&T Education.

- *Curricular/Pedagogical/User Issues—Lecture Room and NAS Auditorium*
- *Logistic/Technology Issues—NAS 150*
- *Economic/Legal Issues—NAS 180*

5:00 PM	**Cocktails and Dinner, the Rotunda and Members Room**
7:00–8:30 PM	**Reports from Break-out Sessions—Lecture Room**

Break-out sessions report back on their findings and recommendations.

Discussion of recommendations from Day 1 that should be included in the report to NSF.

August 8, 1997: Should NSF Sponsor the Establishment of a National Library for Undergraduate SME&T Education?

8:15 AM	**Continental Breakfast - Lecture Room**
8:45 AM	**Overview of Goals and Objectives to be Considered in Break-out Sessions.** *Jack Wilson, Chair*
9:30 AM	**Break-out Sessions**

- *Curricular/Pedagogical/User Issues - Lecture Room*
- *Logistic/Technology Issues - NAS 150 and NAS 250*
- *Economic/Legal Issues - NAS 180*

11:00 AM	**Break**
11:15 AM	**Reports from Break-out Sessions**
12:15 PM	**Final Comments and Discussions from Workshop Participants—Points of Consensus**
12:30 PM	**Adjourn (Box Lunches Provided)**

APPENDIX C: LIST OF WORKSHOP PARTICIPANTS AND NSF OBSERVERS

WORKSHOP PARTICIPANTS

NABIL ADAM
Rutgers University

PRUDENCE ADLER
Association of Research Libraries

TRYG AGER
IBM Almaden Research Center

WILLIAM ARMS
Corporation for National Research Initiatives

STEPHANIE BARRETT
American Geological Institute

HAROLD BILLINGS*
The University of Texas at Austin

TORA BIKSON
RAND Corporation

CHRISTINE BORGMAN
Univeristy of California

ANNE BUCK
California Institute of Technology

JAMES CALLAN
University of Massachusetts

MARY CASE
Association of Research Libraries

SU-SHING CHEN
University of Missouri

JAMES DAVIS
Xerox PARC

ELIZABETH DUPUIS
The University of Texas at Austin

STEPHEN EHRMANN*
American Association of Higher Education

EDWARD FOX
Virginia Polytechnic Institute

GORDON FREEDMAN
California State University, Monterey Bay

RICHARD FURUTA
Texas A&M University

MARGARENT GJERTSEN
North Carolina State University

PETER GRAHAM
Rutgers University Libraries

TIM INGOLDSBY
American Institute of Physics

VICKI JOHNSON
Interconnect Technologies Corporation

JOHN JUNGCK*
Beloit College

JAMES KELLER
Harvard University

DEBORAH KNOX
The College of New Jersey

ROBERTA LAMB
Case Western Reserve University

MICHAEL LESK
Bellcore

ROBERT LICHTER
Camille and Henry Dreyfus Foundation

RICHARD LUCIER
University of California, San Francisco

CLIFFORD LYNCH
Coalition for Networked Information

MIRIAM MASULLO
IBM T.J. Watson Research Center

FRANCIS MIKSA
The University of Texas at Austin

JOAN MITCHELL*
On line Computer Library Center

BRANDON MURAMATSU
National Engineering Education Delivery System

JEANNE NARUM
Project Kaleidoscope

SHAMKANT NAVATHE
Georgia Institute of Technology

LORRAINE NORMORE
Chemical Abstracts Service

JAN OLSEN
Cornell University

ROBERT PANOFF
The Shodor Education Foundation

GILDA PAUL
Princeton University

BARBARA POLANSKY
American Chemical Society

MICHAEL RAUGH
Interconnect Technologies Corporation

RUTH SEIDMAN
Massachusetts Institute of Technology

FRANK SHIPMAN
Texas A&M University

AMANDA SPINK
University of North Texas

RONALD STEVENS
University of California at Los Angeles Medical School

KEITH STUBBS
U.S. Department of Education

DIANE VIZINE-GOETZ*
On line Computer Library Center

NISHA VORA
Association of American Publishers

PAUL WELLIN
Wolfram Research, Inc.

WAYNE WOLF
Princeton University

LEE ZIA
University of New Hampshire

*Authors of commissioned papers who did not attend the workshop

NSF OBSERVERS

LILLIAN CASSEL
National Science Foundation

LLOYD DOUGLAS
National Science Foundation

NORMAN FORTENBERRY
National Science Foundation

STEPHEN GRIFFIN
National Science Foundation

LEE HERRING
American Psychological Society

SUSAN HIXSON
National Science Foundation

DAN HODGE
National Science Foundation

DAVID KEEFE
America Tomorrow Inc.

SUSAN KEMNITZER
National Science Foundation

HERB LEVITAN
National Science Foundation

JAMES LIGHTBOURNE
National Science Foundation

JOY PAUSCHKE
National Science Foundation

JIM POWLIK
National Science Foundation

HAL RICHTOL
National Science Foundation

JANET RUTLEDGE
National Science Foundation

NORA SABELLI
National Science Foundation

FRANK SETTLE
National Science Foundation

GEORGE STRAWN
National Science Foundation

LIZ TELES
National Science Foundation

FRANK WATTENBERG
National Science Foundation

PEGGY WEEKS
National Science Foundation

HOLLIS WICKMAN
National Science Foundation

TERRY WOODIN
National Science Foundation

APPENDIX D: BIOGRAPHICAL SKETCHES OF STEERING COMMITTEE AND WORKSHOP PARTICIPANTS

STEERING COMMITTEE MEMBERS

JACK M. WILSON, RENSSELAER POLYTECHNIC INSTITUTE

Jack Wilson is the Acting Dean of the Faculty; Dean, Undergraduate and Continuing Education; Professor of Physics and Professor of Engineering Science at Rensselaer Polytechnic Institute; and Chairman of the Board of Interactive Learning International (ILINC). Dr. Wilson received his A.B. from Thiel College in 1967, and his M.A. and Ph.D. from Kent State University in 1972. After holding teaching and research positions at Kent State, Sam Houston State, and the University of Maryland among others, he has been with Rensselaer since 1990. Among the many awards he has won, Dr. Wilson received the Pew Charitable Trusts Leadership Award for Renewal of Undergraduate Education in 1996. Dr. Wilson has published numerous papers, the most recent of which is "Re-engineering the Undergraduate Curriculum," a book chapter for *The Learning Revolution* to be published by Anker Publishing Co., 1997.

DENICE D. DENTON, UNIVERSITY OF WASHINGTON

Denice D. Denton is the Dean of Engineering and a professor in the department of electrical engineering at the University of Washington. She received the B.S., M.S. (1982), and Ph. D. (1987) in electrical engineering from the Massachusetts Institute of Technology. Her current interests include plasma deposition of polymers and the use of micromachining in solid state actuator design. Professor Denton was codirector of the National Institute for Science Education in 1995-1996. She is the recipient of the National Science Foundation Presidential Young Investigator Award (1987-1992), the American Society of Engineering Education AT&T Foundation Teaching Award (1991), the

W.M. Keck Foundation Engineering Teaching Excellence Award (1994), the American Society of Electrical Engineers George Westinghouse Award (1995), and the Institute of Electronic and Electrical Engineering Harriet B. Rigas Teaching Award (1995). Dr. Denton is the chair of the NRC's Board on Engineering Education.

JAMES W. SERUM, HEWLETT-PACKARD COMPANY

Jim Serum received a B.A. in chemistry from Hope College and was awarded a Ph.D. in organic chemistry in 1969 from the University of Colorado. His doctorate research was directed toward studies in mass spectrometry. Following his graduate studies, he taught and did research at the University of Ghent, Belgium. He spent a year at Rice University as a Welch Fellow, and then joined the staff at Cornell University as director of the National Institutes of Health High Resolution Mass Spectrometry Facility. Dr. Serum joined the Hewlett-Packard Company in 1973 as applications chemist for mass spectrometry. Since then he has held a number of management positions, including technical support manager for mass spectrometry in Europe (France); marketing manager for mass spectrometry and spectroscopy at the Scientific Instruments Division; research and development manager at the same division; and research and development manager for the Avondale Division (laboratory automation and chromatography instrumentation). Since 1984 he has held positions as operations manager for laboratory automation systems and automated chemical systems, as well as the analytical group research and development manager. Dr. Serum is currently general manager for mass spectrometry, infrared, and protein chemical systems. In addition, he is chairman of Hewlett-Packard's Bioscience Council and vice chairman of the Hewlett-Packard Corporate Research and Development Council.

HARVEY B. KEYNES, UNIVERSITY OF MINNESOTA

Harvey Keynes is a professor of mathematics, past director of education in the Geometry Center, and director of education programs for a new Institute of Technology Center. His research interests are in dynamical systems. Professor Keynes has directed the following projects: The University of Minnesota Talented Youth Program (state and private funding); the National Science Foundation Teacher Renewal Project; the NSF-supported Minnesota Mathematics Mobilization; the Ford Foundation Urban Mathematics Collaborative; the NSF-supported Young Scholars Project; the Bush Foundation Project to increase female participation in the University of Minnesota Talented Youth Program; the NSF-funded Early Alert Initiative; and a new reformed calculus program for engineering students. Professor Keynes has also taught calculus in the University of Minnesota Talented Youth Program, and has been a teacher in the NSF Teacher Renewal Project. He has extensive contacts in Minnesota and national mathematics education and high technology committees. He was a member of the NRC's Mathematical Sciences Education Board and is the recipient of the 1992 Award for Distinguished Public Service of the American Mathematical Society. Professor Keynes has contacts with major mathematics organizations and projects at the international level and throughout the United States.

WORKSHOP PARTICIPANTS AND AUTHORS OF COMMISSIONED PAPERS

NABIL R. ADAM, RUTGERS UNIVERSITY

Nabil Adam is a professor of computers and information systems and the director of the Center for Information Management, Integration, and Connectivity (CIMIC) at Rutgers University and member of the department of computer and information science, New Jersey Institute of Technology. He received his M.S., M. Phil, and Ph.D. degrees from Columbia University Dr. Adam has published a number of technical papers in such journals as *Institute of Electronic and Electrical Engineering (IEEE), Transactions on Software Engineering, IEEE Transactions on Knowledge and Data Engi-*neering, and *Communications of the ACM*, among others. He has co-authored/co-edited nine books including one on database issues in global information systems (GIS) (Kluwer Academic Publisher, 1997), And as part of the Springer Verlag Lecture Notes Series in Computer Science, one on electronic commerce (1996), two on digital libraries (1995, 1996) and one on advanced databases (1993). Dr. Adam is editor-in-chief of the *International Journal on Digital Libraries* and serves on the editorial board of the *Journal of Management Information Systems* and the *Journal of Electronic Commerce*. He served as a guest editor for the *Communications of the ACM, Operations Research*, and *Journal of Management Information Systems*. He is the co-founder and current chair of the IEEE task force on digital libraries. He served as the general chair of the 1997 "IEEE International Conference on the Advances in Digital Libraries (IEEE ADL'97)", the program chair of the 1996 "Forum on Research and Technology Advances in Digital Libraries", the previous year as program co-chair, and the program chair of the 1994 "International Conference on Information and Knowledge Management." He has also served on the program committee of several international conferences. Dr. Adam has lectured on digital libraries and other related topics at several institutions, including the department of computer science, State University of New York at Buffalo (April 1997); The International Conference on the Digital Libraries and Information Services for the 21st Century (KOLISS DL'96), in Seoul, Korea, (September 1996); the Development and Practice of Law in the Age of the Internet, Washington College of Law Centennial Week Symposium (April 1996); and the 2nd International Workshop on Next Generation Info. Technologies and Systems, the Technion and Neaman Institute, Israel (June 1995). His research work has been supported by the Defense Logistics Agency (DLA), the NASA Center for Excellence in Space Data and Information Sciences (CESDIS), and Bellcore. He also serves as a consultant to several organizations, including Bellcore, and Center for Excellence in Space Data and Information Sciences, NASA Goddard Space Flight Center. He is a member of the New York Academy of Science and listed in *Who's Who in America in Science and Engineering*.

PRUDENCE ADLER, ASSOCIATION OF RESEARCH LIBRARIES

Prudence Adler is the assistant executive director of the Association of Research Libraries (ARL). Her responsibilities include federal relations with a focus on information policies, intellectual property rights, telecommunications, issues relating to access to government information, and project management for the ARL GIS Literacy Project. Prior to joining ARL in 1989, Ms. Adler was assistant project director, Communications and Information Technologies Program, Congressional Office of Technology Assessment, where she worked on studies relating to government information, networking and supercomputer issues, and information technologies and education. Ms. Adler has an M.S. in library science and M.A. in American history from the Catholic University of America and a B.A. in history from George Washington University. She has participated in several advisory councils including the Depository Library Council, the Board of Directors of the National Center for Geographic Information and Analysis, and the Alexandria Digital Library Design Review.

TRYG AGER, IBM ALMADEN RESEARCH CENTER

Tryg Ager is the lead of Digital Library Pilots and Prototypes projects at Almaden Research Center. Recent projects include university journal libraries, integration of automated library systems with digital library, countrywide digital library systems, and digital libraries for training and analysis for the Department of Defense. Prior to joining IBM in 1994, Tryg was a consultant for the Institute for Defense Analysis and helped plan and implement worldwide multimedia networking for the Department of Defense Dependents Schools. From 1978 to 1994 Tryg was a senior research scientist at the Institute for Mathematical Studies in the Social Sciences at Stanford University, working on many projects to create, test, and disseminate programs for computer-based instruction in logic and mathematics.

WILLIAM ARMS, CORPORATION FOR NATIONAL RESEARCH INITIATIVES

Bill Arms has been a member of the Corporation for National Research Initiatives (CNRI) since 1995. He leads CNRI's program of research and development in digital libraries. This includes publication of *D-Lib Magazine;* technology development, including a handle system for identifying Internet resources, and repository and registry systems; and implementation projects with the U.S. Copyright Office, the Library of Congress, the Defense Technical Information Center, the Association of American Publishers, the United States Information Agency, and others. Previously, Dr. Arms was vice president for computing at Carnegie Mellon University, and has held faculty positions at Sussex University, the Open University, and Dartmouth College. He has been a member of numerous boards and committees in the field of networking, digital libraries, including chairman of the Educom board, a founder of the Coalition for Networked Information, and is currently vice chairman of the Association of Computing Machinery publications board. Dr. Arms has degrees in mathematics and operational research from Oxford University, the London School of Economics, and Sussex University.

TORA BIKSON, RAND CORPORATION

Tora Bikson is a senior scientist in RAND Corporation's Behavioral Sciences Department. She received B.A., M.A., and Ph.D. (1969) degrees in philosophy from the University of Missouri at Columbia and M.A. and Ph.D. (1974) degrees in psychology from the University of California at Los Angeles. Since 1980, Dr. Bikson's research has investigated properties of advanced information technologies in varied user contexts, addressing such issues as what factors affect the successful incorporation of innovative tools into ongoing activities; how these new work media influence group structures and interaction processes; what impact they have on task and social outcomes as well as user satisfaction; and what individuals and organizations need to know to use them effectively. She has pursued these questions as principal investigator for projects funded by NSF, the Office of Technology Assessment, and the John and Mary R. Markle Foundation. Her work emphasizes field research design, intensive case studies, and large-scale cross-sectional studies addressed to the use of computer-based tools in organizational settings. Dr. Bikson is a member of Data for Development (a United Nation's Secretariat providing scientific guidance on the use of information systems in developing companies) and a technical consultant to the U.N. Advisory Commission on the Coordination of Information Systems.

She is a frequent reviewer for professional papers and has authored a number of journal articles, book chapters, and research reports on the implementation of new interactive media. She is a member of the American Academy of Arts and Sciences, Association for Computing Machinery, American Psychological Association (fellow), Computer Professionals for Social Responsibility, and the Society for the Psychological Study of Social Issues. Dr. Bikson recently served on the NRC's Computer Science and Telecommunications Board committee on information technology and the service society.

*HAROLD BILLINGS, UNIVERSITY OF TEXAS AT AUSTIN

Harold Billings is director of General Libraries, The University of Texas at Austin, a position he has held since 1977. Prior to that appointment he held other administrative positions at UT Austin in the areas of general administration, collection development and technical services. He holds a B.A. degree from Pan American College (now UT Pan American) and the M.L.S. from UT Austin. He was the founding chairman of the Research Libraries Advisory Committee to OCLC (RLAC) and has served on the boards of the Association of Research Libraries, the AMIGOS Bibliographic Council, and the Center for Research Libraries, and has participated in numerous other groups concerned with resource sharing, networking, and preservation. He is the author or editor of works dealing with contemporary literature and bibliography, as well as articles about library cooperation and the electronic information revolution.

CHRISTINE L. BORGMAN, UNIVERSITY OF CALIFORNIA, LOS ANGELES

Christine Borgman holds the Presidential Chair in Information Studies at UCLA. She is a professor of library and information science, and was department chair from 1995 to 1997. She also teaches in the Communication Studies Program at UCLA and is a visiting professor in the Department of Information and Library Studies at Loughborough University, Loughborough, Leicestershire, England (1996-1999). Her teaching and research interests include digital libraries, human-computer interaction, information seeking behavior, and scholarly

communication and bibliometrics, as well as information technology policy in Central and Eastern Europe. Since 1990 she has lectured or conducted research in Australia, Austria, Britain, Croatia, Czech Republic, Denmark, Hungary, Ireland, Lithuania, New Zealand, Poland, Russia, Slovakia, Slovenia, Sweden, and the Ukraine, and has been a Fulbright Visiting Professor at the University of Economic Sciences and at Eötvös Loránd University in Budapest, Hungary, and a scholar-in-residence at the Rockefeller Foundation Study and Conference Center in Bellagio, Italy. Her educational background includes a B.A. in mathematics from Michigan State University, an M.L.S. from the University of Pittsburgh, and a Ph.D. in communication from Stanford University. Prior to her research career, she was a systems analyst, developing automated systems for libraries and information retrieval systems for industry. Professor Borgman has published more than 130 articles, conference papers, reports, and books in the fields of information studies, computer science, and communication. Her books include *Effective On line Searching: A Basic Text* (Marcel Dekker, 1984), *Scholarly Communication and Bibliometrics* (Sage, 1990), and *From Gutenberg to the Global Information Infrastructure* (MIT Press, forthcoming). She is an elected fellow of the American Association for the Advancement of Science and a member of the board of directors of the Council on Library and Information Resources, the advisory board to the Soros Foundation Open Society Institute Regional Library Program, the advisory board to the Electronic Privacy Information Center, and the Association for Computing Machinery Public Policy Committee. She currently serves on the editorial boards of *Communication Research, Journal of the American Society for Information Science, Journal of Documentation, Journal of Computer-Mediated Communication, Computer Supported Cooperative Work, The Information Society*, and the *Journal of Digital Information*.

ANNE M. BUCK, CALIFORNIA INSTITUTE OF TECHNOLOGY

Anne Buck is the Caltech University Librarian. Before coming to Pasadena she was university librarian at the New Jersey Institute of Technology. She was a group supervisor in the Bell Labs Library Network until the breakup of AT&T when she joined Bell Communications Research to build and direct the Bellcore Library Network. She has also been a public library director, consultant, and trustee. Dr. Buck taught library management at Rutgers University and the University of Wisconsin-Madison, and recently contributed chapters to *Professional Writing* and *The Complete Chemical Engineer; A Student Guide to Critical Thinking.* Dr. Buck is vice-president of the Engineering Information Foundation, a director of Engineering Information, Incorporated and a member of the Highsmith Press Editorial Advisory Board. She has served as treasurer of the American Society for Information Science and is listed in *Who's Who in America*, *Who's Who of American Women*, *Who's Who in American Education* and *Who's Who in the West.*

JAMES CALLAN, UNIVERSITY OF MASSACHUSETTS

Jamie Callan is a research assistant professor in the University of Massachusetts, Amherst, Computer Science Department. He is also the assistant director of the UMass Center for Intelligent Information Retrieval (CIIR). He is responsible for obtaining grants, directing graduate student research, advising students and serving on thesis committees, publishing, and teaching. He also helps manage the CIIR's full-time software engineering staff, and its highly successful technology transfer program. Dr. Callan has published papers on a variety of topics in information retrieval, machine learning, and case-based reasoning; he serves on the program committee of the Special Interest Group Information Retrieval (SIGIR) and Text Retrieval Conferences (TREC); and he is the program chair of the 1997 SIGIR workshop on Networked Information Retrieval. He has recently worked on the problem of applying digital library techniques to improve K-12 education. Prior to his academic career, Dr. Callan worked at Digital Equipment Corporation for seven years. He holds a B.A. from the University of Connecticut, Storrs, and M.S. and Ph.D. degrees from the University of Massachusetts, Amherst.

MARY M. CASE, ASSOCIATION OF RESEARCH LIBRARIES

Mary Case is director of the Office of Scholarly Communication of the Association of Research Libraries (ARL). The Office of Scholarly Communication undertakes activities to understand and influ-ence the forces affecting the production, dissemination, and use of scholarly and scientific information. The office seeks to promote innovative, creative, and alternative ways of sharing scholarly findings, particularly through championing evolving electronic techniques for recording and disseminating academic and research scholarship. Before coming to ARL in June 1996, Ms. Case was director of program review in the Office of the Vice President for Administration and Planning at Northwestern University. Prior to that, she was head of Serials and Acquisitions Services at the Northwestern University Library.

SU-SHING CHEN, UNIVERSITY OF MISSOURI-COLUMBIA

Su-Shing Chen received his PhD from the University of Maryland in 1970, and was with the University of Florida until 1985. He then joined the University of North Carolina-Charlotte where he served as the chairman of computer science from 1986-89. Dr. Chen became a professor and chair of computer engineering and computer science of the University of Missouri-Columbia in 1996. He has been a visiting professor at Hong Kong University of Science and Technology (1996), University of North Carolina-Chapel Hill (1990), University of Bonn/Germany (1980), IMPA/Brazil (1980), University of Maryland (1979), and Georgia Tech (1978). He has also been a visiting scientist at IBM Thomas Watson Research Center (1982), IBM Palo Alto Scientific Center (1986), Boeing High Tech Center (1988), and other IBM divisions (1981). He also has served as program director of various research programs at National Science Foundation, such as the program director of geometric analysis (1983-84), program director of intelligent systems (1994-95), program director of knowledge models and cognitive systems (1994-95). From May 1994-August 1995, he was the program director of information technology and organizations. During that period, he was responsible for the establishment of the NSF/ARPA/NASA Research on Digital Libraries Initiative, and was the program director of the initiative.

JAMES DAVIS, PALO ALTO RESEARCH CENTER/XEROX

Jim Davis of Xerox at the Palo Alto Research Center has been working on digital libraries since 1992. He is the original architect of a distributed digital library for computer science technical reports (NCSTRL) which is now in use at 92 institutions worldwide. This same technology is being considered as the basis for an Association for Computing Machinery electronic papers repository for computer science. He also designed CoNote, which provides small groups shared annotation of Web documents, and is now used routinely in CS instruction at Cornell. Dr. Davis received a B.S. and Ph.D. from the Massachusetts Institute of Technology. His graduate work at the Media Lab was in spoken language interaction and computer music.

ELIZABETH DUPUIS, UNIVERSITY OF TEXAS AT AUSTIN

Beth Dupuis is head of the Digital Information Literacy Office, within the Undergraduate Library of the General Libraries, at The University of Texas at Austin. One of her primary responsibilities is to work with faculty, librarians, and students to determine core skills and competencies related to searching, evaluating, saving, manipulating, and organizing information. In her classes, she has taught thousands of undergraduate and graduate students to learn to effectively use core information resources and systems with an emphasis on digital formats and basic skills. Previously she managed the Balcones Library Service Center, a remote library for science and technology-related agencies of approximately 1500 researchers affiliated with The University of Texas at Austin. Ms. Dupuis has published numerous articles and offered conference presentations about digital information and instructional technologies. On campus, she serves on the Multimedia Instruction Committee and the Team Web Planning and Training Group. Currently she is the web administrator and listserv moderator for the Association of College and Research Libraries (ACRL) Instruction Section and will soon begin her responsibilities as associate editor for columns of *Public-Access Computer Systems Review* (PACS-R), an electronic journal about end-user computer systems in libraries. Ms. Dupuis received a B.A. in English and a Master's in library and information science (MLIS) from the University of Illinois at Urbana-Champaign; she holds an Endorsement of Specialization in Special Libraries and Resources from the Graduate School of Library and Information Science at The University of Texas at Austin.

*STEPHEN C. EHRMANN, AMERICAN ASSOCIATION FOR HIGHER EDUCATION

Stephen Ehrmann serves as director of the Flashlight Project at the American Association for Higher Education. Flashlight develops and applies evaluation tools to issues arising from the uses of technology in education. Dr. Ehrmann also is part of the technology projects group that supports the national Teaching, Learning and Technology Roundtable program. His wide ranging experience also includes work on distance education, the economics of courseware, and strategies for employing technology in curricular reform. For eleven years (1985-96) Dr. Ehrmann was senior program officer for interactive technologies with the Annenberg/CPB Projects at the Corporation for Public Broadcasting in Washington, DC. From 1991-94, Dr. Ehrmann also served as senior program officer with the Annenberg/CPB Math and Science Project, an initiative dedicated to improving the teaching of math and science in the public schools. From 1978-85, he was a program officer with the Fund for the Improvement of Postsecondary Education (FIPSE). Prior to that, he served as director of educational research and assistance at The Evergreen State College in Olympia, Washington. His Ph.D. is in management and higher education from the Massachusetts Institute of Technology, where he also received bachelor's degrees in aerospace engineering and in urban planning.

EDWARD A. FOX, VIRGINIA POLYTECHNIC INSTITUTE

Ed Fox holds a Ph.D. and M.S. in computer science from Cornell University, and a B.S. from Massachusetts Institute of Technology. Since 1983 he has been at Virginia Polytechnic Institute and State University (VA Tech or VPI&SU), where he serves as associate director for research at the computing center, and professor of computer science. He directs the Information Access Lab, the Digital Library Research Lab, "Interactive Learning with a Digital Library in Computer Science," "Improving Graduate Education with a National Digital Library of Theses and Dissertations," and a number of other research and development projects. In addition to his courses at Virginia Tech, Dr. Fox has taught more than 25 tutorials in nine countries. For the Association for Computing Machinery (ACM), he served in 1988-91 as a member of the publications board and as editor-in-chief of ACM Press Database Products (responsible for the broad area of electronic publishing including online, CD-ROM, hypertext, interactive multimedia, and developing an electronic library). He also served from 1987-95 as vice chair and then chair of the special interest group on information retrieval, and from 1992-94 as founder and chairman of the steering committee for the ACM Multimedia series of conferences. He serves as chair of the steering committee for the ACM Digital Libraries series of conferences, was program chair for ACM DL'96, and is a member of the editorial board for ACM/Springer *Journal on Multimedia Systems.* He was project director for the Virginia Disc series of CD-ROMs as well as for VPI&SU work on interactive digital video. He is editor for Morgan Kaufmann Publishers book series on Multimedia Information and Systems. He also serves on the editorial boards of CD-ROM Professional, Electronic Publishing (Origination, Dissemination and Design), Information Processing and Management, *Journal of Educational Multimedia and Hypermedia, Journal of Universal Computer Science,* and *Multimedia Tools and Applications.* He has authored or co-authored numerous publications in the areas of digital libraries, information storage and retrieval, hypertext/hypermedia/multimedia, computational linguistics, CD-ROM and optical disc technology, electronic publishing, and expert systems.

GORDON FREEDMAN, CALIFORNIA STATE UNIVERSITY, MONTEREY BAY

Gordon Freedman serves as director for business development at California State University, Monterey Bay, in the university's Center for Science, Technology, and Information Resources. At this new university, funded in part by base conversion funding and devoted to distributed education, Mr. Freedman develops businesses and strategies that bring together knowledge management, learning systems, and appropriate technologies. The university focuses on key relationships in Silicon Valley and Los Angeles to create 21st century learning and knowledge businesses. At a demonstration level, Mr. Freedman designs, develops, and produces interactive, distributed, and media-rich products that fit into the university's strategic mission. Mr. Freedman is the overall designer and producer of the National Science Foundation-funded Virtual Canyon project, which utilizes

the deep sea content and methods of the Monterey Bay Aquarium Research Institute for a K-12 learning system prototype. He developed and supervises hyper design technologies (hdt.net), a university-affiliated private business that develops technology and media-driven knowledge and learning systems. Mr. Freedman coordinates the development of online learning tools with the university and Silicon Graphics, Inc (SGI) and is the operator at Cal State, Monterey Bay of SGI's Authorized Training Partner program. He is part of a start-up university-affiliated business which will be a value-added supplier of distance learning utilities. Mr. Freedman has a background in government, news media, entertainment, software development and publishing. He spent five years on Capitol Hill as a researcher and investigator, including service on the Senate Watergate Committee. Mr. Freedman was a producer for ABC News, 20/20, and Nightline in Washington, D.C., a producer of television drama and feature films in Los Angeles, including the documentary adaptation of Stephen Hawkings best selling book, *A Brief History of Time,* and a developer of CD-ROMs. Before coming to the business development post at Cal State, Monterey Bay, he served as a founding vice president of electronic media at Knowledge Exchange, a multiple media publishing company in business, finance, and economics funded by Michael Milken. Mr. Freedman has co-authored two books and packaged two books. He attended Michigan State University where he studied communication theory.

RICHARD FURUTA, TEXAS A & M UNIVERSITY

Richard Furuta is an associate professor at Texas A&M University in the department of computer science, director of the Hypermedia Research Laboratory, and associate director of the Center for the Study of Digital Libraries. Dr. Furuta's current areas of research include hypermedia systems and models, structured documents and electronic publishing, document structure recognition from bitmapped sources, management systems for three-dimensional-gesture-based user interfaces, and digital libraries. He also has studied applications in computer supported cooperative work, software engineering, and visual programming. He is U.S. editor of the journal *Electronic Publishing: Origination, Dissemination, and Design* (EP-odd), published by John Wiley, and has just completed a term as chair of the ACM Special Interest Group on Hypertext (SIGLINK). He was the conference chair for Digital Libraries '94, the first conference in a new series and the program chair for the next in the series, Digital Libraries '95. Dr. Furuta received the B.A. degree from Reed College in 1974, the M.S. degree in computer science from the University of Oregon in 1978, and the Ph.D. degree in computer science from the University of Washington in 1986.

MARGARET GJERTSEN, NORTH CAROLINA STATE UNIVERSITY

Peg Gjertsen is associate director of the Physics Courseware Evaluation Project. Her duties include maintaining all software, computers, and the website, managing the Novell network both for administrative tasks and teaching functions, training staff on computers, researching new software developments for possible inclusion in her work group and in teaching, maintaining a database of all known physics courseware concerned with teaching physics, and managing the publication of the newsletter. She has been involved in this work since 1984. She is a past editor of the review column for *Computers in Physics* and continues to write the biennial directory of physics courseware for this journal. Mrs. Gjertsen is associate editor of *Physics Academic Software.* Her responsibilities include helping establish and maintaining editorial standards and insuring the quality of the published software and the associated user's manual. Mrs. Gjertsen is associate director of The Academic Software Library, a manufacturing and distribution project for faculty written software. She is responsible for the software and hardware concerns, the day to day running of the office, the production and distribution of the software, and the financial reports at the end of each month. Mrs. Gjertsen received her BS and MS in chemistry from Carnegie Mellon University in 1967 and 1968, and has studied at the University of North Carolina at Chapel Hill.

PETER S. GRAHAM, RUTGERS UNIVERSITY

Peter Graham is associate university librarian at Rutgers, The State University of New Jersey. Since 1987, he has been in charge of acquisitions, cataloging, and networked information services. For three years he was also associate vice president for information services, with responsibility for the uni-

versity's academic and administrative computing and networking. He is a member of the governing bodies of the American Library Association, the Bibliographical Society of America, and the Center for Electronic Texts in the Humanities. Mr. Graham is a working group leader within the Coalition for Networked Information and has spoken there several times. He is an advisor to the Research Libraries Group (RLG) on matters of digital libraries and preservation. He has published widely on issues of scholarly preservation, digital library requirements, and the necessary changes within research libraries. Mr. Graham has submitted a proposal to the National Endowment for the Humanities for a series of Digital Preservation Archiving Workshops with the aim of getting major players (National Science Foundation projects, Research Library Group, National Digital Libraries Federation, National Archives Information Server, Library of Congress, etc.) together to reach consensus on next steps to be taken in digital archiving. A planning grant has already been offered from the Council on Library and Information Resources.

TIMOTHY INGOLDSBY, AMERICAN INSTITUTE OF PHYSICS

Tim Ingoldsby is the director of product development for the American Institute of Physics. This position includes responsibility for the development of AIP online journals and AIP's Online Journal Publishing Service, a digital library platform for many publishers of research journals. He was responsible for AIP's pioneering online journal, *Applied Physics Letters Online,* which became, in January of 1995, the first online full text searchable hyperlinked journal in physics. Prior to assuming his current position in 1993, Mr. Ingoldsby served as AIP's first director of information technology, responsible for upgrading the institute's computing and communications infrastructure. He also led the technology task force that developed the advanced networking and communications capabilities installed into the newly constructed American Center for Physics. Before joining AIP in 1988, Mr. Ingoldsby worked for Grumman Data Systems, Wang Laboratories, and was associate executive officer of the American Association of Physics Teachers (1979-83). He began his career as a classroom teacher of physics and digital electronics.

VICKI JOHNSON, INTERCONNECT TECHNOLOGIES CORPORATION

Vicki Johnson is the president of Interconnect Technologies Corporation. Interconnect Technologies is a Silicon Valley firm specializing in research and development and application of digital library technologies. Ms. Johnson has led technical teams at AT&T Bell Labs and Stanford University, and was product manager for an international commercial online service. At Interconnect she works closely with clients to set strategic directions and lead implementation teams. She holds an M.B.A. in finance from New York University and an M.S. in computer engineering from Stanford University.

*JOHN JUNGCK, BELOIT COLLEGE

John Jungck is the Mead Chair of the Sciences at Beloit College and has been involved in biology education reforms for thirty years. Professor Jungck served as president of the Association of Midwestern College Biology Teachers, is the editor of *Bioscene: Journal of College Biology Teachers*, and has been on the editorial boards of both the *Bulletin of Mathematical Biology* and *BioSystems*. He has participated in projects for the Pre-Service Preparation of College Biology Teachers and for the development of investigative laboratory exercises with the Commission for Undergraduate Education in the Biological Sciences (CUBS). His awards include: an NSTA-Ohaus Award for Innovations in College Science Teaching, a FIPSE Mina Shaughnessy Scholar Award for developing "new approaches to learning from practice," and a year-long Fulbright Scholar Award as a visiting professor to Thailand (with extensions to Sri Lanka and Egypt). In 1986, with Nils Peterson, he started the BioQUEST Curriculum Consortium and became editor of the BioQUEST Library. Dr. Jungck maintains an active research program in mathematical molecular evolution, and the history, philosophy, and social studies of biology. For the past several years he has served on the executive committee of CELS (the Coalition for Education in the Life Sciences) and several national panels devoted to examining college science education. Dr. Jungck received a B.S. and M.S. from the University of Minnesota and a Ph.D. from the University of Miami.

JAMES KELLER, HARVARD UNIVERSITY

James Keller is the associate director and a research associate at the Harvard Information Infrastructure Project. His research interests include the commercialization of the Internet and the federal role in information infrastructure development. His publications include *Converging Infrastructures: Intelligent Transportation Systems and the NII*, MIT Press, 1996 (co-editor with Lewis Branscomb), *Public Access to the Internet*, MIT Press, 1995 (co-editor with Brian Kahin), *Coordinating the Internet*, MIT Press, 1997 (co-editor with Brian Kahin), and *Investing in Innovation* (co-editor with Lewis Branscomb). Prior to joining the Information Infrastructure Project, Mr. Keller was a product planner and member of the Strategic Planning Group at Sprint Data Group, specializing in the evaluation of emerging communications technologies as they related to new business opportunities. Prior to this, Mr. Keller was a member of the Strategic Planning Group at INTELSAT. INTELSAT owns and operates the international satellite communications system. Mr. Keller graduated with honors from the University of Massachusetts, and holds a Masters in Public and Private Management from the Yale School of Organization and Management.

DEBORAH KNOX, THE COLLEGE OF NEW JERSEY

Deborah Knox is an associate professor of computer science at The College of New Jersey. She is an advocate of the use of hands-on laboratories in support of the CS curriculum and has led two Association for Computing Machinery Special Interest Group on Computer Science Education working groups on laboratories for computing courses. She developed the Special Interest Group Computer Science Education Computing Laboratory Repository, a web-based resource center for laboratory materials (http://www.tcnj.edu/~compsci/), and serves as the editor of the site. Dr. Knox received a B.S. in medical technology from Moravian College in 1979, and her M.S. and Ph.D. degrees in computer science from Iowa State University in 1987.

ROBERTA LAMB, CASE WESTERN UNIVERSITY

Roberta Lamb has recently joined the Weatherhead School of Management at Case Western University as an assistant professor of management information and decision systems. Previously she managed the development of application technologies and tools for Platinum Software Corporation, a financial software systems integrator, while completing her Ph.D. degree. Dr. Lamb has written about the organizational use of online information resources, and is particularly interested in the use of digital libraries and scholarly communication systems by the corporate sector. She has participated in digital library workshops and planning forums in the United States and Canada. Dr. Lamb received a B.S. in 1987 and an M.S. in 1989 in computer science and engineering from California State University, Fullerton. She received an M.S. in 1994 and her Ph.D. degree in 1997 in information and computer science from the University of California, Irvine.

MICHAEL LESK, BELLCORE

Michael Lesk is a chief research scientist at Bellcore, and was previously head of the Computer Science Research Department there. He is also visiting professor of computer science at University College London, and is the author of *Practical Digital Libraries: Books, Byte and Bucks*, published by Morgan Kaufmann in July 1997. However, he is probably best known as the author of Unix utilities such as tbl, lex and uucp. He has BA and PhD degrees from Harvard University (1961 and 1969, respectively).

ROBERT L. LICHTER, CAMILLE AND HENRY DREYFUS FOUNDATION

Robert Lichter is executive director of the New York City-based Camille and Henry Dreyfus Foundation, Inc., the only nationally operating private foundation that exclusively supports the chemical sciences. Since 1946, through its special grant program in the chemical sciences, the Dreyfus Foundation has provided over $30 million for support of chemistry education. Previously, Dr. Lichter was vice provost for research and graduate studies at the State University of New York at Stony Brook, a regional director of grants at Research Corporation, and professor of chemistry at Hunter College of the City University of New York, where he also served as department chair. A fellow of the American Association for the Advancement of Science, Dr. Lichter serves on two American Chemical Society committees, is a member and former chair of the board of governors of the National Conferences on Under-

graduate Research, and has chaired the committee on science education of the New York Academy of Sciences. He received an A.B. in chemistry from Harvard University in 1962 and a Ph.D. in chemistry from the University of Wisconsin-Madison in 1967. He did postdoctoral work at the Technische Hochscule Braunschweig, Germany, and the California Institute of Technology.

RICHARD E. LUCIER, UNIVERSITY OF CALIFORNIA, SAN FRANCISCO

Richard Lucier is assistant vice chancellor for Academic Information Management, director of the Center for Knowledge Management, and university librarian at the University of California, San Francisco. His responsibilities include: the management of academic information resources including academic and instructional computing; the university library; and campus-wide policy and planning coordination for information technology in support of education, research, and clinical care. In mid-1995, Mr. Lucier was appointed to lead a University of California planning effort for a digital library which would serve all nine UC campuses. In September 1996, Mr. Lucier began an 18-month, 80% appointment as special assistant for library planning at the UC Office of the President, providing leadership for a university-wide library planning and action initiative whose goals are to: identify organizational, budgetary, and functional changes required to ensure the continued scholarly and economic vitality of UC's libraries; guide library evolution over the next decade; and ensure that immediate actions are taken in support of such changes and evolution. Mr. Lucier holds a B.M. in music and philosophy from the Catholic University of America and an M.L.S. in library science from Rutgers University. He has done extensive graduate work in health policy at the University of North Carolina at Chapel Hill. Mr. Lucier was the co-founder and director of the Laboratory for Applied Research in Academic Information at The Johns Hopkins University from 1986-1991, and spearheaded the development of the genome data base and the online *Mendelian Inheritance in Man*, both in support of the international Human Genome Initiative. The co-originator of the Knowledge Management Model, he has special interests in scientific and scholarly communication, the development and management of scientific databases, digital publishing, and digital libraries, and he has published and lectured widely on these topics.

CLIFFORD LYNCH, COALITION FOR NETWORKED INFORMATION

Clifford Lynch recently became executive director for the Coalition for Networked Information, a joint project of the Association for Research Libraries, CAUSE and Educom focused on the use of information technology and networked information to enhance scholarship and intellectual productivity. Prior to joining CNI, Dr. Lynch spent 18 years at the University of California Office of the President, the last 10 as Director of Library Automation, where he was responsible for public access systems serving the nine campuses and the intercampus TCP/IP network. Lynch, who holds a PhD in Computer Science from UC Berkeley, is a past president of the American Society for Information Science and a fellow of the AAAS. He is also an adjunct professor at UC Berkeley's School of Information Management and Systems.

MIRIAM MASULLO, IBM THOMAS J. WATSON RESEARCH CENTER

Miriam Masullo is a research staff member in the Systems Laboratory at the Thomas J. Watson Research Center, the IBM Yorktown Heights Research Laboratory. She came to this position 15 years ago, with a long held personal interest in education and 16 years of experience in both systems analysis and network engineering from the telecommunications industry. Dr. Masullo received a B.A. degree in architecture and English literature from The City College of New York, an M.S. in computer science from the City College of New York, an M. Phil. and a Ph.D. in computer science for her interdisciplinary work with the departments of computer science and educational psychology from The City University of New York. Her most recent research has focused in the area of building digital libraries and infrastructure for education. She has contributed numerous papers and seminars to further the understanding of that topic on a worldwide basis.

FRANCIS MIKSA, UNIVERSITY OF TEXAS AT AUSTIN

Fran Miksa is professor at the Graduate School of Library and Information Science at The University of Texas at Austin. His specialty areas are 1) the classification of knowledge and (2) systems of control for information-bearing entities. He participated in the first Digital Library Conference in 1994 sponsored by Texas A&M University where with his colleague, Philip Doty, he presented a paper entitled "Intellectual Realities and the Digital Library." He was local arrangements chair for the second such conference in 1995 in Austin. More recently he has published *The Cultural Legacy of the 'Modern Library' for the Future,* JELIS 37 (1996): 100-19 and *The DDC, the Universe of Knowledge, and the Post-Modern Library* (in press, expected summer 1997) on the Dewey Decimal Classification system and the rise of library classification theory in the 20th century. He presented "The Influence of Mathematics on the Classificatory Thought of S. R. Ranganathan" at the recently held 6th International Study Conference on Classification Research (London, 16-18 June 1997). Dr. Miksa earned both Master's and Ph.D. degrees from the University of Chicago. He was on the faculty of the School of Library and Information Science, Louisiana State University from 1972 to 1984 and has been at The University of Texas since 1984.

*JOAN MITCHELL, ON LINE COMPUTER LIBRARY CENTER / FOREST PRESS

Joan Mitchell is the editor in chief of the Dewey Decimal System at the On line Computer Library Center.

BRANDON MURAMATSU, NATIONAL ENGINEERING EDUCATION DELIVERY SYSTEM

Brandon Muramatsu is the project manager for the National Engineering Education Delivery System (NEEDS) with the Synthesis Coalition, an NSF-funded engineering education coalition. Mr. Muramatsu is responsible for building a World Wide Web accessible database of engineering education courseware (www.needs.org). NEEDS locates, catalogs, and stores engineering and engineering-related courseware nationwide. To ensure quality content in NEEDS, he is responsible for developing a two-tiered evaluation system for engineering education courseware. At the base level is a peer review of courseware based on the journal-model. The highest level is a national award competition, the

Premier Award for Excellence in Engineering Education courseware. He has experience developing, using, and evaluating engineering education courseware. As a lecturer in mechanical engineering at the University of California, Berkeley he has taught courses in the development of multimedia case studies. Mr. Muramatsu received an M.S. and B.S. degrees in mechanical engineering from the University of California, Berkeley.

JEANNE L. NARUM, INDEPENDENT COLLEGES OFFICE

Jeanne Narum is the director of the Independent Colleges Office (ICO) and the director of Project Kaleidoscope (PKAL), both based in Washington, D.C. The ICO serves as the Washington representative for the Associated Colleges of the Midwest and a select group of liberal arts colleges across the country, assisting in their relations with federal agencies and programs. Narum, with over 20 years experience with faculty, curricular, and institutional development projects, came to the ICO in 1988 from administrative positions at Augsburg College (VP for college relations), Dickinson College (director of development), and St. Olaf College (director of government and foundation relations). In 1989, she became the founding Director of PKAL, and has continued to have responsibility for developing and coordinating the various facets of PKAL, including the Faculty for the 21st Century Network, the seminars and publications on facilities planning, and the workshops and events on disciplinary, topical, and institutional issues. Narum was publisher for PKAL Volume I, *What Works*, and editor-in-chief for Volumes II, *Resources for Reform* and Volume III, *Structures for Science*. She is a member of the boards of trustees at Lenoir-Rhyne College, the alumni board at St. Olaf College, the steering committee for the Coalition for Education in the Life Sciences, and a councilor in the Council for Undergraduate Research. She has spoken and written widely on the work of transforming the learning environment for undergraduate students in science, mathematics, engineering, and technology.

SHAMKANT NAVATHE, GEORGIA INSTITUTE OF TECHNOLOGY

Shamkant Navathe is a professor at the College of Computing, Georgia Institute of Technology,

Atlanta. He is well-known for his work on database modeling, database conversion, database design, distributed database allocation, and database integration. He has worked with IBM and Siemens in their research divisions and has been a consultant to various companies. He was the general co-chairman of the 1996 International VLDB (Very Large Data Base) conference in Bombay, India. He is an associate editor of Association for Computing Machinery's *Computing Surveys,* and Institute of Electronic and Electrical Engineering *Transactions on Knowledge and Data Engineering.* He is also on the editorial boards of *Information Systems* (Pergamon Press) and *Distributed and Parallel Databases* (Kluwer Academic Publishers). He is an author of the book *Fundamentals of Database Systems* with R. Elmasri (Addison Wesley, Edition 2, 1994), which is currently the leading database textbook worldwide. His current research interests include object-oriented and multimedia databases, intelligent information retrieval, and mobile disconnected databases. Navathe holds a Ph.D. from the University of Michigan and has over 100 refereed publications.

LORRAINE NORMORE, CHEMICAL ABSTRACTS SERVICE

Lorraine Normore is a senior associate research scientist at Chemical Abstracts Service (CAS) where she has been employed since 1983. Her research has focused on exploring ways to determine and better serve the information needs of end user scientists and engineers. She was deeply involved in both the research and product specification phases for SciFinder, CAS's award-winning end user interface. She acted as the CAS liaison for the Chemistry Online Retrieval Experiment (CORE), one of the pioneer electronic library projects. Dr. Normore is an active member of both the Association for Computing Machines' Special Interest Group in Human-Computer Interaction (local and national) and of the Human Factors & Ergonomics Societies' Computer Systems Technical Group, having served in various capacities. She is also a member of Ada Semantic Interface Specification and the American Psychological Association. She received her B.A. (Hons.) degree from McGill University in 1967, her M.L.S. from the University of Toronto in 1975, and her Ph.D. in experimental psychology from the Ohio State University in 1986.

JAN OLSEN, CORNELL UNIVERSITY

Jan Olsen has been an administrator in research libraries within institutions of higher education for the last twenty years. She has represented abroad the United States government and institutions of higher education and carried out consultancies in Brazil, Peru, the Philippines, Spain, and Africa. Dr. Olsen is the director of the Albert R. Mann Library, a major science library at Cornell University. In 1993 the Mann Library won the ALA/Meckler Library of the Future Award. This reflected the successful creation of a working digital research library. Dr. Olsen has conducted a number of research projects exploring the application of electronic technology to the use and storage of scholarly information. As a librarian, she is concerned that scholars and scholarship will be effectively served by the emerging digital library. One of her most recent publications is a book published by the Meckler Press on electronic journal literature and its implications for scholars. Dr. Olsen completed an M. L. S. degree in library science at the University of Wisconsin, a M.Ed. and a Ph.D in administration in higher education at Cornell University.

ROBERT M. PANOFF, THE SHODOR EDUCATION FOUNDATION

Robert Panoff is founder and executive director of The Shodor Education Foundation, Inc., a non-profit education and research corporation dedicated to reform and improvement of mathematics and science education by appropriate incorporation of computational and communication technologies. Shodor is a partner with the National Center for Supercomputing Applications at the University of Illinois at Urbana-Champaign in the new National Computational Science Alliance. As principal investigator on several National Science Foundation grants that seek to explore the interaction of high performance computing technologies and education, he worked to develop a series of interactive simulations that combine supercomputing resources and desktop computers. Besides developing and teaching a new courses in information technologies, Dr. Panoff continues an active research program in computational condensed matter physics while defining and implementing educational initiatives at the Shodor Foundation. His research specialties are stochastic optimization, quantum simulations of strongly-correlated systems, and computational science education. At Kansas State University and Clemson University from 1986-1990, he developed a fully interdisciplinary computational science and engineering course. He served as director of the Carolinas Institute in Computational Science, an NSF-funded initiative in Undergraduate Faculty Enhancement, 1991-1993. His work has won several major science and education awards, including the 1990 Cray Gigaflop Performance Award in Supercomputing, the 1994 and 1995 Undergraduate Computational Science Education Awards from the U.S. Department of Energy, and a 1995 Achievement Award from the Chicago Chapter of the Society for Technical Communication. In 1993-1994, his interactive simulations were used as the basis of an international science collaboration demonstrating network technologies involving four of the schools from the Department of Defense Dependent Schools, for which he received a letter of commendation from the Department of Defense. In recognition of Dr. Panoff's efforts in undergraduate faculty enhancement and curriculum development, the Shodor Foundation was named in 1996 as a foundation partner of the National Science Foundation for the revitalization of undergraduate education. Dr. Panoff has been a consultant at several national laboratories and is a frequent presenter at NSF-sponsored workshops on visualization, supercomputing, and networking. He has served on the advisory panel for Applications of Advanced Technology program at NSF. Dr. Panoff received his B.S. in physics from the University of Notre Dame and his M.A. and Ph.D. in theoretical physics from Washington University in St. Louis, undertaking both pre- and postdoctoral work at the Courant Institute of Mathematical Sciences at New York University.

GILDA PAUL, PRINCETON UNIVERSITY

Gilda Paul is the associate director of the Pew Science Program in Undergraduate Education at Princeton University. The Pew Science Program is committed to the idea that collaborative efforts among faculty should be at the heart of projects to improve undergraduate science and mathematics education. The Pew Science Program has focused particularly on collaborations across institutional boundaries among faculty from liberal arts colleges and research universities. Pew Science Program funding has focused primarily on projects that have the potential to generate substantial improvement in undergraduate science education but that would be difficult, or even impossible, for a single institution to undertake alone. Dr. Paul received a B.A. in psychology from Barnard College in 1975, an M.A. from Columbia University in psychology in 1977, and her Ph.D. degree in developmental psychology from Temple University in 1987.

BARBARA POLANSKY, AMERICAN CHEMICAL SOCIETY

Barbara Polansky is administrator of copyright and special projects for the American Chemical Society's publications division. As an active member of various organizations that deal with copyright issues, she is chair of the electronic information committee and member of the rights and permissions licensing network committee for the Association of American Publishers' Professional/Scholarly Publishing Division, cofounder and past chair of the Copyright Round Table (Washington, DC), and is a member of the copyright committee of International Association of Scientific, Technical and Medical Publishers (STM). Ms. Polansky was executive director of the American Copyright Council from 1985-1986. She is a lecturer and author of various papers and book chapters on copyright, and is co-editor of the book, *Modern Copyright Fundamentals*; Weil, B.H.; Polansky, B.F., Eds., Revised Edition, Learned Information, 1990. Ms. Polansky received a B.S. in Operations Management from the Pennsylvania State University in 1975 and did graduate coursework in library science at the University of Illinois, as well as continuing legal education at the Practicing Law Institute in New York.

MICHAEL RAUGH, INTERCONNECT TECHNOLOGIES CORPORATION

Mike Raugh is vice president and chief technology officer of Interconnect Technologies Corporation. Interconnect Technologies is a Silicon Valley firm specializing in research and development and application of digital library technologies. Dr. Raugh has worked in advanced technology at Stanford University and Hewlett-Packard Labs. Before joining Interconnect, he served as chief scientist at the Research Institute for Advanced Computer Science

where he developed innovative methods for organizing online information. He leads Interconnect's products and services for information organization and analysis.

RUTH K. SEIDMAN, MASSACHUSETTS INSTITUTE OF TECHNOLOGY

Ruth Seidman is head of the Engineering and Science Libraries at the Massachusetts Institute of Technology, where she has led the librarian staff in innovative partnering with faculty to teach information competencies in the undergraduate engineering design curriculum. She previously served as Director of the Air Force Geophysics Laboratory Research Library. Ms. Seidman is the editor of the Haworth Press, Inc., quarterly *Science & Technology Libraries*. In 1990-1991, she was President of Special Libraries Association; she is also a member of the American Library Association, the Association of College and Research Libraries, the American Society for Engineering Education, and Phi Beta Kappa. Ms. Seidman has given presentations widely on library automation, library management, and international librarianship. She is the author of the 1993 monograph, *Building Global Partnerships for Library Cooperation*. Her Web home page is <http://web.mit.edu/rks/www/>. Ms. Seidman holds a bachelor's degrees with highest honors from Brown University, master's degrees from Harvard University and from Hebrew College of Brookline, Massachusetts, and a master's degree in library science from Case Western Reserve University, where she was elected to Beta Phi Mu.

FRANK M. SHIPMAN III, TEXAS A&M UNIVERSITY

Frank Shipman is an assistant professor in the Department of Computer Science and Center for the Study of Digital Libraries at Texas A&M University. He has been pursuing research in the areas of hypermedia, computer-supported cooperative work, and intelligent user interfaces since 1987. Dr. Shipman's doctoral work at the University of Colorado and subsequent work at Xerox PARC and Texas A&M has investigated combining informal and formal representations in interfaces and methods for supporting incremental formalization. He manages two on-going research projects in the areas of spatial hypertext and computers and education.

AMANDA SPINK, UNIVERSITY OF NORTH TEXAS

Amanda Spink is assistant professor of information science at the University of North Texas. Dr. Spink has numerous funded and industry projects and publications in the area of user modeling research for digital libraries and interactive information retrieval. Her research includes developing a digital library for cattle ranchers. Dr. Spink is also an associate editor of the journal *Information Processing and Management*. She received a B.A. from the Australian National University, a postgraduate degree in information from the University of New South Wales, an M.B.A in information technology management from Fordham University and a Ph.D. in information science from Rutgers University.

RONALD STEVENS, UNIVERSITY OF CALIFORNIA AT LOS ANGELES

Ron Stevens received his Ph.D. from Harvard University in microbiology and molecular genetics in 1971 and is professor of microbiology and immunology and professor of education. For 15 years he directed an immunology research laboratory and authored/co-authored over 100 articles in basic and clinical immunology. He is also the developer and original programmer of the Interactive Multimedia EXercises (IMMEX) problem-solving software which is used for evaluating the problem-solving performances of students from elementary schools through medical schools. Additional analytic software tools allow an electronic re-construction of the strategies that students' employ as they solve the problems allowing a determination of not only if the problem was solved, but how the problem was solved. Dr. Stevens has authored over a dozen educational research papers based on his use of IMMEX for evaluating students. He is currently using artificial neural networks in conjunction with the students' problem-solving performances to identify strategic problem-solving patterns that can discriminate within the novice-expert continuum. Dr. Stevens is the principal investigator on a major grant from the National Science Foundation to use the IMMEX software system to help integrate technology and problem-solving into all the science classrooms of the middle and high schools of Los Angeles.

KEITH STUBBS, U.S. DEPARTMENT OF EDUCATION

Keith Stubbs' current responsibilities as Director of the National Library of Education's Resource Sharing and Cooperation Division include the U.S. Department of Education's Web site, the Education Resources Information Center (ERIC) and its 30+ Web sites (which include AskERIC and the National Parent Information Network), and plans for a resource sharing network for educational libraries and information providers. Mr. Stubbs initiated ED's Internet presence in 1992, launched ED's Web site in March 1994, led an award-winning Web redesign and wrote ED's Web Server Standards & Guidelines in 1995, and recently conducted one of the first OMB-sanctioned Internet customer surveys. He co-chairs ED's Internet Working Group and represents ED on the interagency World Wide Web (WWW) Federal Consortium and the Federal Internet-Based Education Resources (FIBER) initiative. Currently he is directing several cross-site indexing, cataloging, and searching projects to help people find the information they seek among the exploding volume of education material scattered across thousands of Internet sites.

*DIANE VIZINE-GOETZ, ON LINE COMPUTER LIBRARY CENTER

Diane Vizine-Goetz joined On line Computer Library Center in 1983 as post-doctoral fellow to continue research in database quality begun as an OCLC research assistant and doctoral student. Since then she has conducted research on the application and use of Library of Congress subject headings in online bibliographic systems and on automated classifier-assistance tools. Her research interests include cataloging and classifying print and electronic resources. She is principal research investigator on a project to enhance the usefulness of the direct digital control as a knowledge organizing tool. Dr. Vizine-Goetz received her Ph.D. from the School of Information and Library Science, Case Western Reserve University.

NISHA VORA, ASSOCIATION OF AMERICAN PUBLISHERS

Nisha Vora is currently the deputy director of copyright and new technology for the Association of American Publishers. She is responsible for AAP's International Enforcement Program, the Rights and Permissions Advisory Committee, and the International Copyright Information Center. She is also the public liaison for the Electronic Publishing Special Interest Group, and helps to coordinate meetings of AAPs Enabling Technologies and Copyright Committees. Ms. Vora works with the U.S. government, including the U.S. Trade Representative, the Copyright Office, and the United States Information Agency for the protection of American copyrights here and abroad. Ms. Vora works with the International Intellectual Property Alliance, an umbrella organization of seven associations, to represent the U.S. copyright-based industries in bilateral and multilateral efforts to improve international protection of copyrighted works. She is responsible for the operation of AAP's copyright enforcement campaign in ten countries, and assists in coordinating copyright enforcement efforts in the United States. Ms. Vora earned her B.A. in communications from Virginia Tech, and has been with AAP since 1994.

PAUL WELLIN, WOLFRAM RESEARCH

Paul Wellin is the director of Corporate and Academic Affairs for Wolfram Research, Inc., maker of the technical computing software Mathematica. In this role, he serves as the liaison between Wolfram Research and industry and academia. Prior to joining Wolfram Research, Dr. Wellin was in academia, teaching mathematics in California. He is the author of two books (one on programming and another on computer simulations) and is the founder (and editor for its first five years) of the paper and electronic journal *Mathematica in Education and Research* (Springer-Verlag). He is chair of the Mathematics Advisory Board for Wolfram Research, and is a member of the Corporate and Foundation Alliance of the National Science Foundation.

WAYNE WOLF, PRINCETON UNIVERSITY

Wayne Wolf is associate professor of electrical engineering at Princeton University. Before joining Princeton, he was with AT&T Bell Laboratories. He received the B.S., M.S., and Ph.D. degrees in electrical engineering from Stanford University in 1980, 1981, and 1984, respectively. His research interests include computer-aided design of VLSI and embedded computing systems, video signal processors, and video libraries. He is a senior member of the Institute of Electronic and Electrical Engineers and a member of the Association for Computing Machinery and the International Society for Optical Engineering.

LEE ZIA, UNIVERSITY OF NEW HAMPSHIRE

Lee Zia is an associate professor of mathematics at the University of New Hampshire. He has been involved in a range of activities concerning undergraduate education, including the use of computational and visualization tools in differential equations, linear algebra, and scientific computing. Dr. Zia serves on the Education Committee for the Society for Industrial and Applied Mathematics (SIAM) and is an associate editor for the education section of SIAM Review. In 1995 and 1996 he was a program director with the National Science Foundation's (NSF) Division of Undergraduate Education, where a primary area of responsibility concerned information technology issues and their impact on undergraduate education. Dr. Zia received a B.S. in mathematics from the University of North Carolina in 1978, an M.S. degree in mathematics from the University of Michigan, and a Ph.D. in applied mathematics from Brown University in 1985.